Le PIGEON

COOKING AT THE DIRTY BIRD

GABRIEL RUCKER and
MEREDITH ERICKSON
with **LAUREN** and **ANDREW FORTGANG**

Photographs by **DAVID L. REAMER**

TEN SPEED PRESS

Berkeley

Le Pigeon

CONTENTS

Foreword by Tom Colicchio *viii*

Introduction: Five Years of Le Pigeon *1*

LETTUCE AND SUCH

TONGUE

FAT LIVER

{Gabriel's Love Letter to Plymouth Valiants} *72*

LITTLE BIRDS

FOREWORD

There is a moment in time in the career of a chef that is unlike any that has come before or will come again. You're not yet known. Perhaps you're a sous-chef, bouncing around from restaurant to restaurant. Then you take a risk and open a small kitchen and suddenly you're cooking whatever you want, coming up with four new dishes a day inspired by anything and everything— a wild mushroom you found backpacking over the weekend, a news item about Bavaria from that morning—it's a wildly creative time. From early morning until very, very early the next morning, you're working . . . and you're having the time of your life. It's a small window of time during which this all happens, after you plunk down the rent on your little space and before *Food & Wine* magazine discovers you and everything changes.

Soon there will be more expectations from the press and from the food industry. You suddenly realize that you're now responsible for the liveli-hoods of a lot of people who are counting on you to keep this thing going. And all these considerations begin to encroach on your ability to create, to make decisions based solely on what you want to do with food. You must begin to not only allow these decisions to influence the food you make, but also to take up time that was previously devoted to creativity. Now there is a lot more to your work as a chef than simply getting into a kitchen, banging around a lot of pots and pans, and being creative. There's no going back, and you need to find new ways forevermore to remain relevant.

I think this process happens for people in any creative field, by the way. It's ironic that the very thing that will sustain your ability to create—a modi-cum of recognition—often leads to growth that then, in turn, inhibits your ability to create. Business factors aside, you start becoming self-conscious, more deliberate. It's important to recognize this shift so you can figure out a way to preserve the playfulness and fearlessness of that time when all you had to do was bring yourself—all of yourself—into the kitchen and play.

Gabriel Rucker is living in this moment and loving it. Le Pigeon has provided a showcase for Rucker's daily inspirations for the last five years, and through this book, we get a front-row seat to the evolution of a chef—and a restaurant—on the cusp of very big changes. The wild creativity that happens during this period in a chef's career is often fast, furious, and unpredictable. That Gabriel has managed to put these first few years of recipes down on paper is a feat by itself and a spectacular benefit to Le Pigeon and Little Bird's legions of loyal fans. It's great when you can actually recognize that you're living this moment while you're in it. Gabriel does, and that's what he's celebrating in this cookbook. It's clear that he has found a way to keep his food irreverent and fun.

But there's a sub-story here, too. One that starts with a scrappy fifteen-year-old who showed up in my kitchen some years ago, insisting that he wanted to work with me for the summer. He seemed bright, and so I gave Andy Fortgang a chance. He *was* bright. He was also hardworking, trustworthy, and not at all shy about taking initiative. Andy worked in my restaurant kitchen over summers and vacations throughout high school and post college, after he realized that he'd found his calling in the front of the house. When Andy told me that he had an opportunity to be part of something new in Portland, I was sad for me and excited for him.

I wasn't surprised to learn that Gabriel hired Andy over the phone and put him to work at Le Pigeon the very first day they met. I suppose Andy just has that effect on chefs. And it's to Gabriel's credit that he recognized in Andy the other half of the equation that equals a successful restaurant (or two . . . and some day, maybe more). Andy has created the structure that allows Gabriel to focus on the food. And along with that structure, he brought along his talented wife, Lauren, who became the pastry chef at Le Pigeon and Little Bird.

Gabriel and Andy have been going through this crazy time of round-the-clock uninhibited inventiveness together: Andy is the Packard to Gabriel's Hewlitt, the Orville to his Wilbur, the Jerry to his Ben (the Stimpy to his Ren? Fill in your own partnership—you get the point), and they've chosen to preserve a luscious, frenetic, passionate snapshot of it. You're holding it in your hands.

INTRODUCTION
FIVE YEARS OF LE PIGEON

Andrew Fortgang and Gabriel Rucker met through Craigslist. True story.

As Gabriel tells it: It was 2007 and I had been running Le Pigeon (aka LP) for a little more than a year with my partners in crime, Erik Van Kley and Su Lien Pino. Each day was a marathon, starting with brunch and ending (later and later) at the B-Side bar next to LP drinking Powers Whiskey, exhausted and staring at each other with disbelief that we had pulled off another night of ninety-plus covers (we're tiny, only thirty-five seats). The phone was ringing nonstop and local and national press were beginning to descend. But I was so busy I hardly noticed.

I posted a manager position in the "Casual Encounters" section (or maybe it was under "Food and Hospitality"?). Either way, I was completely desperate for a manager. Leif Sundstrom, who had been the manager until that point, was leaving. He had helped build Le Pigeon, but he wanted to get into the wine business, and I needed someone to tighten the service. Le Pigeon has a small dining room with an open kitchen, and I could actually hear the waitstaff asking, "Who's got the chicken?" as they plopped down the plates in front of the guests.

I didn't have time to deal with seat numbers (which tell the servers who ordered what); we were constantly packed. Just as we were recovering from brunch, the lines were beginning to form for dinner. I knew the nonstop work-party-work-party-work-party approach had an expiration date, and that it was near approaching. I needed a Mr. Wolf for my restaurant clean-up duty. I needed the Jerry to my Kramer.

Andy had just visited Portland, and unbeknownst to me, had eaten at Le Pigeon. He and his wife, Lauren, were considering a move to the West Coast because they wanted a more relaxed life than they had in New York.

Two days after arriving back in New York (where he was born and raised), Andy saw the Craigslist posting. We talked on the phone a few times over the next couple of months, but the first time we met in person was his first day as manager.

But let's rewind. I was twenty-five, and this was not supposed to be my trajectory.

I grew up in Napa, California—not the French Laundry, wine-guzzling, home-to-millionaires Napa—but blue-collar suburban California. And I loved it. So much so that when I failed math in junior college and was told I should "learn a trade," I happily took on a year of cooking school. I dropped out when I got my first cooking gig at the age of nineteen at the Silverado Country Club doing banquets for hundreds of people a day. I was a sponge and learned a lot of the basics, but I was bored with my hometown.

My next stop was the Southern Exposure Bistro, a run-of-the-mill joint in the coastal town of Santa Cruz that served lasagna, filet mignon, and mashed potatoes piped from a bag. The restaurant wasn't much, but it was during this time that I began to understand cooking on an intuitive level. The customers didn't have high expectations, but I did, and I started to push myself. I would fall asleep at night reading *The French Laundry Cookbook* (which had just been published) and replaying the evening at the bistro: what had gone well, what had been a disaster, and what I wanted to cook the next day.

This was at the tail end of the rave era, and my two years in Santa Cruz passed quickly in a haze of techno music, in-line skating, baggy jeans, and fourteen-hour shifts at the restaurant. I wanted to move to a bigger pond and desperately hoped it would be San Francisco, but I couldn't afford the city. My friend David Reamer, a funny, eccentric guy from New Jersey who also cooked at the bistro (and who took the photographs in this book), suggested that we move to Portland. We visited PDX one weekend, found a really shitty house in the southeast, and moved the next week. Looking back, it's amazing how quickly it all happened.

I grew up in Napa—not the French Laundry, wine-guzzling, home-to-millionaires Napa—but blue-collar suburban California.

When I arrived in Portland, I noticed a few things (that are the city's calling card now): the jeans were tighter, rent was so affordable that young people not only owned homes but also owned businesses, and, most importantly, people knew how to eat. Through complete happenstance, the first job I landed was at Paley's Place, one of the first restaurants in Portland to focus on local products and farmers. Although I was thrilled, I didn't realize what a coup this was at the time. The food was *way* above my level of expertise. I was nervous before every shift, worried about my skill level and convinced that my *poseur-dom* would be revealed. But we rotated stations regularly, and I was so completely engaged that the nervousness would subside simply because I didn't have time to think about it. It was at Paley's that I learned the beauty of shellfish stock, how to work with bone marrow, how to clarify a consommé, and to how to slow down and just *make food well*.

Paley's was the cooking school I never finished.

Within two years I hit my stride, and I was so thankful to be left in charge when Vitaly Paley and the sous-chef, Bennie Bettinger, were out of the restaurant attending or cooking at events.

By this time it was 2003, and I was cooking alongside Jason Barwikowski (currently the chef at Woodsman Tavern), a talented friend with a quiet intensity. That year Jason and I went to a Christmas party where we met Tommy Habetz, a fellow cook who had just come to Portland after working under Mario Batali in New York. Tommy and Naomi Pomeroy (from Beast in Portland) were working for a now-defunct restaurant group and asked me to come on as sous-chef at their new project, Gotham Tavern. I remember that I was wearing a cream-colored leisure suit at the time; the fact that they still offered me the job should have been an ominous sign.

For many reasons (including, perhaps, that I was drinking a bottle of Pernod every night, thus being knighted "Pernod-chio" by my peers), Gotham failed. But it was while working at Gotham that I learned how to manage a kitchen, work the line, expedite two hundred covers per night, and run (and *not* run) a business.

After that, I wandered the PDX streets like a lost mutt, but Cathy Whims was kind enough to take me in at Nostrana, where I made pizza but mostly just licked my wounds from Gotham. One day I received a call from Paul Brady. Paul is truly a Portland character, a Mr. Fix-It, computer whiz, flamenco singer, and Burning Man regular. He had experienced a financial windfall and decided to sink the money into a small restaurant on East Burnside, a gritty strip across the river from downtown. At the time, the prostitutes and drug dealers working the neighborhood were less than subtle. Paul was also on the rebound, as the restaurant Paul acquired was more of a cook's fantasy wonderland than a real, operating business—there were KitchenAids in every color, each meal was made to order, all dairy came from the artisanal Norris Farms—you get the picture. Paul gave me three months to turn it around.

First, we needed a name. One day Tommy and I were hanging out at the new space, and we looked down at the cacophony of tattoos on my arm: a flock of birds, a gnarly shark, and the words *le pigeon*. The birds brought to mind a calming aviary vibe, which was somehow better than a bloody-toothed, poorly drawn shark. Tommy said, "Le Pigeon, that's it." And it was.

Paul then called his friend Ian Lynam, an amazing graphic designer, and begged him to help with a logo. Ian came through with the killer one you see on the cover of this book. For staff, my first call was to Erik Van Kley, who still hadn't found a home since Gotham; he joined as sous-chef. Another Gotham alum, Su Lien, came on next. The tone was set; it felt like

the band was back together, and this is when we really started writing hits. We broke even in two months and filled the restaurant almost nightly for the next year.

Which brings us back to Andy Fortgang: a straight-talking New Yorker who should have been a lawyer but was discovered by (one could also argue, *lost to*) Tom Colicchio. He did his time at Gramercy Tavern and then Craft. During our first phone call, I could already tell that Andy was dedicated to service, was adamant about balancing books and keeping order, and was all in all the front-of-the-house ninja we desperately needed. When Andy first started, I was utterly shocked by his professionalism. I constantly worried that he wouldn't find our place to be professional enough and would leave. The same was true with his wife, Lauren Fortgang, who was (and is) one of the best pastry chefs I've worked with (you can see her handywork for yourselves in the desserts chapter, where Lauren takes over the recipe controls).

Andy understands that you can maintain a relaxed vibe while still providing service at a high level, giving more to our guests without making a show of it. He also understands the importance of looking after our staff; within months of his arrival, he made sure we were providing health insurance to our employees. Although Andy's hand in Le Pigeon may not be obvious or exciting to outsiders, without him we would all be lost.

Andy has really enjoyed his transition from New York to Portland. He may be the only guy in Portland who packs his linen slacks away when Labor Day rolls around, but he is also oddly comfortable sitting around a

With the five-year anniversary of the restaurant behind us, we thought it would be a good time to look back, to get all nostalgic and shit about the early days . . .

dive bar drinking Miller High Life while wearing seersucker pants with his shirt tucked in.

And that reminds me . . . everyone at Le Pigeon has a nickname.

One day I was calling for a runner to bring food to a table, sternly saying, "Pick up, pick up, someone pick up, pickles, pickles." Instead of the runner, Andy walked by and picked up the food. "That's it," I said, "your nickname is Pickles." He glared at me, as only Andy can, and claimed that "Pickles" lacked gravitas. And so it became "Mr. Pickles." That's the name by which people both inside and outside LP know Andy: Mr. Pickles. A funny name for a straight guy—and that's why it works.

A lot of people thought Le Pigeon would fail. We were broke to start; Paul was even offering coupons in the phone book those first few weeks. We had unmatched china, the music was way too loud, there was a club upstairs (see "The Basement Tapes" on page 123), and we had zero credit with purveyors (see "Gabriel's Love Letter to Plymouth Valiants" on page 72). We were known as an offal den back then, but that wasn't the image we were *trying* for. Honest to god, we were pushing offal so hard partly because of inspiration from guys like Fergus Henderson, but mostly because those are the cheap bits, and cooking things that most people throw in the garbage was the easiest (and most creative) way to ensure we would have enough money to stay open the following week.

Still, those first three years were really a golden time at Le Pigeon. We were shooting from the hip with our wild finds and the hits were coming nonstop: Rabbit and Eel Terrine (page 110), Buffalo Sweetbreads (page 220), Duck Nuggets (page 92), Lamb Tongue Fries (page 45), Rabbit Spanakopita (page 116), and Foie Gras Profiteroles (page 316). Erik was constantly pushing me and coming up with Pigeon legends, such as Jacked Pork Chops (page 188) and the Lamb Belly BLT (page 244). It was during this period that LP went from the tiny underdog on a rough street in Portland to a nationally recognized restaurant.

When you own a restaurant and have the great fortune to work with someone like Erik, who is amazing both in and out of the kitchen, at some

point you end up with a metaphysical gun to your head: do you let him go, or do you build another place for him to do his thing? For me, the answer was clear. Our team was growing and becoming too big for the nest on East Burnside. In 2010, we built Little Bird right across the river from LP on 6th Avenue, and the "A" team shifted there. I brought in a new motley crew for LP, with big talent and fresh nicknames: Taffy, Fistopher, Chavez, and the rest. And although we flirt with the fantasy of opening a chicken shack or a tiny taco stand, I can tell you straight-faced that an empire we will never be.

As we write this book, it's six years after opening night, and Portland is now known for its restaurants as much as its "Put a bird on it" motto. LP has changed a bit, but really not much. We're still serving our cracked-out mountain food, but with a (slightly) refined edge (for example, Beef Cheeks Bourguignon, page 206, is still on the menu, but instead of heaped fried potatoes, it's served with a cocotte of gratin with a side of black garlic and carrot salad). The music is probably still too loud, there are still freaks in our back stairwells, and the communal table ensures you will wind up talking to the stranger beside you.

And although I still feel like the kid who started this place, the truth is that Andy and I both have kids of our own now. With the five-year anniversary of the restaurant behind us, we thought it would be a good time to look back, to get all nostalgic and shit about the early days, and to get these recipes down on paper before we forget them—a challenge for me because "winging it" isn't just a bad pigeon reference, it's actually how I come up with new dishes. Along with the recipes, we wanted to tell some fun stories and introduce a few of the interesting characters we've gotten to know over the years (lord knows we've had our fair share of those).

What you're holding in your hands is a tome of our "best-of's," a retrospective of Le Pigeon's hits. We hope you like it.

How to Use This Book

FROM ANDY: You will notice that some dishes in this book have beverage pairings (called "The Pigeon Pours"), and many others do not. We decided that rather than tell you what you should be drinking with each dish, we would highlight some pairings that we feel very strongly make eating the dish better. One of our golden rules in the resturant is that if the wine is good and the food is good, you are going to be okay! So follow your gut when pairing wine, or go to your local wine shop, tell them what you are having for dinner, and ask for a suggestion. Or call me at the restaurant and I'll give you a suggestion. I mean it.

FROM GABRIEL: The food world is a giant wave that all of us chefs are riding and trying to stay atop. Sometimes you are on the crest and sometimes you are swimming to catch up. I have spent almost my whole career behind the stove at 738 East Burnside, and I've grown and constantly evolved my style by learning from colleagues, from my employees, and from my travels. You might notice that the dishes in this book vary in technique, plating, and flavors. That is because I really wanted you to get a feel for what we were cooking at different times in the Pigeon's history. You can, for instance, make our Bone Marrow, Caramelized Onion Sandwich (page 233)—a simple, over-the-top indulgent, in-your-face dish that graced our early menus—or prepare a more refined Beef Carpaccio (page 227)

with soft-boiled eggs and trout roe. Two different dishes and two different approaches, but both delicious and served out of the same kitchen.

Seasoning a dish is like constructing a building: you want to start from the ground floor and work your way up. By seasoning the ingredients in increments throughout the process (rather than seasoning the entire dish only at the end), you build depth and give the end result a multidimensional flavor. Making risotto is a great example of how this works. You season the onions, then season the rice, and then season it again after the addition of the wine. You're probably going to add Parmesan (another form of seasoning) too, so when you give it a final taste, it won't need much else.

The process for balancing acidity is similar. Sometimes I'll use multiple vinegars and a vinaigrette in a dish, and other times I reduce a single vinegar down to a syrup and finish the dish with a final hit of the liquid. Herbs are another instance where you can build the flavor with multiple layers. I will sometimes use the same herb in fresh and dried forms in the same recipe. Or, if using tarragon, for example, I might include tarragon vinegar to add a third layer.

The number one thing to remember when using this book, or cooking anything, is to have fun. If things get a little stressful, take a deep breath and have a nice sip of the cooking wine that is sitting on the counter. I can tell you that's what I'm doing when I'm in the kitchen.

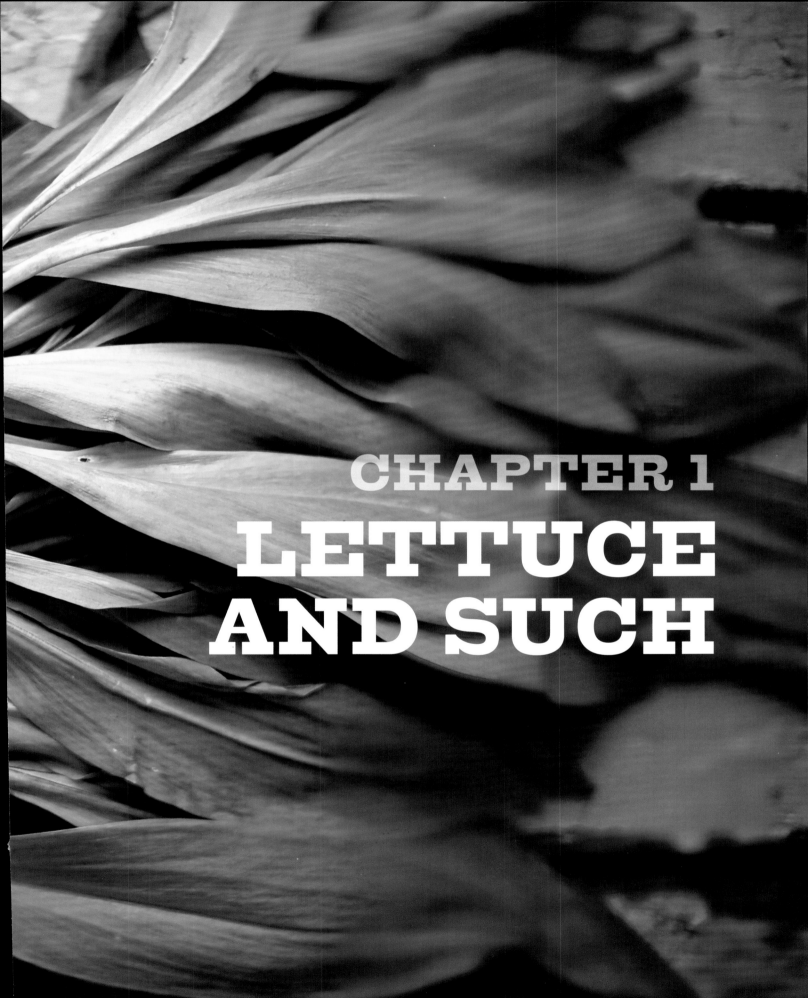

CHAPTER 1
LETTUCE AND SUCH

The idea of cooking a piece of celery root on the grill and brushing it with a Beaujolais BBQ sauce seemed *very* Pigeon, and the result didn't disappoint. The meaty celery root, served hot with one of our favorite cheeses melting over the top, is great on its own; add some fresh mâche leaves and sweet currant vinaigrette to round it out and you have our favorite fall salad.

Note: You can make the sauce up to 2 weeks in advance and the vinaigrette up to 1 week. Store both in airtight containers in the refrigerator. {SERVES 4}

BBQ CELERY ROOT, MÂCHE, DULCE DE BOURGOGNE

BBQ Sauce
1 bottle (750 ml) Beaujolais
½ cup (125 ml) LP Ketchup (page 324) or any ketchup
½ cup (125 ml) red wine vinegar
¼ cup (60 ml) honey
1 teaspoon paprika
1 teaspoon freshly ground black pepper

Currant Vinaigrette
½ cup (125 ml) Beaujolais (reserved from making the BBQ sauce)
2 tablespoons dried currants
¼ cup (60 ml) vermouth vinegar or red wine vinegar
1 tablespoon minced shallot
½ cup (125 ml) extra-virgin olive oil
Kosher salt and freshly ground black pepper

4 slices peeled celery root, each about ¼ inch (6 mm) thick
Extra-virgin olive oil for brushing
Kosher salt and freshly ground black pepper
4 (1-ounce/30g) pieces Dulce de Bourgogne or other triple cream cheese, at room temperature
2 large handfuls of mâche

1. To make the BBQ sauce, in a small saucepan over medium heat, combine all but ½ cup (125 ml) of the Beaujolais, the ketchup, red wine vinegar, honey, paprika, and pepper. Cook slowly, stirring occasionally, until the sauce is sweet and thickened, about 15 minutes. Remove the sauce from the heat, let it come to room temperature, and set aside until you're ready to use it.

2. To make the currant vinaigrette, in a small saucepan over medium heat, warm the reserved Beaujolais with the currants. Simmer until the currants are plump and all of the liquid has evaporated, about 5 minutes. Remove from the heat and stir in the vinegar and shallot. Let stand for 5 minutes so the flavors mingle. Stir in the oil and season with salt and pepper.

3. Preheat a gas grill or prepare a charcoal grill for cooking over medium heat. Generously brush the celery root slices with olive oil and season with salt and pepper. Grill until just cooked through, about 5 minutes on each side, occasionally brushing the slices with the BBQ sauce: think BBQ chicken. You want to cook the celery root but not kill it. There should be just a touch of resistence when pierced with a fork. If you are cooking over open coals, make sure to place the celery root off to the side or on a spot that is not too hot, as it can burn.

4. Once the celery root is cooked through, transfer to plates and immediately top each slice with a piece of the cheese. While the cheese is melting, toss the mâche with the currant vinaigrette and place a nice handful of mâche next to the celery root. There will be some currants left in the bowl. Scoop them up, sprinkle them around the plate to garnish, and serve.

A lot of people soak radicchio in salted or ice water to remove the bitterness, but we would rather complement the bitterness than contort it. Enter BCD. Our *titular* (see sidebar below) homemade blue cheese dressing was originally developed for The Le Pigeon Burger (page 234), but it has so many other applications, including this one right here. {SERVES 4}

RADICCHIO, PEARS, HAZELNUTS, BLUE CHEESE DRESSING

1 head radicchio, cored and cut into thick strips

½ cup (75 g) coarsely chopped toasted hazelnuts

1 pear, peeled, cored, and cut into strips ⅛ inch (3 mm) thick

1 tablespoon grappa

A squeeze of fresh lemon juice

Kosher salt

½ cup (125 ml) Blue Cheese Dressing (page 321)

In a large bowl, combine the radicchio, hazelnuts, pear, and grappa. Add the lemon juice and season with salt. Add the dressing, toss well to combine, and serve.

MAKE IT TITULAR

Titular, according to *Merriam-Webster*: "Having the title and usually the honors belonging to an office or dignity without the duties, functions, or responsibilities."

Titular, according to Le Pigeon: Better than good. *Perfect*. As in, "Make it titular."

Yes, I'm aware that our use of the word *titular* is incorrect. The Upright Citizens Brigade performs a skit where they use the word *titular* incorrectly, over and over again. It's stupid funny. After my fellow chef Jason Barwikowski and I saw the skit, we also started using the word incorrectly, nonstop, while working at Paley's Place. Once we started we couldn't stop, and it went from dumb to dumber. If you eat at Le Pigeon, you're bound to hear the word *titular* at least once.

We admit it: when most people think of Le Pigeon, "salad" isn't the first image they conjure up. That's not why the lines form outside our modest restaurant. That's not the reason that eyes light up at our menu. But we would like to think it could be. Beautiful gems of vegetables and bright salads should be more integral to a meal, than, say, Zantac is. And so here we have a beautiful butter lettuce salad with a dressing that works with anything green. And though kale chips do nothing for Gabriel, ramps? Yes. The leaves get nice and crispy, and the bottom roasts just perfectly. This is one of the few times when a garnish was the catalyst for a dish. {SERVES 4}

BUTTER LETTUCE, PICKLED GARLIC, RAMPS

Pickled Garlic Dressing
¼ cup (60 ml) Pickled Garlic
    (page 325)
¼ cup (60 ml) champagne vinegar
2 egg yolks
1 tablespoon chopped fresh tarragon
¼ teaspoon kosher salt
A dash of espelette pepper
1 cup (250 ml) neutral oil

12 ramps
1 teaspoon extra-virgin olive oil
Kosher salt
2 heads butter lettuce, leaves
    separated
40 fresh tarragon leaves

1.   To make the pickled garlic dressing, add the garlic, vinegar, egg yolks, tarragon, salt, and pepper to a blender. Set the blender to puree and, with the blender running, add the oil in a thin, steady stream to create an emulsion. When the dressing is smooth, turn off the blender and set the dressing aside.

2.   Preheat the oven to 425°F (220°C). In a bowl, toss the ramps with the olive oil and a sprinkling of salt. Spread the ramps evenly on a baking sheet and roast for 10 to 12 minutes, turning the ramps over after about 3 minutes. The green parts should be crispy, similar to a kale chip, and the bottoms of the ramps should be cooked through.

3.   Toss the butter lettuce with the dressing and divide among four plates. Sprinkle the tarragon leaves over the salads, top with the crispy ramps, and serve.

 THE PIGEON POUR: Salads can be tricky to pair with wine. I look for wines with grassy or herbaceous flavors. Loire Valley sauvignon blanc, grüner veltliner, and some lighter rosés are good starting points. With this salad, try a Pouilly-Fumé, Sancerre's funky cousin. It's grassy and minerally, with bright, tart fruit to complement the sweet and savory character of the pickled garlic and ramps.

Here we combine fennel pollen, a beautiful aromatic that you can find in most specialty food stores, and licorice root powder, another aromatic that seems to be put on this earth to pair with fennel. A splash of Pernod in the dressing adds to the fresh lemon flavor. And because we don't cook out the alcohol, you get the full effect of the liqueur. In the lemon confit preparation, we use a simple syrup containing Pernod, giving you another taste of the same spirit.

{SERVES 4}

BUTTER LETTUCE, LEMON CONFIT, GRAPES, SPICED BRIOCHE

Pernod Dressing
2 egg yolks
Juice of 2 lemons
2 tablespoons Pernod
1 teaspoon fennel pollen
¼ teaspoon licorice root powder
¾ cup (180 ml) neutral oil
Kosher salt

3 lemons
½ cup (125 ml) Pernod
¼ cup (60 g) sugar
2 slices brioche, torn into small pieces
1 tablespoon unsalted butter
¼ teaspoon fennel pollen
¼ teaspoon licorice root powder
¼ teaspoon kosher salt
3 heads butter (or Bibb or Boston) lettuce, leaves separated
½ cup (100 g) red seedless grapes, halved

1. To make the dressing, add the egg yolks, lemon juice, Pernod, fennel pollen, and licorice root powder to a blender. Set the blender to puree, and with the blender running, add the oil in a thin, steady stream to create an emulsion. When the dressing is smooth, turn off the blender and add salt to taste. Set the dressing aside.

2. Supreme 2 of the lemons by peeling them with a knife and cutting along the membrane to separate each segment. Place the segments into a bowl.

3. In a small saucepan over medium heat, combine the Pernod and sugar. Warm the mixture until the sugar is dissolved and the liquid is *just* about to come to a boil. Pour the Pernod syrup over the lemon segments in the bowl and set aside.

4. Preheat the oven to 350°F (180°C). Put the brioche pieces in a food processor and pulse until it forms fine crumbs, about the size of sand.

5. In a medium saucepan, melt the butter with the fennel pollen, licorice root powder, and salt. Toss the brioche crumbs in the melted butter to coat, and then spread the brioche on a baking sheet. Bake in the oven until golden brown, about 5 minutes.

6. In a large bowl, toss the butter lettuce with the dressing and grapes. Taste and adjust the acidity and salt if necessary.

7. To form the lettuce before you serve it, collect a quarter of the leaves in your hand, arranging them to re-create the shape of a head of lettuce. Simple but impressive. Repeat with the remaining lettuce and place one "head" of lettuce on each of four plates. Divide the lemon segments among the plates and drizzle with some of the Pernod syrup, sneaking a couple drips for yourself. Sprinkle with brioche crumbs and serve.

This is a classic example of working with what's on the shelves, on the fly. When local critic and author Karen Brooks came to the restaurant to procure a recipe for inclusion in her book about the Portland food scene called *The Mighty Gastropolis*, Gabriel (surprise!) had forgotten she was coming and had nothing prepared. Luckily, he's most comfortable when he's cooking on the fly. Potatoes, six squabs (including innards), and the usual condiments later, and there it was: a very dirty potato salad. We've modified this recipe to include chicken livers for more simplicity and less squab decapitation (but they're still optional). {SERVES 6}

DIRTY POTATO SALAD

1½ pounds (680 g) small Yukon gold potatoes
1 (4-pound/1.8 kg) box rock salt
1 tablespoon red pepper flakes
5 sprigs tarragon
5 sprigs thyme
Peel of 1 orange, cut into strips
4 green onions, thinly sliced
2 celery stalks, thinly sliced
2 red jalapeños, seeded and thinly sliced
½ cup (125 ml) mayonnaise
2 teaspoons spicy mustard
1 teaspoon Sriracha hot sauce
Kosher salt
Juice of 1 lemon
¼ cup (60 ml) BBQ Sauce (page 12)
½ cup (113 g) chicken livers (optional)
1 tablespoon olive oil (optional)
1 teaspoon balsamic vinegar (optional)

1. Preheat the oven to 400°F (200°C). Place the potatoes in a large roasting pan and cover them with all of the rock salt, the red pepper flakes, tarragon, thyme, and orange peel. Cover with aluminum foil and roast until the potatoes are tender, about 45 minutes. Remove from oven and let cool.

2. When the potatoes are still warm but cool enough to handle, remove each potato from the roasting pan, brushing off the salt and discarding the orange and herbs. Save the rock salt for another use.

3. On a cutting board, use your palm to gently smash the potatoes. They will crumble into pieces of different size and look quite rustic. In a bowl, combine the potatoes, green onions, celery, and jalapeños. Stir in the mayonnaise, mustard, Sriracha, 1 teaspoon of salt, the lemon juice, and the BBQ sauce.

4. Season the livers well with salt. In a small sauté pan, heat the olive oil over high heat and add the livers. Sauté until medium rare, about 1 minute on each side. Remove the livers from the pan and mince with a knife. In a small bowl, toss the chopped livers with the balsamic and then fold the livers into the salad. Divide the salad among six plates and serve. Now it's dirty.

If we don't have time to go to Gino's for the best Caesar in Portland (or anywhere, really*), this is the Caesar salad I make for my family.

{SERVES 4}

LE PIGEON CAESAR

Dressing
4 egg yolks
4 cloves garlic
3 anchovy fillets
½ cup (40 g) grated Parmesan
¼ cup (60 ml) freshly squeezed
    lemon juice
2 teaspoons Dijon mustard
1 teaspoon white wine vinegar
½ teaspoon freshly ground black
    pepper
A dash of Tabasco
¾ cup (180 ml) neutral oil

Croutons
2 cups cubed day-old baguette
¼ cup (60 ml) extra-virgin olive oil
2 cloves garlic, finely minced

2 hearts of romaine, trimmed
Parmesan shavings to finish
Freshly ground black pepper

1.   To make the dressing, add the egg yolks, garlic, anchovy fillets, Parmesan, lemon juice, mustard, vinegar, pepper, and Tabasco to a food processor. Set to puree and, with the motor running, add the oil in a thin, steady stream to create an emulsion. When the dressing is smooth, turn off the machine and set the dressing aside.

2.   To make the croutons, in a bowl, toss together the bread, olive oil, and garlic and combine well. In a large sauté pan over medium-high heat, toast the bread until golden brown. (We do it like this rather than in the oven so that the bread turns out crispy outside but remains soft inside.)

3.   Place the whole romaine hearts in a bowl, add the dressing, and toss with tongs to combine. Add the croutons and a few shavings of Parmesan. Using the largest pepper grinder you can find (for effect only), season well with pepper and serve.

* Trust me, Gino's has the most killer Caesar anywhere. As you are eating your intensely garlicky salad, there is a waiter peeling a huge pile of garlic on the bar right next to you. And the people at the table beside you are eating a fragrant garlicky aioli with cod. Then you see the woman across the room wearing garlic earrings. Not really, but you get the idea.

These sweet and pulpy ripe tomatoes dressed with a simple black pepper vinaigrette are an easy three-pointer if you need a quick dish for a summer barbecue or picnic. We like to serve this alongside the Simple Roast Pork Loin (page 194) in summer, when all we want to do is cook in the backyard. There are so many heirlooms to choose from now, but we prefer Green Zebra and Brandywine. {SERVES 4}

TOMATOES, PLUMS, WATERCRESS

1 pound (450 g) ripe heirloom
    tomatoes
1 pound (450 g) ripe plums
¼ cup (60 ml) extra-virgin olive oil
Juice of 2 lemons
1 teaspoon minced fresh tarragon
1 teaspoon freshly ground black
    pepper
2 cups (60 g) watercress leaves,
    wild if possible
Maldon flake salt

1. Cut both the tomatoes and plums into bite-sized wedges. In a large bowl, combine the tomatoes and plums with the olive oil, lemon juice, tarragon, and pepper and toss.

2. Immediately before serving, add the watercress leaves to the bowl and toss gently to coat. Spread the salad on a nice serving platter and sprinkle with a generous amount of Maldon salt before serving.

In this recipe, hearts of romaine are grilled to a nice char on one side, giving you a hot-and-cold effect on the plate. We use a couple of different techniques with lemon here: *roasting*, for a bright vinaigrette to drizzle on the plate, and *preserving*, to brighten a creamy dressing. This salad is all about depth of flavor and contrast: Hot versus cold. Preserved versus roasted. Acidic versus creamy. {SERVES 4}

GRILLED ROMAINE, PRESERVED LEMONS

Preserved Lemon Dressing

3 egg yolks
2 cloves garlic, minced
2 white anchovies (boquerones)
¼ cup (20 g) grated Parmesan
2 tablespoons minced Preserved Lemons (page 326)
2 tablespoons freshly squeezed lemon juice
½ teaspoon freshly ground white pepper
½ teaspoon kosher salt
¾ cup (180 ml) extra-virgin olive oil

Honey Lemon Vinny

4 lemons, halved
4 sprigs thyme
3 cloves garlic
2 shallots, sliced ¼ inch (6 mm) thick
2 tablespoons water
1 tablespoon freshly ground black pepper
1 teaspoon kosher salt
½ teaspoon red pepper flakes
¼ cup (60 ml) honey
½ cup (125 ml) olive oil

2 hearts of romaine, trimmed
3 tablespoons olive oil, plus more for brushing
Kosher salt and freshly ground black pepper
Juice of ½ lemon
2 teaspoons Seasoned Bread Crumbs (page 327)
½ cup (30 g) Parmesan shavings

1. To make the dressing, add the egg yolks, garlic, anchovies, Parmesan, preserved lemon, lemon juice, white pepper, and salt to a food processor. Set to puree and, with the motor running, add the oil in a thin, steady stream to create an emulsion. It should be the consistency of a loose aioli, very creamy. When the dressing is smooth, turn off the machine and set the dressing aside. Store leftovers in the refrigerator for up to 1 week.

2. Preheat the oven to 375°F (190°C).

3. To make the honey lemon vinny, in a Dutch oven, toss together the lemons, thyme, garlic, shallots, water, black pepper, salt, and red pepper flakes. Roast in the oven, uncovered, until the lemons are browned, about 45 minutes. Remove from the oven and, using a ladle, push the mixture through a chinois, trying to extract as much liquid as you can. Let the liquid cool to room temperature.

4. Add the cooled liquid and honey to a blender or food processor. Set to puree and, with the motor running, add the oil in a thin, steady stream to create an emulsion. You want a deep lemon flavor, slightly sweet. Turn off the machine and set aside.

5. Preheat a gas grill or prepare a charcoal grill for cooking over very high heat. Remove a few outer leaves from the romaine hearts and slice them thinly crosswise, into a chiffonade. You should have about 1 cup (40 g). Cut the romaine hearts in half, brush them with oil, and season with salt and pepper. Grill the romaine, cut side down, until the lettuce has grill marks and the edges look nice and charred, about 3 minutes.

6. Toss the sliced romaine with the lemon juice and 3 tablespoons of olive oil. Season with salt.

7. In the center of a plate, spoon a nice circle of the preserved lemon dressing. Top with the sliced romaine. Toss the grilled romaine hearts in a bowl with the remaining preserved lemon dressing and place, grilled side up, on top of the sliced romaine. Drizzle the salad with the honey lemon vinny and sprinkle with bread crumbs. Top with shaved Parmesan and serve.

What says Portland more than salmon and timber? Here in the Pacific Northwest cedar-planked salmon is what, say, lobster rolls are to Maine. The smell of salmon being cooked on fresh cedar wafts throughout backyards all over Stumptown all summer long.

For a light option on our menu, we cook marinated zucchini on cedar shingles, which you can buy at almost any cookware store or lumberyard (in which case make sure that the wood is untreated). Paired with sweet balsamic vinegar and spicy toasted almonds, this is a vegetarian's BBQ dream.

Note: Use a cedar plank about 5 by 10 inches (13 by 25 cm). Do not soak the plank before using; simply rub it down with a couple tablespoons of olive oil. {SERVES 4}

CEDAR-PLANKED ZUCCHINI, CHÈVRE, ALMONDS

¼ cup (30 g) blanched slivered almonds
1 tablespoon unsalted butter, melted
¼ teaspoon espelette pepper
2 zucchini, each 8 ounces (225 g), ends trimmed and halved lengthwise
2 tablespoons extra-virgin olive oil
4 cloves garlic, minced
½ teaspoon minced fresh thyme
Kosher salt
½ cup (125 ml) Goat Cheese Vinny (page 323)
2 tablespoons Herb Pistou (page 324)
Juice of 1 lemon
Maldon flake salt
1 cup (40 g) frisée
¼ cup (10 g) fresh flat-leaf parsley
12 thin rings red onion
2 tablespoons aged balsamic vinegar (the quality matters here; use aged if you're able to)

1. Preheat the oven to 350°F (180°C). Toss the almonds with the butter and espelette pepper. Spread evenly on a baking sheet and toast until lightly browned, about 8 minutes. Remove from the oven and let cool. The almonds will keep, covered, for about 4 days, but definitely do not refrigerate them, or they will become chewy.

2. Increase the oven temperature to 450°F (230°C). Place the oiled cedar plank on a baking sheet and preheat in the oven for 7 or 8 minutes to get that cedar aroma going. (Turn on your kitchen fan, as there will be some smoke. You want this; it smells great.)

3. While the shingle is warming, toss the zucchini with the olive oil, garlic, and thyme. Season with salt. Place the zucchini cut side down on the shingle and bake until cooked through but still slightly firm to the touch, 8 to 10 minutes. Remove from the oven and set aside.

4. Spoon about a tablespoon of the goat cheese vinny on each of four plates. Place a piece of zucchini, cut side up, on top of the vinny. Drizzle the zucchini with the pistou and lemon juice. Sprinkle with the Maldon salt. In a bowl, toss the frisée with the toasted almonds, parsley, red onion, and the remaining goat cheese vinny. Season with kosher salt. Top the zucchini slices with the salad, drizzle each plate lightly with the balsamic vinegar, and serve.

We love aged Gouda. Just ask Steve Jones, owner of Portland's best cheese shop, The Cheese Bar (see page 254). When Gouda is aged just past five years, it crystallizes, and you wind up with little ice-creamy shards breaking in your mouth.

This dressing is like our blue cheese dressing (BCD; page 321), but with Gouda, so we call it GCD. You want to flex your cheese muscles with this salad, so use a decent aged Gouda if you're going to make this. This isn't a fussy salad, and we like to serve it on a platter, family style, so everyone can serve themselves a wedge or two. The dressing will last a week in the fridge. {SERVES 4}

LITTLE GEM LETTUCE, GOUDA CHEESE DRESSING

GCD
4 ounces (125 g) aged Gouda
1 cup (250 ml) sour cream
¼ cup (60 ml) Moscatel vinegar
¼ cup (60 ml) buttermilk
½ teaspoon freshly ground black pepper
Kosher salt
A squeeze of fresh lemon juice

½ cup (125 ml) Moscatel vinegar
¼ cup (60 ml) sweet white wine, such as riesling
½ cup (65 g) dried currants
4 heads Little Gem lettuce, each halved and cored

1.   To make the dressing, use a vegetable peeler to remove about 16 shavings of Gouda and set aside for garnish. Grate the remaining Gouda and add it along with the sour cream, vinegar, buttermilk, and pepper to a blender or food processor. Puree until it forms a pourable consistency. The dressing is not going to be perfectly smooth. Taste and add salt and lemon juice to taste.

2.   In a small saucepan over medium heat, combine the vinegar, riesling, and currants and heat until the currants have plumped and the liquid has evaporated, 8 to 10 minutes. Essentially you're "undrying" the dried currants here.

3.   Reserve a few tablespoons of the GCD for drizzling. In a large bowl, toss the lettuce with the remaining dressing. Pile the salad on a big platter and sprinkle with the currants and the Gouda shavings. Drizzle the reserved dressing on top and serve.

 THE PIGEON POUR: With this salad, I like a local rosé. Two that work well are those by Matello and Division Winemaking Company. Both are made entirely from pinot noir and are super vibrant, but with a little roundness on the tongue. Salads that have a dried fruit component can really sing with rosés.

We like to cure our own meats when we can, but certain things are above our skill level when it comes to charcuterie, and, simply put, there are a host of Portlanders who can do it better. The guy on the top of that list is Eli Cairo at Olympic Provisions. Eli makes a killer mortadella and, since one of their locations is just a few blocks from the restaurant, it's a total no-brainer that we bring it into LP.

Based in a historic cereal mill, Olympic Provisions (www.olympic provisions.com) is the kind of place where the menu (especially the charcuterie) is exactly what you feel like eating, the light through the massive widows shines in just right, and the wine list is full of gems. In the few years that they have been in operation, they've become one of the nation's leading producers of salumi, and you can now find their products in many specialty stores and online. {SERVES 4}

MORTADELLA, MUSTARD GREENS, SWISS CHEESE

Croutons
1 cup very thin slices day-old baguette
2 tablespoons extra-virgin olive oil
2 tablespoons grated Parmesan
¼ teaspoon paprika
¼ teaspoon garlic powder
¼ teaspoon onion powder

Toasted Pistachios
2 tablespoons sugar
½ cup (60 g) shelled roasted pistachios
1 clove garlic, minced
1 teaspoon Moscatel vinegar
1 teaspoon Maldon flake salt

1. To make the croutons, preheat the oven to 350°F (180°C). Toss together the baguette slices, olive oil, Parmesan, paprika, garlic powder, and onion powder. Spread out the slices evenly on a baking sheet and bake until browned, about 5 minutes. Remove from the oven and set aside.

2. To make the toasted pistachios, turn the oven up to 400°F (200°C) and line a baking sheet with a silicone baking mat. In a small, heavy saucepan over medium heat, heat the sugar until it begins to caramelize and turn a nice amber color, 2 or 3 minutes. Add the pistachios, garlic, and vinegar and continue to cook for 1 minute more, stirring constantly.

3. Spread the pistachios on the prepared baking sheet and toast in the oven for 5 minutes. Remove from the oven and sprinkle with the Maldon salt. When cool, coarsely chop with a knife. Set aside.

Dressing

2 tablespoons minced shallot

3 tablespoons white wine vinegar

3 tablespoons Dijon mustard

1 egg yolk

1 cup (250 ml) neutral oil

1 tablespoon minced fresh oregano

Kosher salt

12 slices mortadella

1 tablespoon olive oil

A squeeze of fresh lemon juice

Kosher salt and freshly ground
    black pepper

Maldon flake salt

4 cups (120 g) coarsely chopped
    heirloom mustard greens

½ cup (60 g) julienned good-quality
    Swiss cheese

¼ cup (25 g) sliced red onion

¼ cup (30 g) thinly sliced prunes
    (dried plums)

4.   To make the dressing, in a bowl, combine the shallot and vinegar; let sit for 5 minutes. Add the Dijon mustard and egg yolk and, using a whisk, whisk in the oil in a thin, steady stream to create an emulsion. Stir in the oregano, season with salt to taste, and set aside.

5.   In a bowl, toss the mortadella with the olive oil and lemon juice; add kosher salt and pepper to taste. Arrange the mortadella on one side of a serving platter and sprinkle with Maldon salt. In a bowl, toss together the mustard greens, Swiss cheese, red onions, prunes, toasted pistachios, and croutons with the dressing. Season with kosher salt and pepper to taste and arrange the salad on the other side of the platter to serve.

CHAPTER 2
TONGUE

Lamb's tongue can be hard to come by, so if you are planning on making this dish you should give your butcher some lead time. Here in Oregon we are lucky enough to have lamb farmers who frequent the farmers' markets. If at all possible, buddy up with a farmer and sweet talk him or her into selling you the tongue. If not, try www.uswellnessmeats.com. They stock frozen lamb's tongues and will ship them to you directly.

Note: Lamb's tongue usually comes with a little bone attached to the bottom; ask your butcher to remove it. {SERVES 4}

GRILLED LAMB'S TONGUE, CREAMED PEAS, MORELS

Lamb's Tongue

4 lamb's tongues
1 cup (250 ml) white wine
½ yellow onion, thinly sliced
6 cloves garlic, crushed
4 bay leaves
1 bunch thyme
2 tablespoons kosher salt
1 teaspoon ground mace
1 teaspoon truffle oil
A squeeze of fresh lemon juice

Sauce

1 tablespoon truffle butter
½ red onion, diced
¾ cup (180 ml) braising liquid (reserved from making the Lamb's Tongue)
½ cup (125 ml) LP Ketchup (page 324) or purchased ketchup
⅓ cup (75 g) firmly packed brown sugar
⅓ cup (80 ml) balsamic vinegar
½ teaspoon Tabasco
¼ teaspoon truffle oil

Morels

4 ounces (125 g) morel mushrooms (about 2 cups)
1 tablespoon unsalted butter, melted
1 shallot, thinly sliced
3 cloves garlic, thinly sliced
1 tablespoon aged balsamic vinegar
¼ teaspoon truffle oil
Kosher salt

1. To make the tongues, preheat the oven to 350°F (180°C). In a Dutch oven, combine the lamb's tongues, white wine, onion, garlic, bay leaves, thyme, salt, mace, and truffle oil. Braise in the oven until fork-tender, about 3 hours. When it is done it will look almost like a stock with some tongues swimming in it and smell gamy and earthy from the truffle oil. Let cool slightly in the braising liquid, about 20 minutes, then remove the tongues and set aside.

2. When the tongues are cool enough to handle, peel off the outer layer (see sidebar on page 34). Split the tongues lengthwise and set aside. Strain the braising liquid, discarding the solids and reserving the liquid for the sauce.

3. To make the sauce, in a small saucepan over medium heat, melt the truffle butter. Add the onion and sauté until slightly translucent, about 4 minutes. Add the reserved braising liquid, the ketchup, brown sugar, balsamic vinegar, Tabasco, and truffle oil. Continue to cook, stirring occasionally, until it has the consistency of barbecue sauce, about 30 minutes. Remove from heat and set aside.

4. To make the morels, preheat the oven to 450°F (230°C). In a bowl, toss the mushrooms with the melted butter, shallot, garlic, aged balsamic vinegar, and truffle oil. Add a dash of salt. Spread the mushroom mixture out on a baking sheet and roast in the oven until the edges of the mushrooms are slightly crisp, 12 to 15 minutes. Set aside and keep warm.

5. To make the creamed peas, prepare an ice water bath and set it aside. Bring a large pot of salted water to a rolling boil over high heat. Add the peas and cook until soft but not mushy, about 90 seconds (remove one pea

{Continued}

Creamed Peas

Kosher salt
1 cup (155 g) green peas
2 tablespoons truffle butter
¼ cup (60 ml) crème fraîche
1 tablespoon chopped chives
A squeeze of fresh lemon juice

Semolina Onion Rings (page 327)

and taste; if it's not ready, cook for 30 seconds more). Using a slotted spoon, transfer the peas from the pot to the ice water bath to chill for 5 minutes. Drain the peas and pat dry. In a small sauté pan over medium heat, warm the truffle butter. Add the peas and cook for 1 minute, using the back of a fork to coarsely smash the peas; they should look rough and rustic. Add the crème fraîche and cook for 2 minutes more; it should look like creamed spinach. Stir in the chives and lemon juice and adjust the salt; remove from the heat.

6.   Preheat a gas grill or prepare a charcoal grill for cooking over very high heat. When the grill is super-hot, toss the tongue pieces in ½ cup (125 ml) of the sauce and place the tongues on the grill cut side down. Grill for about 1 minute. Turn and continue cooking on the second side for 1 minute more. You're not trying to cook the tongues, just caramelize them on the grill. Once your tongues are *titular* (see sidebar on page 14), remove them from the heat and give them a good squeeze of lemon juice.

7.   Spoon a mound of creamed peas onto each of four plates. Top peas with a few slices of grilled tongue. Arrange the morels in a nice pile next to tongue, top with the onion rings, and serve.

THE PIGEON POUR: Loire Valley Cabernet Franc gets the love at Le Pigeon. And this dish especially calls for it, with the sweet peas, truffly earthy goodness, and the char of the grill on the tongue. There are a few appellations for Cab Franc in the Loire, but for this dish, we look to a Bourgueil, as it tends to be the earthier and gamier of Loire Valley Cab Francs. Producers to look for are Domaine de la Butte, Domaine du Mortier, or Catherine and Pierre Breton.

**HOW TO PEEL
A TONGUE**

Using a paring knife, start at the bottom of the tongue and remove the outer layer in strips; it should be about the same thickness as chicken skin. If the tongue is still warm, it should peel right off. If you let the tongue cool completely, it will be nearly impossible to peel, but you can rewarm it in cooking liquid and then peel it.

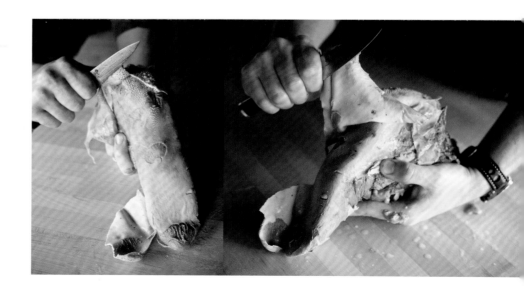

This dish first hit the menu in 2009 when we were having fun twisting American classics—like beef stroganoff, mac and cheese, broccoli with cheese sauce, and corn bread—by reworking them with offal. If you're buying elk, you might as well request the tongue and make this hearty Oregonian fall dish. You can always request just the tongue, too. Elk is the true test of this recipe, but if you really cannot find it, then substituting beef is okay.

Note: The tongue has to braise for 3 to 3½ hours for this dish. {SERVES 4}

ELK TONGUE STROGANOFF

1 elk tongue, about 1 pound (450 g)
2 cups (500 ml) red wine
½ yellow onion, sliced
10 black peppercorns
2 bay leaves
2 juniper berries, crushed
2 tablespoons red wine vinegar
1 tablespoon kosher salt
2 teaspoons sugar
¼ teaspoon red pepper flakes
2 tablespoons unsalted butter
Pretzel Spaetzle (page 183), with the
    baking powder omitted
1 cup (70 g) pearl onions (preferably
    red), blanched, peeled, and halved
¾ cup (180 ml) crème fraîche
2 tablespoons prepared horseradish
1 tablespoon chopped fresh flat-leaf
    parsley
Kosher salt

1. Preheat the oven to 350°F (180°C).

2. Place the tongue, red wine, onion, peppercorns, bay leaves, juniper berries, red wine vinegar, salt, sugar, and red pepper flakes in a Dutch oven and cover. Braise in the oven until the tongue is easily pierced with a fork, 3 to 3½ hours.

3. Remove the tongue and peel while still warm (see sidebar on page 34). Cut into ¼-inch (6mm) slices and set aside. Strain the braising liquid, discard the solids, and put the liquid in a small saucepan over medium heat. Cook until the liquid is reduced and thickened so that it coats the back of a spoon, about 15 minutes.

4. While the sauce is reducing, in a heavy sauté pan over medium heat, melt the butter. When it begins to bubble, add the spaetzle and cook, flipping occasionally, until nicely browned, about 3 minutes. Add the tongue and the pearl onions and cook about a minute longer. Add the crème fraîche and cook to reduce to a nice creamy consistency, about 2 minutes; you want it just a little runny. Add the horseradish and parsley. Toss to combine, season with salt, and serve family-style from the Dutch oven with the sauce drizzled over the top.

By no means are we the first restaurant to come up with corned beef tongue, but corned beef tongue Reuben? Maybe.

Normally, we would have brined the tongue anywhere from 5 to 12 days, but we were so itching to get this on the menu the next day that we slowly poached the tongue in the brine instead. And what do you know? It yielded perfect flavor and texture—a rare instance where taking the shortcut paid off. Note that you can prep the cabbage balls and dressing the day before, which will cut this recipe from about a 3½-hour endeavor to 2 hours. {SERVES 4}

BEEF TONGUE REUBEN

Tongue
1 pound (450 g) beef tongue
1 head garlic, halved
2 quarts (2 l) water
¾ cup (105 g) kosher salt
2 tablespoons sugar
1½ tablespoons pickling spice
1 teaspoon pink curing salt
Neutral oil for frying
1 egg
2 tablespoons water
Crumbs from 1 slice rye bread

Cabbage Balls
1 head savoy cabbage
2 tablespoons unsalted butter
½ yellow onion, thinly sliced
2 juniper berries, crushed
1 (12-ounce/375ml) bottle ale
4 slices of rye bread, cubed
½ cup (60 g) grated Swiss cheese
½ teaspoon ground caraway seed
2 eggs
½ cup (125 ml) heavy cream
Kosher salt and freshly ground
    black pepper

Slaw
½ cup (75 g) shredded red cabbage
A couple sprigs of curly parsley
A squeeze of fresh lemon juice
1 tablespoon good-quality olive oil
Kosher salt

Titular Island Dressing (page 329)

1. To make the tongue, in a large pot or Dutch oven over high heat, combine the beef tongue, garlic, water, salt, sugar, pickling spice, and curing salt. Bring to a boil, then reduce the heat to a simmer and cover. Simmer until the tongue is fork-tender, 3 to 3½ hours.

2. Scoop the tongue out of the braising liquid with a slotted spoon and discard the liquid. When cool enough to handle, peel off the outer layer of tongue (see sidebar on page 34); it will feel a bit like peeling the plastic off a photo album page. Chill the tongue for 1 hour. When the tongue is cool, cut into 1½-inch-thick (4cm) pieces and set aside.

3. To make the cabbage balls, remove 4 nice outer leaves from the savoy cabbage and set aside; core and thinly slice the inner leaves. In a sauté pan over medium heat, melt the butter. Add 1 cup (150 g) of the sliced cabbage leaves, the onion, and the juniper berries and sauté until lightly sweated. Add the ale and continue to cook until the ale is completely evaporated and the vegetables are soft, about 5 minutes. In a large bowl, combine the rye bread, the cabbage mixture, the Swiss cheese, and caraway seed. In a separate bowl, whisk together the eggs and cream. Fold the egg mixture into the bread mixture. You should have a thick consistency that you can work with your hands. Season to taste with salt and pepper.

4. Cut four squares of plastic wrap, each about 12 inches (30 cm) square. Bring a large saucepan of water to a boil and prepare a large bowl of ice water. Blanch the reserved outer cabbage leaves in the boiling water and immediately transfer to the bowl of ice water to stop the cooking. Dry between paper towels. Trim the leaves to the size of a bread plate, roughly 5 inches (13 cm) in diameter. Spoon ¼ cup of the bread mixture into the center of each leaf. Scoop the edges of the leaves up and form a ball. Place a piece of the plastic wrap under the ball and wrap the ball as tightly as possible. (See photos on pages 38–39.)

{Continued}

Beef Tongue Reuben, *continued*

5.   Prepare a steamer for cooking, or, if you don't have one, fashion one yourself. Simply find a pot big enough to hold your smallest colander and fill it with 2 inches (5 cm) of water. Place the colander in the pot, making sure the water level is no higher than the lowest point in the colander. Put the pot over medium heat and wait for the water to simmer. Place the plastic-wrapped cabbage balls in the colander, cover the pot, and steam for 15 minutes. Remove from the steamer and reserve.

6.   To finish the tongue, in a deep sauté pan, heat about ¼ inch (6 mm) of oil over medium-high heat. Set up an egg wash assembly line. In a shallow dish, beat together the egg and water. In another shallow dish, put the rye crumbs. Dip one side of the beef tongue pieces in egg wash and dredge in the crumbs. Put the tongue in the sauté pan, crumb side down, and cook until browned, about 2 minutes. Flip and fry the side without the crumbs for 30 seconds. Transfer to a plate lined with paper towels.

7.   To make the slaw, in a bowl, toss together the red cabbage, parsley, lemon juice, and olive oil. Season with salt.

8.   Carefully remove the plastic wrap from each cabbage roll and put one on each of four plates. Spoon the dressing over each cabbage ball. Place the tongue next to each cabbage ball, top with the slaw, and serve.

Here we take a simple beef tongue and brine it in the traditional flavors used to cure bacon: salt, brown sugar, sage, and black pepper. To pump it up, we use actual bacon as well. You may call it cheating; we call it "bacon performance enhancement." After 4 days in the brine, the tongue will start to smell like delicious bacon. And from there a nice slow smoke will turn a cheap (and usually unwanted) cow tongue into a fabulously rich and complex piece of meat. Feel free to experiment with any leftover tongue. It works particularly well with sandwiches (a BLT, perhaps?) and breakfast.

We typically make four accompaniments to serve along with the tongue: a subtle celery aioli, rich bacon butter, cornichon relish, and eggs pickled in bacon vinegar. At the restaurant, we give the eggs 3 days to brine, but you can get away with 2 days at home. We serve all of the above atop bacon-toasted brioche, which gives this dish the quintessential over-the-top Pigeon feel. {SERVES 6}

TONGUE BACON, BRIOCHE, CELERY, CAPERS

1 cup (160 g) diced bacon
½ yellow onion, sliced
2 quarts (2 l) water
½ cup (70 g) kosher salt
½ cup (100 g) firmly packed brown sugar
10 tablespoons black peppercorns
1 bunch sage
1 teaspoon pink curing salt
1 pound (450 g) beef tongue
Neutral oil for frying
1 tablespoon capers
4 slices brioche, each ¼ inch (6 mm) thick
Bacon Butter (page 42)
Celery Aioli (page 43)
Bacon Pickled Eggs (page 43)
A squeeze of fresh lemon juice
Maldon flake salt
Cornichon Relish (page 43)

1. In a heavy pot over medium heat, sauté the bacon until it starts to release its fat and the flavor blooms, about 5 minutes. Add the onion, water, kosher salt, brown sugar, peppercorns, sage, and curing salt and bring to a boil. As soon as the liquid boils, take it off the heat and immediately chill over an ice water bath for about 30 minutes.

2. Using a skewer poke, the tongue all over. Take your anger out on that tongue and just poke the shit out of it. We want the brine to get in deep! Place the tongue in the brine, cover, and refrigerate for 4 days.

3. Remove the tongue from the refrigerator and transfer the tongue and its brine to a large pot. Over medium heat, simmer the tongue in the brine, covered, until tender, about 2 hours. We want to cook this guy a little less than other tongue preparations because it will be sliced and panfried later, and we don't want it falling apart.

4. Remove the tongue from the pot with a slotted spoon and let it cool until it is just cool enough to handle. Peel the tongue (see sidebar on page 34). If you have a smoker, prepare it according to the manufacturer's instructions. Place the tongue in the smoker and smoke until you have a sweet, smoky aroma and the color has darkened considerably, about 1 hour. If you don't have a smoker, light a small fire in the corner of a grill and toss a handful of applewood chips on the fire. Place the tongue on the grill as

{Continued}

far away from the fire as possible and close the lid. Smoke, checking every 10 minutes or so to make sure there is plenty of smoke and to add more wood chips as needed. Remove the tongue from the smoker or grill and refrigerate until chilled, about 1 hour. Once chilled, slice the tongue into pieces about ¹⁄₁₆ inch (2 mm) thick (about the thickness of a quarter).

5. In a small sauté pan over high heat, heat ½ inch (12 mm) of oil. The oil is hot enough when a caper thrown into the oil hisses. Dry the capers on paper towels. Add the capers to the oil and fry; they will pop and spit at first. You know they are done when they puff up, about 30 seconds. Remove the capers from the oil with a slotted spoon and place on a plate lined with paper towels.

6. Brush the brioche with the bacon butter. In a sauté pan over medium heat, toast the brioche until browned on both sides, about 1 minute per side. In another sauté pan over high high, heat a thin film of oil. Add the sliced tongue and fry until crisp, about 1½ minutes per side. The tongue might want to curl up on you; if that happens, turn it more frequently.

7. To serve, spread 1 tablespoon of celery aioli on a serving plate. Top with the toasted brioche. Using an egg slicer, slice 4 bacon pickled eggs (if you made five just in case one broke, then you are a bad-ass cook and you get to eat the extra egg). Fan the sliced egg out over the brioche and arrange slices of crispy tongue bacon on top and around. Add a good squeeze of lemon juice, a sprinkle of Maldon salt, and a spoonful of relish and enjoy.

A NOTE ON GOOD VINEGAR

Olive oil expert and man about town Jim Dixon turned us on to Katz Vinegars, our favorite vinegars to keep on hand at the restaurant as well as at home. Our three favorites are Gravenstein Apple Cider Vinegar (basically, the best ever), Sauvignon Blanc Agrodolce (a sweet and sour vinegar), and our absolute favorite, the Late Harvest Viognier Honey Vinegar, which I could drink like a bottle of wine.

Bacon Butter

¼ cup (40 g) chopped bacon
2 tablespoons unsalted butter

MAKES 2 TABLESPOONS

In a medium sauté pan over low heat, combine the bacon and butter. Simmer them together until your kitchen is filled with that mouthwatering bacon aroma and the chopped bacon pieces have rendered their fat, about 15 minutes. Strain and reserve the melted butter. (Keep the bacon bits around for snacking while you cook.) The butter will keep in the fridge for up to 1 month. Aside from making the most delicious toast, the butter is great for scrambling eggs and is a quick way to make a chicken breast taste *titular* (see sidebar on page 14).

Celery Aioli

½ cup (125 ml) celery juice
A pinch of ground celery seed
2 egg yolks
½ cup (20 g) fresh flat-leaf parsley
Small pinch of vitamin C powder
½ cup (125 ml) neutral oil
Kosher salt

MAKES 1½ CUPS (375 ML)

In a small saucepan over medium heat, combine the celery juice and celery seed and cook until reduced to 1 tablespoon liquid, 3 to 4 minutes. Transfer the reduced liquid to a blender and add the egg yolks, parsley, and vitamin C powder. Puree until the parsley is very finely chopped and then, with the motor running, add the oil in a thin, steady stream to create an emulsion. If it becomes too thick, add a couple of drops of water and blend again. Season with salt to taste. The aioli will keep in the refrigerator, covered, for 3 days.

Bacon Pickled Eggs

2 quarts (2 l) water
5 farm-fresh eggs
¼ cup (40 g) chopped bacon
1 shallot, diced
1 clove garlic
5 sage leaves
2 bay leaves
1 cup (250 ml) champagne vinegar
¼ cup (60 ml) water
3 tablespoons sugar
1 tablespoon kosher salt
1 teaspoon black peppercorns

MAKES 5 EGGS

Bring the water to a boil over high heat. Gently place the eggs in the boiling water and cook for 14 minutes. Using a slotted spoon, remove the eggs from the water and transfer to an ice water bath until cool. Carefully peel the eggs and set aside in a heatproof bowl. In a small saucepan over high heat, combine the bacon, shallot, garlic, sage, bay leaves, vinegar, water, sugar, salt, and peppercorns. When the mixture comes to a boil, carefully pour it over the eggs. Cover and refrigerate for at least 2 days. The eggs will keep for up to 1 month refrigerated in the pickling liquid in an airtight container.

Cornichon Relish

1 tablespoon finely diced bacon
¼ cup (45 g) very finely diced celery
¼ cup (40 g) very finely diced red onion
1 tablespoon finely diced cornichons
2 teaspoons chopped celery leaves
1 tablespoon Katz Trio Red Wine Vinegar or other good-quality red wine vinegar (see sidebar on page 42)
Kosher salt

MAKES ¾ CUP (180 ML)

In a sauté pan over medium-high heat, sauté the bacon until crisp. Add the celery and onion to the pan and toss to combine. Add the cornichons and celery leaves, stir in the vinegar, and season to taste with salt. Remove from the heat and let cool to room temperature. The relish can be made up to 2 days in advance. If storing, cover and keep refrigerated until 1 hour before serving.

We had these fries on the menu for about one week when Andy Ricker, the chef-owner of Pok Pok, came in to eat. He was loving the fries—until he bit into the bullet that had taken down that particular lamb. He politely put it on a bread plate and handed it back to Eric, our sous-chef. All this is to say we're extremely fastidious when cleaning our tongues, and even more so now, if that's possible. And you should be too.

Note: The tongues have to braise for 4 hours and then chill for 2 hours for this dish. {MAKES 1 LARGE BOWL OF FRIES}

LAMB TONGUE FRIES, ROSEMARY KETCHUP

10 lamb's tongues
4 cups (1 l) water
2 cups (500 ml) white wine
½ yellow onion, sliced
1 head garlic, halved
3 sprigs rosemary
1 teaspoon red pepper flakes
2 tablespoons kosher salt

3 eggs
½ cup (125 ml) whole milk
1½ cups (185 g) all-purpose flour
2 cups panko
Rice oil or vegetable oil for deep-frying
Spicy Rosemary Ketchup (page 324) for serving

1. Preheat the oven to 350°F (180°C).

2. In a large Dutch oven, combine the tongues, water, wine, onion, garlic, rosemary, red pepper flakes, and salt. Cover and braise in the oven until the tongue is very tender when pierced with a paring knife, about 4 hours. Remove the tongues from the braising liquid and discard the liquid. When the tongues are cool enough to handle, peel off the outer layer (see sidebar on page 34). Refrigerate the tongues for 2 hours and then remove them from the fridge and quarter lengthwise.

3. In a small, shallow bowl, whisk together the eggs and milk. Set up three bowls: the first with the flour, the second with the egg wash, and the final one with the panko. Working in batches, about five pieces at a time, coat the tongues in flour, shaking off any excess. Dip the floured pieces in the egg wash and then dredge them in the panko. Repeat until all pieces are breaded. In a deep pot over medium high heat, pour oil to a depth of 8 inches (20 cm). When the oil reaches 350°F (180°C) on a candy thermometer, carefully add the breaded tongues, working in batches of 8 at a time, and fry for 2 minutes. Remove the tongues from the pot with a slotted spoon and drain on paper towels.

4. Serve immediately with the ketchup.

Maybe it's because Gabriel grew up in California, but he loves Mexican food, which is also some of his favorite food to cook. This is a dish with unapologetically Mexican flavors—with a punch of pork flavor cut by brightly pickled radishes and poblano *crema*—but we use lentils rather than the traditional pinto beans to cut back on the heaviness and starch. {SERVES 4 TO 6}

GRILLED PORK TONGUE, REFRIED BEANS, LARDO

Tongue

2 pork tongues, each about 12 ounces (375 g)
3 bay leaves
1 teaspoon freshly ground black pepper
1 teaspoon ground cumin
1 head garlic, halved
1 cup (250 ml) dry white wine
1 cup (250 ml) water
1 tablespoon kosher salt

Lentils

2 tablespoons lard or unsalted butter
½ yellow onion, diced
2 tablespoons chopped sun-dried tomatoes
1 teaspoon sambal chile paste
1 teaspoon ground bay leaves
¼ teaspoon cayenne pepper
1 cup (220 g) French green lentils
2 teaspoons kosher salt
4 cups (1 l) chicken stock
¼ cup (60 ml) cider vinegar

Neutral oil for brushing
12 thin slices lardo
Poblano Crema (page 326)
Pickled Radish (page 326)
1 lime
Cilantro sprigs for garnish

1. Preheat the oven to 350°F (180°C).

2. To make the tongue, combine the pork tongues, bay leaves, pepper, cumin, garlic, wine, water, and salt in a small ovenproof dish. Cover and braise in the oven until the tongues are easily pierced with a paring knife, about 3½ hours. Remove the tongues from the liquid and discard the liquid. When the tongues are cool enough to handle, peel off the outer layer (see sidebar on page 34). Note: Pork tongue is a $#@% to peel. I know, because I've peeled every kind of tongue there is. Have patience and *scrape* rather than peel, as the outer layer does not peel the same way other tongues do. Cut the tongues in half lengthwise and set aside.

3. To make the lentils, in a large, heavy sauté pan over medium heat, melt the lard. Add the onion and sauté until aromatic, 4 minutes. Add the sun-dried tomatoes, sambal chile paste, ground bay leaves, and cayenne and continue cooking, stirring occasionally, for 5 minutes more. Add the lentils and salt and cook, stirring well, for 1 minute longer. Add the stock and vinegar and bring to a boil. Reduce the heat to a slow simmer and cook, stirring frequently to keep the lentils from scorching, until the lentils are very soft and most of the liquid has evaporated, about 1 hour. Don't be alarmed if it seems like there is too much liquid in the pot as you are cooking the lentils. We are actually trying to *overcook* them to make them look and feel like refried beans. Remove the pan from the stove. The lentils will keep for 3 days covered in the refrigerator if need be.

4. Preheat a gas grill or prepare a charcoal grill for cooking over high heat. Brush the tongues with a little neutral oil and place the pieces, cut side down, on the grill. Grill until nicely charred (we're looking for deep grill marks here), about 3 minutes, and then flip and grill until soft and warmed through, about 2 minutes more. Remove from the grill and top each tongue half with three slices of lardo. If necessary, reheat your lentils and place a nice-sized scoop in the center of each plate. Top with the tongue. Give each tongue a scoop of poblano crema and scatter a few pickled radishes around. Squeeze lime juice over each plate and top with a sprig of cilantro.

We're lucky to have a strong Asian community in Portland and thus a plethora of Asian grocery stores. Incorporating Asian flavors into the food at Le Pigeon feels natural and is a habit that we really enjoy. In fact, we're so smitten with this influence in our dishes that we actually plan to decorate the whole restaurant as a Chinese food joint called the Broccoli Knuckle and create a new menu, complete with dishes like this one right here. The recipe below calls for a half pound of beef tongue; if you can only find larger tongues, use the leftover to make chow mein, beef with broccoli and oyster sauce, or any sort of stir-fry, really. Just look at your local Chinese takeout menu and improvise. {SERVES 4}

BBQ BEEF TONGUE, FRIED RICE

½ pound (225 g) beef tongue
1 cup (140 g) diced yellow onion
6 cloves garlic, crushed
6 cups (1.5 l) water
1 cup (250 ml) plus 1 tablespoon soy sauce
4 tablespoons (60 ml) hoisin sauce
1 tablespoon plus 1 teaspoon minced fresh ginger
½ teaspoon red pepper flakes
Kosher salt
4 tablespoons (60 ml) neutral oil
¼ cup (40 g) frozen green peas
½ cup (90 g) corn kernels
2 eggs, lightly beaten
2 cups (320 g) cooked and chilled long-grain white rice
2 green onions, chopped, plus 2 green onions thinly sliced on the diagonal

1. Preheat the oven to 350°F (180°C).

2. In a large Dutch oven or deep baking dish, combine the tongue, ½ cup of the onion, 4 of the garlic cloves, the water, 1 cup of the soy sauce, 2 tablespoons of the hoisin sauce, 1 tablespoon of the ginger, the red pepper flakes, and 1 tablespoon salt. Cover and bake about 3 hours, checking at the 2½-hour mark for doneness. If the tongue is easily pierced with a fork or a paring knife, then you are good to go; if not, cover and continue to cook, checking every half hour. Remove the tongue from the liquid with a slotted spoon and discard the liquid. When the tongue is cool enough to handle, peel the outer layer (see sidebar on page 34). Transfer the tongue to a plate and refrigerate for 30 minutes.

3. Cut the tongue into about four slices, each 2 inches (5 cm) thick. Rub with the remaining 2 tablespoons of hoisin sauce. In a large nonstick pan or wok over high heat, heat 1 tablespoon of the oil. Add the remaining ½ cup diced onion, the remaining 1 teaspoon of ginger, and the remaining 2 cloves garlic. Season with a dash of salt and sauté until lightly cooked and very aromatic, 3 to 4 minutes. Add the peas and corn and cook until all of the flavors have melded, about 3 minutes longer. Remove from the heat, transfer to a bowl, and set aside.

4. Add another 1 tablespoon of the oil to the pan and add the eggs. Lightly scramble until just set, about 2 minutes. Transfer the eggs to the bowl with the vegetables.

5. Turn the heat down to medium-high and add the remaining 2 table-spoons of oil. Let the oil get hot, then add the rice. Toss to coat the rice well with the oil and then let the rice sit, without stirring, for about a minute to get the rice on the bottom nice and crispy. Stir and repeat three more times. Add the remaining tablespoon of soy sauce, the chopped green onions, and the reserved vegetable and egg mixture back to the pan, toss to combine, and season to taste with salt.

6. Preheat a gas grill or prepare a charcoal grill for cooking over high heat, or heat a grill pan on the stove top. Oil the grill or pan well. Place the hoisin-rubbed tongue on the grill or in the pan and grill until the hoisin caramelizes and becomes super-tasty (think of ribs on a grill), about 3 minutes per side. Remove from the grill.

7. Divide the rice mixture among four bowls. Top with the beef tongue and the thinly sliced green onions, and serve.

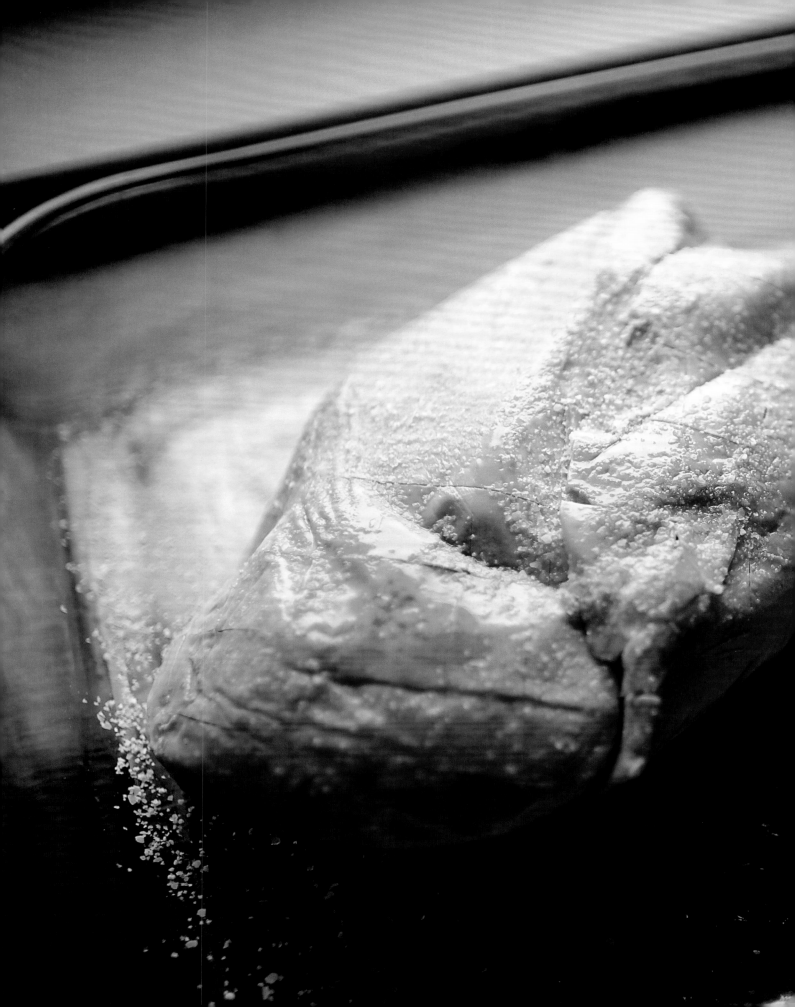

CHAPTER 3
FAT LIVER

When purchasing foie gras, please buy smart. Our favorite resource, D'Artagnan (www.dartagnan.com), is also the easiest for you. Here you can buy foie gras in small quantities and in slices or cubes rather than a whole lobe. Cleaned and deveined, this foie gras comes as little pucks that are ready to be seared and served. It's a smaller commitment for a much more reasonable expense.

Su Lien has been with us since day one, and she's an integral part of our team. She has taken the role of sous-chef at Little Bird, but when she was at the Pigeon, she was our go-to person for preparing torchon of foie gras. To say she had it down to a science would be an understatement. Like any torchon, this is best served with sweet jam and toasted brioche. We also use it in our Venison, Creamed Spinach, Yorkshire Pudding (page 228). {MAKES 1 TORCHON}

SU LIEN'S FOIE GRAS TORCHON

1 lobe foie gras, about 1¼ pounds (600 g), cleaned and deveined (see sidebar below)

Kosher salt

HOW TO CLEAN AND DEVEIN FOIE GRAS

Tightly seal the lobe of foie gras in a vacuum bag or a large resealable plastic bag, pressing as much air out of it as possible. Place the bag in a shallow dish and add lukewarm water to cover. Soak the foie gras until you can separate the lobes, about 1 hour. Using a butter knife, separate the lobes and gently remove any large veins. The veins begin at the back and run like spider webs through the lobes. Working with one lobe at a time, find the start of the vein on the back side and gently scrape (not cut) the foie gras away from the veins, working your way down the lobe. The veins will become thinner and more fragile toward the front of the lobe. Try to expose all the veins and then gently lift off the network of veins, starting at the back where they are the thickest. Give the lobe a once-over to get any stragglers, and then repeat this process on the other lobe. Once the veins have been removed, gently fold the lobes back into their original shape as much as possible.

1. Cut two pieces of butcher's twine: one 10 inches (25 cm) long and the other 12 inches (30 cm). Place the foie gras on your work surface, outer side up, and generously salt. Let sit for 1 hour, then gently pick up the lobe and thoroughly rinse under very cold running water. Shake off as much of the water as possible. (Note: The foie gras needs to be just above room temperature. If it's too cold, it won't roll up correctly. And if it's too warm, it won't hold its shape in the cloth. Leave the foie on your work surface for a while after rinsing if it's too cold, or put it in the refrigerator for a few minutes to chill if it has become too warm.)

2. Place the desired size portion onto a smooth piece of cloth (perhaps a cloth napkin) on the end closest to you. Roll into a log shape, both pushing in the sides to keep the log compact and running your hands along its length to create a cylinder of even diameter.

3. Once you reach the other end of the cloth, pick up your log with both hands and twist the cloth in opposite directions like a Tootsie Roll. This will take a good amount of pressure. Using the shorter piece of string, tie off one end; this will be the bottom of your torchon. Using one hand, pick up the untied end along with the end of the longer piece of string. Using your other hand, wrap the string around the cloth above the torchon, applying an ample amount of pressure downward onto the torchon as you wrap the string tightly. This will make your torchon denser; the more pressure you apply, the better your torchon. Continue wrapping until the torchon feels tight. The wrapped string will extend about ¼ inch (6 mm) above the torchon.

4. Hang from a rack in the refrigerator, like you would a fresh sausage, to maintain the cylinder shape. Refrigerate overnight and enjoy the next day.

We don't consider ourselves to be locavores, but we do buy white bread made by Franz, a Portland institution that has been around for 100 years. In the first few months after opening, Gabriel had the idea to make a foie gras PB&J. His initial attempt was to mix the foie with actual peanut butter, but (as you can imagine) it was a flop. The next effort was straight foie mousse instead of the peanut butter and roasted peanuts as a garnish. Not the most avant-garde of dishes, but the perfect (decadent) snack. We like to make this using strawberry, raspberry, or apricot jelly, but you can use whatever type you like. {MAKES 4 SANDWICHES}

TOASTED FOIE GRAS AND JELLY

½ cup (115 g) Foie Gras Mousse
  (page 322)
¼ cup (75 g) of your favorite jelly
8 slices white bread
2 tablespoons unsalted butter
¼ cup (30 g) chopped roasted peanuts

1. Remove the foie mousse from the fridge and let it come to room temperature. Assemble your sandwich, spreading the foie mousse and the jelly on the bread as you would for a PB&J.

2. In a sauté pan over medium heat, melt the butter. Toast the sandwich in the butter, turning once, like you would grilled cheese, until lightly browned. Sprinkle the peanuts on top and serve.

A note from Gabriel: I love making terrines and have been particularly into foie terrines since my early days in the kitchen. Sous-vide is the best technique for this recipe, but for most people it's not an option, so we've also provided a more traditional approach that will still yield a delicious result.

After years of serving this terrine with the classical toasted brioche, I wanted a new combo. One of our cooks had just made a batch of wheat bread at home and brought some in for us to try. It was amazing, rich, salty, and slightly sweet, and I thought it would be great with foie. So I decided to make wheat muffins, but the first batch was missing something. Standing in the kitchen one day, the answer was staring me in the face: a jar of black bean paste, which is available at almost any Asian grocer. It adds a great salty-sour taste that complements the sweetness of the figs.

Note: If you can't find a decent Sauternes, a good alternative is Sainte-Croix-du-Mont. Same style, much cheaper. {SERVES 12}

FIG AND FOIE GRAS TERRINE

1 cup (150 g) thinly sliced dried figs
2 cloves garlic, finely minced
¼ teaspoon espelette pepper
¼ cup (60 ml) Sauternes or Sainte-Croix-du-Mont
1 lobe foie gras, about 1½ pounds (720 g), cleaned and deveined (see sidebar on page 52)
Kosher salt
12 fresh black Mission figs, halved
2 tablespoons good-quality balsamic vinegar
1 teaspoon fermented black bean paste
Fermented Black Bean Muffins (page 56)
Maldon flake salt

1. In a bowl, toss the dried figs with the garlic, pepper, and Sauternes. Set aside to marinate for 1 hour.

2. Coarsely cut the foie gras into cubes the size of ping-pong balls and season well with kosher salt. Keep any scraps of foie; you're going to want them for the muffins. In a bowl, toss the marinated figs and foie gras together and let marinate, covered, in the fridge for 2 hours. Spoon the mixture into a 10 by 3½-inch (25 by 9cm) terrine mold, spreading it evenly and smoothing it out as you work. When it's all in, firmly press to get rid of any spaces or air bubbles.

3. If you have the tools for sous-vide cooking, place the terrine in a vacuum bag and vacuum pack using the high setting. Place the bag in a water bath at 118°F (48°C) for 40 minutes. Remove from the water and chill in an ice water bath. Once cool, open the bag and remove the terrine mold. Skip to step 5 to unmold the terrine and proceed.

4. If you do not have the tools for sous-vide, heat the oven to 250°F (120°C) and cover the terrine mold with a lid of aluminum foil. Place the terrine in a roasting pan and pour hot water in the pan to come halfway up the sides of the terrine mold. Cook until a thermometer inserted into the middle of the terrine reads 120°F (50°C), about 45 minutes. Remove from the oven. Cut a piece of cardboard to fit just inside the top of the terrine mold. Wrap the cardboard with foil and place on top of the terrine, pressing

it lightly so the terrine is firm. Find a weight (such as a couple of soup cans) and place them on top, and set aside overnight. There will be a nice gelée that comes over the top. Remove it and save, as this is a bonus and should be frozen for other uses, like making foie gras vinaigrette or poaching scallops.

5.   To unmold the terrine, run a knife under hot water and then run it along the edges of the terrine mold. Invert the mold onto a plate and carefully remove the terrine. If you're not enjoying it now, it can be wrapped in plastic wrap and stored for up to 3 days in the fridge.

6.   Toss the fresh figs with the balsamic vinegar and the black bean paste. Set aside to marinate for 20 minutes.

7.   Cut a thick slice of the terrine and sprinkle with Maldon salt. Place some figs next to the foie and drizzle the fig marinade around the plate. Serve with the fermented black bean muffins.

{Continued}

THE PIGEON POUR: The rich, sweet, and earthy flavors of this dish had us grabbing for one of our favorite fortified wines. When we want sweetness and balance we look to Madeira. Made only on the tiny island of the same name, Madeira is one of the wine world's marvels. It is made by subjecting the wine to all the things wine isn't supposed to be subjected to: heat, light, and temperature variation. By the time it is in the bottle, it has become an indestructible liquid of delight. Made from one of several white grapes, the end product is a deep amber color and has a flavor reminiscent of tawny port, but with a backbone of acidity and minerality you don't often fine in port. A nice thing, too, is that a bottle of Madeira doesn't deteriorate after being opened, so we sell a series of them by the glass. We usually pour five or six different vintages that date back to the 1920s. They aren't cheap, but how often do we drink something from the time of the Coolidge administration?!

In addition to being great with desserts and awesome served with cheese, Madeira is ideal for savory dishes that want some sweetness. The three most common types of Madeira are Sercial, the driest of the three; Bual; and Malmsey or Malvasia, the sweetest of the three. One that we usually carry is the Rare Wine Company's Boston Bual. If you were eating at Le Pigeon, this is what you would be drinking with this dish . . . unless you wanted to spring for the D'Oliveiras '22.

Fermented Black Bean Muffins

2½ cups (310 g) whole wheat flour
2 teaspoons baking powder
1 teaspoon baking soda
1 teaspoon kosher salt
1 egg
½ cup (125 ml) molasses
¼ cup (60 g) brown sugar
¼ cup (60 g) unsalted butter, melted
¾ cup (180 ml) buttermilk
1 tablespoon fermented black bean paste
4 ounces (120 g) foie gras scraps from making the terrine, diced
Salted butter for serving

MAKES 12 MUFFINS

Preheat the oven to 375°F (190°C). Grease a muffin pan with butter. In a large bowl, combine the flour, baking powder, baking soda, and salt. In a separate bowl, mix the egg, molasses, sugar, butter, buttermilk, and black bean paste until well combined. Fold the wet ingredients into the dry and combine well with a spatula. Fold in the scraps of foie and mix well. Fill the muffin cups with the batter and bake until a toothpick inserted into one of the muffins comes out clean, about 15 minutes. Spread with butter and serve.

This is our take on bacon and eggs. The foie gras is cured like bacon and then lightly smoked. We slice it, sear it, and serve it with salt-cured egg yolks and a nice little composed salad. The acidity of the salad is necessary to cut the saltiness. It's an annual Pigeon favorite, but something we can't make more often because it's both expensive and labor-intensive. As you'll see, this needs to be made over 2 days.

If the idea of making your own brioche is the straw that breaks the camel's back, it's fine to buy a Pullman loaf or something similar. For this recipe you're going to need a Little Chief Smoker or some other smoking device. {SERVES 8 TO 10}

FOIE GRAS BACON, BRIOCHE

Cured Foie
2 cups (280 g) kosher salt
½ cup (100 g) firmly packed brown sugar
½ cup (125 ml) maple syrup
Leaves from 1 bunch sage, cut into long, thin strips
1 lobe foie gras, about 1 pound (480 g), cleaned and deveined (see sidebar on page 52)

Candy Cap Vinaigrette
¼ cup (60 ml) Candy Cap Jam (page 61)
1 egg yolk
3 tablespoons sherry vinegar
½ cup (125 ml) neutral oil
A squeeze of fresh lemon juice
A pinch of kosher salt

Sherried Onions
2 tablespoons unsalted butter
2 yellow onions, thinly sliced
1 teaspoon minced fresh thyme
¼ cup (60 ml) honey
¼ cup (60 ml) good sherry vinegar

Salad
1 cup (40 g) frisée
3 tablespoons fresh flat-leaf parsley

Brioche (page 60)
Salt-Cured Egg Yolks (page 60)

1. To make the cured foie, in a bowl stir together the salt, brown sugar, maple syrup, and sage. Cover the foie gras lobe well with the rub. You will have some rub left over. Either discard it or save it for next time. Wrap the foie tightly in plastic wrap and refrigerate for 24 hours.

2. The next day, remove the foie lobe from the fridge and, under cool running water, carefully rinse off the cure. Gently pat dry. You'll need two large bowls. Fill one with ice cubes, and put the foie in the second bowl. Place the bowl with the foie atop the bowl of ice to keep the foie cool while you prep the smoker.

3. If you're using a smoker, prepare it according to the manufacturer's instructions using applewood chips. Pour yourself a glass of something while you wait for the chips to start smoking. Place the bowl of ice and the bowl of foie on the middle rack, and smoke until the smoke stops streaming from the box (keeping the foie on ice prevents it from rendering while it is smoking). Repeat this process twice with fresh applewood chips, adding fresh ice to the bowl as necessary. Remove the foie from the smoker and chill for at least 1 hour in the refrigerator.

4. If you're using a charcoal grill, get a small amount of coals very hot on one side of the grill. Once they have burned down to embers, add about 2 cups of applewood chips and wait for them to start smoking. Once a good smoke is going, place the bowl of ice and the bowl of foie on the grill as far from the fire as possible. Cover the grill with the lid. Check the foie after 10 minutes: when you stop seeing smoke, add another 2 cups of chips. The foie will be adequately smoked after 2 batches of chips (remember to add fresh ice to the bowl as necessary). Remove the foie from the grill and chill it for at least 1 hour in the refrigerator.

5. Warm a very sharp knife under running hot water. Separate the lobe into two pieces and clean it of any sinew. Warm your knife under the hot

HOW TO SEAR
FOIE GRAS

Score the foie gras about
1/16 inch (2 mm) deep in a cross-
hatch pattern. To sear the foie
gras, in a dry, heavy sauté pan
over high heat, place the foie
scored side down. Allow the
foie to render its fat, about
1 minute, and then flip it over.
Using a spoon, baste the foie
gras with the rendered fat in
the pan until medium-rare,
about 3 minutes. The foie gras
is ready when the tip of a knife
inserted into the foie meets little to no resistence; the consistency should be like a stick of
butter from the refrigerator.

water again and then cut the foie into pieces the size of hockey pucks, about
2 ounces (60 g) each. Transfer to a plate.

6. To make the vinaigrette, in a blender, combine the jam, egg yolk, and vinegar and puree. With the motor running, add the oil in a thin, steady stream to create an emulsion. Season to taste with lemon juice and salt.

7. To make the onions, in a sauté pan over medium heat, melt the butter. Turn the heat down to low, add the onions and thyme and sauté, stirring occasionally, until the onions are translucent, about 5 minutes. Stir in the honey and vinegar. Let simmer until the liquid has evaporated and the onions are honey-lacquered, about 3 minutes. Set aside.

8. To make the salad, in a large bowl, toss together the frisée and parsley. Dress with the vinaigrette, leaving a bit for garnish. Arrange the salad on a plate and spoon the sherried onions alongside.

9. To serve, sear the foie gras as described in the sidebar (at left). Brown the brioche in the remaining foie gras fat. Set it atop the sherried onions. Set the foie gras atop the brioche. Spoon a bit of candy cap vinaigrette over the top of the foie gras and grate the salt-cured egg yolks over all.

 THE PIGEON POUR: Like any breakfast dish, this foie gras recipe wants a glass of OJ! Or at least something sweet and bright. So we figured that the fresh-squeezed OJ of the wine world was Riesling Auslese from Germany. When this dish was on the menu, we paired it with a riesling from Dr. Loosen from the Mosel.

{Continued}

Brioche

1 package (2¼ teaspoons) active
    dry yeast
2 tablespoons warm water
5 cups (625 g) bread flour
⅓ cup (90 g) sugar
7 eggs
1 teaspoon kosher salt
2 cups (500 g) cold unsalted butter,
    cubed

MAKES ONE (13 BY 4-INCH/33 BY 10CM) PULLMAN LOAF

1.   Activate the yeast by mixing it in a small bowl with the water. Let it sit for 5 minutes, or until the yeast has dissolved.

2.   Meanwhile, put the flour and sugar in the bowl of a stand mixer fitted with the dough hook. Start mixing on the lowest speed, then add the eggs and yeast. Mix for 10 minutes. After 10 minutes, add the salt and half of the butter. When the butter is almost incorporated, add the second half. After all of the butter has been added, keep mixing the brioche until the dough peels away from the sides of the bowl. Place the dough in a large oiled bowl and cover with plastic wrap. Put the bowl in a warm place to rise. When the dough has doubled in size, about 2 hours, punch it down and cover again. Place the bowl in the refrigerator overnight. Pull it out the next day and let it come almost to room temperature before shaping

3.   Preheat the oven to 375°F (190°C).

4.   To shape the dough, press the dough into a 13 by 4 by 4-inch (33 by 10 by 10cm) rectangle, or a rectangle that is as long as your bread pan or pans. Starting along one long side, roll up the dough to form a loaf. Pinch the seam closed. Bring the ends over the seam and pinch closed. Roll the loaf over so that the seam is on the bottom.

5.   Place the loaf in the pan. Cover the loaf with the lid of the pan and let rise until double in size, about 2 hours. It will be about 1 inch (2.5 cm) from the top of the pan. Bake for 15 minutes. Rotate the pan and bake for another 15 minutes. Take the lid off of the pan and continue to bake for 22 minutes. Remove from the oven and flip the bread out of the pan and onto a cooling rack. Tap the top of the bread. It will sound hollow if it's done. If not, put it back into the pan and back in the oven for another 5 to 10 minutes. Once the bread is cool, it can be stored, wrapped in plastic wrap, in the refrigerator for up to 4 days or in the freezer for up to a month.

Salt-Cured Egg Yolks

2 cups (280 g) kosher salt
2 egg yolks

MAKES 2 EGG YOLKS

In a small, airtight container, pour 1 cup (140 g) of the salt. Gently place the egg yolks on top of the salt. Carefully cover the yolks with the remaining 1 cup (140 g) of salt, seal the container, and refrigerate for 48 hours. Remove the container from the fridge and gently dig the yolks out of the salt; they will be firm with the texture of a stiff gum drop. Gently rinse off the salt and pat dry. The salt-cured yolks can be stored in an airtight container in the refrigerator for up to 2 weeks

Everyone loves chanterelles, and that's especially true here in Oregon, where it's the state mushroom. Although the chanterelle season runs from summer through the fall and into early winter (see The Weird and Wonderful World of Lars Norgren on page 198), this dish is best served in the fall, when the northwest wind is biting and there's a ready excuse for nipping at the cooking sherry to warm your belly.

Candy cap mushrooms—elusive little guys that taste of maple syrup—are used to make a jam for the sandwiches. Although they are tough to find, your efforts will be rewarded tenfold if you do manage to get your hands on some. We get ours from Mikuni Wild Harvest (www.mikuniwildharvest.com), but they may need a few days lead time to source them for you. {SERVES 8}

CHANTERELLE SOUP, FOIE GRAS, CANDY CAP SANDWICH

Candy Cap Jam
¼ cup (50 g) dried candy cap mushrooms
½ yellow onion, thinly sliced
½ cup (125 ml) cream sherry
¼ cup (60 g) firmly packed brown sugar
1 teaspoon kosher salt
¼ teaspoon espelette pepper

Chanterelle Soup
¼ cup (60 g) unsalted butter
1 large yellow onion, diced
6 cloves garlic, chopped
Kosher salt
2½ pounds (1.25 kg) chanterelle mushrooms
1 tablespoon chopped fresh thyme
¼ cup (60 ml) sherry vinegar
1 cup (250 ml) dry sherry
1 cup (250 ml) cream sherry
2 quarts (2 l) chicken stock
1 russet potato, peeled and roughly chopped
1 cup (250 ml) heavy cream

½ cup (115 g) Foie Gras Mousse (page 322)
16 slices white bread, each cut into a 2-inch (5cm) circle
2 tablespoons butter, softened
1 tablespoon minced chives

1. To make the jam, in a medium saucepan over low heat, combine the dried mushrooms, onion, sherry, brown sugar, salt, and pepper. Cook for 1 hour, stirring frequently. Remove from the heat, transfer to a food processor, and carefully puree until you have a nice smooth consistency. Set aside while you work on the soup.

2. To make the soup, in a 12-quart pot over medium heat, melt the butter. Add the onion and garlic. Season with salt and sauté until the onions are translucent, about 2 minutes. Add the chanterelles and thyme and cook, stirring occasionally, for about 10 minutes. The mushrooms should release a good amount of liquid. Add the sherry vinegar, dry sherry, and cream sherry. Continue to cook for 2 to 3 minutes so the alcohol evaporates. Add the chicken stock and potato and bring to a simmer. When the potatoes are fork-tender, after about 20 minutes, remove from the heat and let cool for a couple of minutes. Transfer the soup to a blender and puree until smooth. Stir in the cream and season to taste with salt. (Refrigerated, the soup will keep for 3 days.)

3. Spread 1 tablespoon of the mousse on each of eight slices of bread. Spread 1 tablespoon of candy cap jam on the remaining eight slices. Press together the slices to form eight sandwiches. Spread the butter on the outside of each sandwich. In a large sauté pan over medium heat, toast the sandwiches until golden brown on both sides. To serve, divide the soup among eight bowls and garnish with the chives. Place a sandwich alongside each bowl and enjoy.

Peaches happen a little late in the season here, but when they finally come around they are spectacular. Late August is our favorite time to bite into a fresh Oregon peach (we get ours from Viridian Farms). This recipe takes those fresh peaches and turns them into a lightly cooked chutney bolstered by the addition of foie gras butter and sweet Moscatel vinegar. Filling rich flaky puff pastry with chutney and serving it warm provides a perfect balance of sweet, sour, rich, and warm, yet it still tastes like the freshest peach. The peach chutney is delicious on its own yet made even better by a piece of perfectly seared foie gras. {SERVES 4}

FOIE GRAS, PEACH CHUTNEY PUFF PASTRY

½ cup (125 g) sugar
½ cup (125 ml) Moscatel vinegar
½ yellow onion, diced
4 cloves garlic, minced
2 tablespoons yellow mustard seeds
¼ teaspoon red pepper flakes
Kosher salt
2 packed cups (470 g) diced peaches
4 foie gras cubes, each about 2 ounces
   (60 g) (see page 51)
2 pieces of puff pastry, each
   4 by 10 inches (10 by 25 cm)
4 foie gras slices, each about 2 ounces
   (60 g) (see page 51)

Egg Wash
2 eggs
¼ cup (60 ml) milk

1.   In a heavy saucepan over medium heat, melt the sugar. When the sugar has melted and turned light brown, add the vinegar. It will seize up and spit, so be careful! When everything comes back to a liquid state, add the onion, garlic, mustard seeds, and red pepper flakes. Season with a dash of salt. When the onion and garlic have become translucent, after 2 or 3 minutes, add the peaches and stir well. When the peaches have some give but still retain their shape, after 5 to 6 minutes, remove the pan from the heat. Add the foie gras cubes and stir to combine. (You want the foie gras to soften and melt slightly while still retaining its shape.) Transfer to a bowl and refrigerate until completely chilled, about 1 hour.

2.   Preheat the oven to 400°F (200°C)

3.   If you're using purchased puff pastry, it will probably come folded in three, like a letter; this works out well for you. You will need two of these rectangles. On a lightly floured surface roll out each rectangle of dough to increase the size by 1 inch (2.5 cm) on all sides. Lay one of your rolled-out rectangles onto a baking sheet. Spoon the filling into the center, leaving 1 inch (2.5 cm) of dough exposed all around the edges.

4.   To make the egg wash, in a small bowl, whisk together the eggs and milk. Brush the exposed dough with egg wash and place the other pastry rectangle on top. Gently pat the top layer of dough down and use a fork to crimp the edges together to form a tight seal. Using a sharp knife, trim away any ragged edges to give you nice clean sides. Cut about five slits in the top layer to let the steam escape while baking. Transfer the pastry to a baking sheet and refrigerate for 20 minutes.

5. Brush the top of the pastry with the egg wash and place in the oven. Bake until flaky and golden brown, about 15 minutes. Remove from the oven and let rest for 15 minutes.

6. Sear the foie gras slices as described on page 59. Remove from the heat and set aside.

7. Cut the chutney-filled pastry into four pieces, top each with a piece of seared foie gras, and serve.

As we were writing this chapter of the book, we noticed that we present foie gras mostly in three forms: seared, as a torchon, or in a terrine. So we came up with this recipe. It's a carpaccio, cured for 24 hours with salt, sugar, and cardamom and then sliced paper thin. We make our own puffed quinoa at the restaurant, but you can buy it—along with the Saba grape syrup—at any specialty food market.

{SERVES 6 TO 8 AS AN APPETIZER}

FOIE GRAS CARPACCIO

Cure
½ teaspoon green cardamom seeds
2 tablespoons kosher salt
¼ teaspoon pink curing salt
2½ teaspoons sugar
½ teaspoon ground cardamom, plus more for serving
1 lobe foie gras, about 1 pound (480 g), cleaned and deveined (see sidebar on page 52)

Pickled Onions
4 pearl onions
¼ cup (60 ml) champagne vinegar
2 tablespoons water
1 tablespoon sugar
1 teaspoon kosher salt

Maldon flake salt
½ cup (100 g) seedless green grapes, peeled and sliced
¼ cup (50 g) puffed quinoa
1½ cups (325 ml) Saba grape syrup
Fresh chervil springs for garnish

1. To make the cure, in a small, dry saucepan over medium heat, toast the cardamom seeds, shaking the pan constantly, until aromatic, about 2 minutes. Remove the pan from the heat and let the seeds cool. Pour the seeds into a spice grinder and grind into a powder.

2. In a small bowl, mix together the ground cardamom seeds, the kosher salt, curing salt, sugar, and ground cardamom. Rub the cure all over the foie gras, letting any excess fall off. Place the coated foie in a resealable plastic bag, pressing as much air out of the bag as possible. Cure in the refrigerator for 24 hours.

3. The next day, place a serving platter in the refrigerator to chill. To make the pickled onions, peel the pearl onions and slice them into thin rings. Place the rings in a small bowl and set aside. In a small saucepan over medium heat, combine the vinegar, water, sugar, and salt and bring to a simmer. Pour the vinegar mixture over the onions and let them cool to room temperature. (They can be stored in an airtight container in the refrigerator for up to a month.)

4. Remove the foie lobe from the fridge and, under running cool water, carefully rinse off the cure. Gently pat dry. (At this point, the foie can be stored in the refrigerator in an airtight container for up to 4 days.)

5. To serve, warm a very sharp knife under running hot water and dry it with a towel. Gently slice the foie gras into very thin slices and layer them across the cold platter. Sprinkle the foie carpaccio with a pinch each of Maldon salt and ground cardamom. Scatter the grapes and pickled onions on top of the foie and sprinkle with the puffed quinoa. Drizzle the grape syrup over the top and garnish with the chervil.

While working at Paley's Place, I learned how to make oxtail consommé, something so flavorful yet so clear that it's possible to see all the goodies in it on the bottom of the bowl. I then decided to try making a grilled eel consommé to use as a light base for an Asian-influenced pot-au-feu. Because this is Le Pigeon, you can guess that it didn't turn out to be your standard pot-au-feu. It's carrot-less and bouquet garni–less, and it includes fruit (Bosc pears to be exact).

This recipe can be followed from beginning to end, or it can be read as a concept, offering encouragement rather than a precise recipe. All the components are prepared separately up until the last 5 minutes. This means that you can work on them days apart, if you like. The pears, for example, will last up to 4 days in the refrigerator.

Note: You should be able to find unagi at any Asian supermarket or specialty food shop. If not, there is always www.seafood.com. {SERVES 4}

FOIE GRAS, EEL POT-AU-FEU, PEARS, DUMPLINGS

Eel Consommé

1 yellow onion, diced
1 celery stalk, chopped
4 cloves garlic, crushed
1½ teaspoons tomato paste
1 piece unagi (freshwater eel), about 12 ounces (375 g), skinned and shredded
1 cup (250 ml) dry sherry
1½ tablespoons sherry vinegar
1 sprig thyme
2 bay leaves
1 tablespoon black peppercorns
½ teaspoon red pepper flakes
1 cup (11 g) bonito flakes
4 cups (1 l) chicken stock
2 cups (500 ml) fish stock
1 cup (250 ml) water
Kosher salt
4 ounces (126 g) ground chicken
¼ cup (35 g) diced onion
¼ cup (40 g) diced celery
¼ cup (40 g) diced carrot
4 egg whites

1. To make the eel consommé, in a large pot over medium heat, sauté the onion, celery, garlic, tomato paste, and eel for about 5 minutes. Be sure to continually stir it to keep it from sticking. Add the dry sherry and sherry vinegar and cook for 3 minutes more. Add the thyme, bay leaves, peppercorns, red pepper flakes, bonito flakes, chicken stock, fish stock, water, and 1 teaspoon salt. Bring to a boil, turn down to a simmer, and cook, tasting occasionally, until it tastes like eel dashi, sweet and with a strong flavor of umami. It should take about 1 hour. Strain the liquid, discarding the solids. Refrigerate until ready to use.

2. In a food processor combine the ground chicken, onion, celery, and carrot and season with 1 tablespoon of salt. In a large bowl, whisk the egg whites until they start to foam and almost reach soft peaks. Add the chicken mixture to the bowl and gently fold together with the egg whites. In a large, heavy pot over medium heat, combine the eel broth and the chicken and egg white mixture and stir to combine. Warm to a very gentle simmer, stirring occasionally, until a raft forms. You will know that this has happened when it looks like a dirty mess of cooked egg whites on top of the liquid (ignore your intuition: this is a good thing).

3. Once the raft forms, use a wooden spoon to poke a 1-inch (2.5cm) hole in it so the stock can bubble up through it. *Do not stir, or it will turn the stock cloudy.* Continue to simmer for about 20 minutes. You will know you are there when a spoonful of the consommé that is bubbling up through the raft is clear.

Foie Glaze
1 tablespoon honey
1 tablespoon sherry vinegar

Eel Dumplings (page 69)
Pear Balls (page 69)
Sautéed Mushrooms (page 69)
4 hard-boiled quail eggs, halved
    vertically
¼ cup (60 ml) water
4 slices foie gras, each 3 ounces (90 g)
Kosher salt
Maldon flake salt

4. Using the finest strainer you have lined with a cloth napkin, gently create a larger hole in the raft with a ladle and ladle the liquid out and through the napkin. Be careful to not get the raft with your consume. If it seems a little cloudy, strain twice. Set aside.

5. Preheat the oven to 350°F (180°C).

6. To make the foie glaze, in a small bowl whisk together the honey and sherry vinegar mixture until smooth.

7. To assemble the dish, in a Dutch oven, combine the eel dumplings, pear balls, mushrooms, quail eggs, and water. Heat in the oven until warmed through, about 5 minutes.

8. Season the foie gras with kosher salt and sear as described on page 59. Drain the fat from the pan and add about a tablespoon of the foie glaze to the pan. Toss to coat the foie and remove from the heat. Set aside.

9. To serve, in each of four deep soup bowls, arrange two dumplings, two pear balls, one quail egg, and a quarter of the mushrooms; top with the seared foie. Sprinkle with Maldon salt. Pour about ⅓ cup (80 ml) hot consommé into each bowl from a creamer tableside for a nice effect.

THE PIGEON POUR: Dishes like this one call for something different. Its depth, richness, and subtle complexity call for a wine that also has depth and richness. Something really sweet or bright would be jarring. The consommé is an extra challenge for the wine as well. Many wines taste odd against a consommé because of their acids and tannins. A dry oloroso sherry is the way to go. A great one is the 15 años bottling from El Maestro Sierra. Another great, and more widely available, option is the Don Nuño bottling from Lustau.

{Continued}

Eel Dumplings

½ cup (60 g) all-purpose flour
¾ teaspoon baking powder
Kosher salt
1 tablespoon unsalted butter
3 tablespoons bonito flakes
¼ cup (60 ml) whole milk
1 piece unagi (freshwater eel),
    1 to 2 ounces (30 to 60 g),
    skinned and shredded
Neutral oil

MAKES 12 GUMBALL-SIZED DUMPLINGS (ENOUGH TO SNACK ON WHILE PREPARING THE REST OF THE RECIPE)

In a mixing bowl, combine the flour, baking powder, and ½ teaspoon salt. In a small saucepan over medium heat, melt the butter with the bonito flakes and add to the flour mixture along with the milk. Add the eel and stir to make a loose dough. Refrigerate for 30 minutes.

Bring a large pot of salted water to a boil and lightly oil a baking sheet. Using your hands, roll the dough into 12 pieces the size of gumballs. Place them in the boiling water and cook until they puff up, about 3 minutes. Cut into one to make sure they are cooked through, and continue cooking another minute if necessary. Using a slotted spoon, transfer the dumplings to the prepared baking sheet. The dumplings will keep in the refrigerator, covered, for up to 2 days.

Pear Balls

½ cup (125 ml) white wine
¼ cup (60 ml) water
¼ cup (60 g) sugar
¼ cup (60 ml) rice wine vinegar
1 teaspoon truffle oil
2 Bosc pears, peeled, cored, and
    formed into 8 balls using a melon
    baller

MAKES 8 MINI PEAR BALLS

In a small saucepan over medium heat, combine the white wine, water, sugar, rice wine vinegar, and truffle oil. Bring to a boil. Meanwhile, put the pear balls in a heatproof bowl. When the liquid begins to boil, very carefully pour it over the pears. Let the pears cool in the liquid until ready to serve.

Sautéed Mushrooms

Neutral oil for sautéing
4 ounces (125 g) cleaned beech
    mushrooms
Kosher salt

MAKES ½ CUP (125 G)

In a sauté pan over high heat, heat a thin film of oil. Add the mushrooms, season with salt to taste, and sauté until the mushrooms are cooked through, about 3 minutes. Keep warm until ready to use.

Gabriel grew up eating spinach-artichoke dip with tortillas and watching San Francisco Giants games on the television in his parents' den. This is one of those home dishes we adapted for the restaurant. At Le Pigeon, we serve this dip in a brioche cup with seared foie gras, kind of like those bread bowls that people liked to serve in the 1980s, but you can also serve it with tortilla chips or toasted slices of baguette. {SERVES 10 AS A SNACK}

SPINACH, ARTICHOKE, FOIE GRAS

3 tablespoons unsalted butter
2 yellow onions, diced
5 cloves garlic, sliced
2 pounds (900 g) spinach
1 3-pound (1.4 kg) can cooked
    artichoke hearts, drained
Kosher salt and freshly ground black
    pepper
1¼ cups (310 ml) sour cream
½ cup (125 ml) Aioli (page 321)
2 cups (160 g) grated Parmesan
1 pound (480 g) foie gras cubes
    (see page 51)
½ teaspoon Tabasco
Zest of 1 lemon

1.   In a large pot over medium heat, melt the butter. Add the onions and garlic and sauté for 4 minutes. Add the spinach (in batches if necessary, adding more as the spinach cooks down) and cook until the leaves are wilted, 2 to 3 minutes. Add the artichoke hearts and cook until any excess liquid is evaporated, 6 to 7 minutes more.

2.   Remove the pot from the heat and season the spinach with salt and pepper. Stir in the sour cream, aioli, Parmesan, foie gras cubes, Tabasco, and lemon zest. Transfer to a food processor and puree until you have a nice dip consistency. Adjust the seasoning and serve warm.

This makes a great side when you want to take a simple dish—say Venison (page 228), Simple Roast Pork Loin (page 194), Simple Roasted Pigeon (page 76), or Elk Filet (page 217)—to another, perhaps even more satisfying, level.

Note: This should be enjoyed the same day you make it.

{MAKES 2½ CUPS (500 G)}

FOIE-CREAMED SPINACH

2 tablespoons unsalted butter
1½ cloves garlic, thinly sliced
2 tablespoons dried currants
1 pound (450 g) spinach
¼ cup (60 ml) crème fraîche
1 teaspoon kosher salt
A pinch of freshly grated nutmeg
4 egg yolks
¼ cup (120 g) panko
3 ounces (90 g) foie gras cubes
   (see page 51)

1. Preheat the oven to 350°F (180°C).

2. In a heavy sauté pan over medium heat, melt the butter. Add the garlic and currants and sauté for 1 minute. Add the spinach and sauté until the leaves are wilted, about 3 minutes. Add the crème fraîche, salt, and nutmeg. Continue cooking, stirring with a wooden spoon, until the mixture is the consistency of creamed spinach, about 5 minutes.

3. Transfer the mixture to a food processor and, with the motor running, add the egg yolks, panko, and foie gras and process until you have a smooth puree, about 30 seconds.

4. Transfer the mixture to a small baking dish and bake until a nice crust has formed and it's bubbling along the edges of the dish, about 12 minutes. Serve warm.

GABRIEL'S LOVE LETTER TO PLYMOUTH VALIANTS

My first car was a cream-colored 1969 Plymouth Valiant. My dad talked me into it, saying that for $1,600 it was a better deal than a Camaro or a Chevelle. His logic was that there is not a sturdier car or more solid engine than a slant six.

He was right. Since 1997, I've had five Valiants.

I ran the first two into the ground completely (repairing them was not an option on a cook's salary). I also had a 1964 (again, cream-colored) two-door that was nicknamed "The Ace and Gary Mobile" because my sous-chef, Erik Van Kley, and I were always together, riding around making pickups. This is what I was driving when we opened Le Pigeon. At that time, LP was too small to have our ingredients delivered, so we had to make runs to our suppliers—Sheridan Fruit Company, Nicky USA, Newman's Fish, Provista, and various farm-ers' markets—in the Valiant.

We would load it up so full that the suspension eventually gave way, and any speed bump would nearly take out the under-side. Ultimately, the car was such a menace that we joked that we should just strap the bags of flour to the top and cut them open if we needed a smokescreen to stay out of trouble.

Also, because the seals were leaking, and because of the ubiquitous Portland rain, the car was essentially a fog machine on wheels. My solution was to always have a pair of underwear handy to wipe the windshield. Eventu-ally (and understandably), no one would ride with me. This forced a brief yet thought-provoking break from Valiants. I moonlighted briefly with a Cadillac, but it didn't feel right. Not the same smell, not the same feel; a loss of identity ensued.

And so, in 2010, I was ecstatic when I saw a 1964 Plymouth Bar-racuda for sale at Johnny B's, the diner across the street from my old house. (The Plymouth Valiant Barracuda first appeared in 1964. The "Valiant," part was dropped

in 1966, when it was renamed the Plymouth Barracuda in hopes of appealing to muscle car enthusi-asts. It didn't work. And in 1974 Plymouth stopped making the Barracuda.)

Three years later, and after having sunk more than double what it originally cost into repairs, I'm still driving the Barracuda, with the practical addition of childproofing.

Even though doing mundane things, like running to the Plaid Pantry for milk, becomes an hour-long ordeal because every old dude wants to bro-down about the details of the car, and even though almost all of the supplies for LP are now delivered to the restaurant, I still enjoy taking trips to the farmers' market or Nicky USA to load the car up with pro-duce or veal heads.

I just have to be careful of that suspension.

CHAPTER 4
LITTLE BIRDS

Gabriel likes cooking pigeons.

So much so that he tattooed pigeons on his body. So much so that he opened a restaurant called Le Pigeon. We joke that our pigeons come from under the Burnside Bridge, but we actually get them from Palmetto Farms in South Carolina via Nicky USA (www.nickyusa.com). They come to us with their heads and feet still on, with all the goodies still inside, hence our use of hearts and livers. Pigeons have just the right amount of gaminess (similar to duck, but slightly lighter), yet they still allow for over-the-top accompaniments. You can even stuff the bird with figs, spinach, or foie gras. If you have yet to try pigeon, now is your chance. Enjoy this simple dish on its own, or serve it with the bacon-roasted cipollini onions from the Sturgeon au Poivre recipe (page 169). Eats best medium rare. {SERVES 4}

SIMPLE ROASTED PIGEON

4 pigeons, cleaned, with or without the head and feet attached
Kosher salt
A pinch of ground cloves
A pinch of freshly grated nutmeg
4 sprigs thyme
4 cloves garlic, smashed
3 tablespoons unsalted butter

1. Preheat the oven to 450°F (230°C).

2. Season the pigeons inside and out with salt. Sprinkle the skin with a touch of cloves and nutmeg. Stuff the cavity of each bird with a sprig of thyme and a clove of garlic. Truss the birds with butcher's twine (see illustration opposite).

3. In a heavy pan over medium-high heat, melt the butter until it becomes foamy. Add the trussed birds breast side down and cook until gently browned on the bottom, about 2 minutes. Flip the birds and brown on the second side, 2 minutes more. Sit the birds in the pan breast side up and roast in the oven until they are a nice medium-rare, 8 to 10 minutes.

4. Once the birds come out of the oven, baste with the butter and juices in the pan and let rest for 4 to 5 minutes before serving.

 THE PIGEON POUR: If pigeon (often known as squab) were wine, it would be red Burgundy, and if Burgundy were a meat it would be pigeon. Pigeon has pronounced flavors; it's meaty, gamy, sweet, and livery, but all in a subtle way. Red Burgundy is the same; it has fruit, earth, flowers, and mushrooms, but they're all subtle. The direction you take piegeon in a dish will dictate the Burgundy you drink.

With simple roasted pigeon, you can't go wrong with a nice village-level wine. One we love is Monthelie from Domaine Roulot. For Burgundy, don't just look for the big name appellations like Vosne-Romanée, Chambolle, or Volnay. There are also lots of little appellations to consider, such as Ladoix, Monthelie, Auxey-Duresses, Fixin, or Santenay, all of which are a great value.

HOW TO
TRUSS A PIGEON

Buy a fresh pigeon and cut off its head and feet.

Position breast side up and lay a piece of twine or string under the legs and tailbone.

Circle string around legs and tailbone.

PULL TIGHT!

Loop string around legs, pulling tight, and wrap around front, securing wings tight against the body.

With wings tight, loop string back around to legs, and around.

Tie off end and cut remaining string.

Place in baking dish with assorted herbs and cook.

Enjoy!

If the cover of this book didn't give it away, you can see that little birds with little bones are what we like to eat. This dish is perfect for a quick and dirty dinner or brunch, and the duck confit hash is fitting for any hangover: it's quick, fatty, and delicious. {SERVES 4}

MAPLE-LACQUERED SQUAB, DUCK CONFIT HASH

Duck Confit Hash

1 pound (450 g) Yukon gold potatoes, peeled and diced the size of breakfast-style potatoes

¼ cup (60 ml) plus 2 tablespoons neutral oil

Kosher salt

1 cup (85 g) shredded Duck Confit (page 322)

½ cup (70 g) diced yellow onion

½ cup (12 g) sliced green onions, green parts only

Cherry Vinegar

1 cup (250 ml) cider vinegar

½ cup (125 ml) maple syrup

½ cup (125 g) sugar

1 tablespoon kosher salt

12 cherries, pitted but stems left intact

¼ cup (40 g) chopped pitted cherries

Squab

2 tablespoons neutral oil

4 squab (aka, pigeons), cleaned and halved, backbone removed

Kosher salt and freshly ground black pepper

¼ cup (60 ml) maple syrup

4 poached eggs

1. Preheat the oven to 350°F (180°C).

2. To make the hash, toss the potatoes with 2 tablespoons of the oil and salt to taste. Put the potatoes in a baking dish and roast until they are barely cooked through (you don't want soft and mushy), about 10 minutes. Remove the potatoes from the oven but leave the oven on.

3. To make the cherry vinegar, in a small saucepan over high heat, combine the vinegar, maple syrup, sugar, and salt. When it comes to a boil, pour half of the liquid into a heat-proof bowl with the whole pitted cherries. Reduce the heat to low, return the pan to the stove, and simmer the remaining liquid until it thickens and forms a syrup, about 5 minutes. Keep a close eye on it, because it can burn if reduced too much. Remove the pan from the heat and stir in the chopped cherries. Set aside.

4. To make the squab, heat the oil in a large sauté pan over high heat. Season the squab with salt and pepper and sear, skin side down, for 3 minutes. Flip them over and brush with the maple syrup. Place the pan in the oven and bake until a meat thermometer reads 135°F (57°C) for medium-rare, about 5 minutes. Remove from oven and let rest while you finish the hash.

5. Heat a large, heavy sauté pan over high heat with the remaining ¼ cup (60 ml) oil. Add the potatoes and sauté until crispy, about 3 minutes. Stir in the confit and the yellow and green onions. Continue to cook for 3 minutes, mixing well. Season to taste with salt.

6. To serve, create a little mound of the hash on each of four plates, top with a poached egg, then add the squab. Drizzle with the cherry vinegar and add three of the stem-on cherries to each plate before serving.

 THE PIGEON POUR: With the Maple-Lacquered Squab grab a Chambolle-Musigny. The ones from Robert Groffier are complex and bursting with purity of fruit. One of the first Burgundies I remember twisting my head around was a Groffier Chambolle Amoureuses, a top *premier cru*. For a few bucks less, look for his Haut Doix, another *premier cru* located next to Les Amoureuses.

Gabriel's mom, probably like yours, always made green bean cas-serole for Thanksgiving. One thing she did not do is include duck hearts. Green beans are at their best in the peak of summer. Thus, summer is when we make this dish at Le Pigeon. So this actually has nothing to do with moms or Thanksgiving.

Duck hearts in this quantity can be a little tough to find, even for me. Hopefully you have developed a good relationship with your butcher and can ask him or her to save some for you. This might take a little planning ahead, but it will be worth it. {SERVES 6 TO 8}

DUCK HEART, GREEN BEAN CASSEROLE

Heart Jus

Neutral oil for sautéing
1 pound (450 g) duck hearts, rinsed under cold water and squeezed dry
½ yellow onion, thinly sliced
5 cloves garlic, crushed
2 tablespoons black peppercorns
1 bottle (750 ml) ruby port
2 tablespoons molasses
½ cup (60 g) sliced prunes (dried plums)

Casserole

Neutral oil for sautéing
2 pounds (900 g) duck hearts, rinsed under cold water and squeezed dry
2 yellow onions, thinly sliced
2 heads garlic, peeled and sliced
1 teaspoon red pepper flakes
Kosher salt
½ cup (125 ml) red wine
½ cup (125 ml) crème fraîche
3 tablespoons unsalted butter
2 red onions, thinly sliced
1 head black garlic, peeled and coarsely chopped (see sidebar below)
1 cup (120 g) sliced prunes (dried plums)
2½ pounds (1.25 kg) green beans, trimmed and halved
Freshly ground black pepper
1½ cups (375 ml) chicken stock
Juice of 2 lemons
½ cup (60 g) Seasoned Bread Crumbs (page 327)

1. Make the heart jus first to get it out of the way: In a medium saucepan over high heat, heat a thin film of oil. Add the duck hearts and sear them, stirring occasionally, for about 5 minutes. They should look quite caramelized, and any liquid they released should have evaporated. Add the onion, garlic, and peppercorns. Continue to cook, stirring frequently, for another 3 minutes. Add the port, molasses, and prunes. Reduce the heat to medium and continue cooking until the liquid has reduced by three-quarters, 20 to 30 minutes. Strain the liquid and discard the solids.

2. The cooking of the casserole is a two-part process. It sounds more difficult than it actually is, we assure you. First, in a large sauté pan over high heat, heat a thin film of oil. Add the duck hearts and sear for 5 minutes. Add the yellow onions, half of the sliced garlic, and the red pepper flakes. Season with salt. Turn the heat down to medium and cook, stirring frequently, until the onions are soft, about 10 minutes. At this point, add the red wine and crème fraîche and continue to cook another 5 minutes. What you should have is a thick, creamy mess. But wait, it gets better: add the contents of the pan to a food processor and pulse repeatedly to make a coarse puree. Not exactly smooth, but not too chunky.

3. Next, in the same pan over medium heat, melt the butter. Add the red onions, the remaining head of sliced garlic and the chopped black garlic, the prunes, and green beans and season well with salt and pepper. Cook, stirring frequently, about 5 minutes. Add the pureed heart mixture and continue to cook for another 5 minutes. Add the stock and continue to cook until you have a thick green bean stew of sorts, about 10 minutes. At this point add the lemon juice and taste it. It will probably want a pinch more of salt and a couple grinds of pepper.

4. Preheat the oven to 400°F (200°C).

5. Transfer the bean mixture to a 12 by 19-inch (30 by 48cm) baking dish and top with bread crumbs. Bake until the top is golden and crispy, about 10 minutes.

6. Serve with some of the heart jus alongside in a gravy boat so people can serve themselves. (We like it with a lot of heart jus.)

GABRIEL'S NOTE ON BLACK GARLIC

When I had my first taste of black (i.e., fermented) garlic, it was a huge revelation. As a cook I had used garlic every day with different techniques and goals, but I had never tasted anything like this. The gears started turning immediately, and there has been no turning back. Imagine garlic with the flavor of dried fruit. Soft, like roasted garlic, it is sweet and earthy, yet it is much milder than raw garlic.

Duck confit salad, duck liver vinaigrette, and pan-roasted squab—
or, as we say, Duck, Duck, Pigeon. It's all in the title. {SERVES 4}

DUCK, DUCK, PIGEON

Duck Liver Vinaigrette

½ cup (125 ml) plus 1 tablespoon
   neutral oil
4 good-sized duck livers, about
   4 ounces (130 g) each
Kosher salt
¼ cup (60 g) unsalted butter
1 large shallot, thinly sliced
2 cloves garlic, thinly sliced
¼ teaspoon red pepper flakes
¼ cup (60 ml) champagne vinegar
1 lemon

1. Preheat the oven to 400°F (200°C).

2. To make the vinaigrette, heat a small sauté pan over medium-high heat and add 1 tablespoon of the oil. Season the duck livers liberally with salt and add to the pan. Be careful, as they are likely to spit at you. Sear for about 1 minute and turn over; you want to keep them medium-rare, because there's nothing worse than overcooked livers, which become grainy and have an overwhelming iron flavor, like biting into a rusty pipe. Remove the livers from the pan and turn the heat down to medium. Add the butter, shallot, garlic, and red pepper flakes and sauté until the shallot is soft, 3 to 4 minutes. Deglaze the pan with the champagne vinegar.

Pan-Roasted Pigeon

2 pigeons, cleaned and halved, backbone removed

Kosher salt and freshly ground black pepper

2 tablespoons neutral oil

2 cloves garlic, crushed

2 sprigs thyme

1 tablespoon unsalted butter

Duck Salad

3 cups (120 g) frisée

1 cup (200 g) seedless red grapes

¼ cup (55 g) roasted walnuts

¼ cup (10 g) fresh flat-leaf parsley

2 tablespoons chives, cut into 1-inch (2.5cm) lengths

1 tablespoon tarragon leaves

½ cup (45 g) shredded Duck Confit (page 322)

Maldon flake salt

1 lemon

Good-quality balsamic vinegar for drizzling

3. Transfer the liver mixture to a blender and puree, adding the remaining ½ cup (125 ml) oil in a thin, steady stream; the protein in the liver provides the base for the emulsion in this recipe. Hit it with a good squeeze of lemon and a pinch of salt. Check the consistency and add water if needed; it should be the consistency of a nice, thick salad dressing. Set aside until you're ready to finish the dish. It will last 5 days in the fridge, although it will firm up when cold, so take it out at least 2 hours before you use it.

4. To make the pigeon, season the pigeon halves with salt and pepper. In a heavy sauté pan over high heat, heat the oil. Once the oil is just at the smoking point, add the pigeons, skin side down, and sear until the skin is browned, about 2 minutes. Turn the birds over and add the garlic, thyme, and pat of butter. Tilt the pan back toward you and, using a spoon, continuously baste with the butter, which should be nice and foamy, for another minute. Place the pan in the oven and cook until a meat thermometer reads 135°F (57°C) for medium-rare, another 4 to 5 minutes. You don't want to overcook the pigeons or they will taste livery, and I don't mean in a good way. The ideal internal temperature of pigeon is 140°F (60°C). Remove from the oven, transfer the pigeons to a plate, and let rest while you assemble the salad.

5. To make the salad, toss the frisée, grapes, walnuts, parsley, chives, and tarragon together. Toss in the duck confit and season to taste with Maldon salt. Dress the salad with 3 tablespoons of the duck liver vinaigrette. Give a squeeze of lemon and divide the salad between four plates. Arrange a pigeon half next to the salad and drizzle some more vinaigrette on top. Finish with a drizzle of good balsamic vinegar and serve.

It sucks to wake up and cook brunch for a bunch of hungover people, especially if you yourself are hungover. We did brunch for the first year at LP and promptly stopped for that reason. (One thing we used to serve at brunch was the East Burnside Mimosa, which was orange soda mixed with Miller High Life. It was very popular, but Andy won't let us serve it anymore. He cringes at the mere mention of it.)

Lucky for us, there are plenty of places to have brunch in Portland. There is The Roost, Broder, The Woodsman Tavern, Tasty n Sons . . . all amazing options for that hazy weekend afternoon.

Gabriel grew up on Eggos, served both at breakfast and after school. Adding the optional foie maple syrup to this recipe makes the waffles seem (wrongly, perhaps) more adult. {SERVES 4}

CHICKEN-FRIED QUAIL, EGGOS, FOIE MAPLE SYRUP

¼ cup (60 g) plus 1 tablespoon unsalted butter, softened
½ teaspoon espelette pepper
¼ teaspoon Maldon flake salt, plus more for sprinkling
4 semiboneless quail
Kosher salt
1 cup (250 ml) buttermilk
3 cups (375 g) all-purpose flour
1 cup (60 g) fresh bread crumbs, from 4 slices of bread
1 teaspoon paprika
1 teaspoon mustard powder
½ teaspoon freshly grated nutmeg
Neutral oil for frying
4 Eggo Waffles
Foie Maple Syrup (optional; opposite)

1. In a small bowl, combine ¼ cup of the butter, the pepper, and the Maldon salt and set aside. Season the quail with kosher salt. Put the quail in a small bowl with the buttermilk (it should just cover the quail) and set aside to soak.

2. In a large bowl, combine the flour, bread crumbs, paprika, mustard powder, nutmeg, and 1 tablespoon kosher salt. Transfer the flour mixture to a lunch-sized paper bag. Drain the quail well and, one at a time, add them to the paper bag. Shake well to thoroughly coat the quail with the flour mixture, then transfer the quail to a plate.

3. Pour oil to a depth of ½ inch (12 mm) in a cast-iron pan large enough to hold the quail in a single layer. Heat the oil over high heat. When the oil is hot, add the quail along with the remaining tablespoon of butter. Turn down the heat to medium and fry until the quail is browned and cooked through to medium, 2 to 3 minutes on each side. Set the quail aside to rest on a plate lined with paper towels.

4. Toast the waffles. Spread the butter and espelette pepper mixture over the waffles.

5. Arrange one waffle and one quail on each of four dishes. Drizzle the foie maple syrup on top. Sprinkle with Maldon salt and serve.

Foie Maple Syrup

6 ounces (180 g) foie gras cubes
(see page 51)
½ cup (125 ml) maple syrup

MAKES ¾ CUP (180 ML)

In a small saucepan over low heat, melt the foie gras with the maple syrup until the mixture is thick and sticky, 10 to 15 minutes. Carefully strain the liquid, discarding the foie bits and reserving the syrup. The syrup will keep for up to 2 weeks in the refrigerator.

Serving pheasant feels indulgent and makes us happy. It conjures a
real Bacchus feeling: whole pheasants being served on faïence plat-
ters, Caravaggio-esque colors, and big goblets of wine. Here we serve
it with a bit of gnocchi and pears drowned in booze. {SERVES 4}

PHEASANT GNOCCHI, SAKE PEARS

Pheasant

1 pheasant, about 2 pounds (900 g),
    halved
Kosher salt
1 yellow onion, thinly sliced
5 cloves garlic, crushed
3 sprigs thyme
1 tablespoon black peppercorns
6 cups (1.5 l) water
¼ cup (60 ml) rice wine vinegar
¼ cup (60 ml) brown miso
1 tablespoon Sriracha hot sauce
1 bottle (750 ml) dry sake

Sake Pears

1 Bosc pear, peeled, cored, and cut
    into ¼-inch (6mm) wedges
¼ cup (60 ml) dry sake (reserved from
    making the pheasant)

Gnocchi

¾ cup (180 g) unsalted butter
Kosher salt
2 cups (250 g) all-purpose flour
6 eggs

1 tablespoon unsalted butter
½ cup (70 g) peeled and finely diced
    parsnips
3 cloves garlic, thinly sliced
⅛ teaspoon espelette pepper
¼ cup (65 g) Parsnip Pear Butter
    (page 325)
A squeeze of fresh lemon juice
2 tablespoons chopped chives
¼ cup (5 g) thinly sliced shiso leaves
½ cup (125 ml) Shiso Oil (page 328)

1. Season the pheasant well with kosher salt and place in a large stockpot over high heat. Add the onion, garlic, thyme, peppercorns, water, vinegar, miso, and Sriracha. Set aside ¼ cup (60 ml) of the sake and add the rest of the bottle to the stockpot. Season with a little additional salt. Bring to a boil, then reduce the heat to a simmer. Cover and cook until the leg meat is falling off the bone, about 35 minutes.

2. While the bird is cooking, toss the pear pieces with the reserved sake. Let marinate in the refrigerator for 30 minutes.

3. To make the gnocchi, in a heavy saucepan over high heat, combine 1½ cups (375 ml) of water with the butter and 1 tablespoon salt. Bring to a boil, then reduce the heat to medium. Add the flour all at once and stir rapidly with a wooden spoon until the dough pulls away from the sides of the pan. The bottom of the pan should be clean, with no dough sticking to it. Continue to stir for 1 to 2 minutes more. Transfer the dough to the bowl of a stand mixer fitted with the paddle attachment. Let cool for 5 minutes. Turn the mixer on low and add the eggs one at a time. Allow the eggs to incorporate fully each time before adding the next.

4. Bring a large pot of salted water to a boil over high heat. Meanwhile, lightly oil a baking sheet. Fill a pasty bag fitted with a medium (⅝-inch/1.5cm) tip with the dough. If you don't have a pastry bag, you can shape the gnocchi using two tablespoons instead. Turn the water down to a simmer. Hold the pastry bag over the pot with one hand and a small knife in the other, squeeze out 1-inch (2.5cm) segments and cut them off with the knife into the water. The gnocchi will sink to the bottom. When they rise to the top, they're done, after 1 to 2 minutes. You have to be quick here; work in batches and don't bite off more than you can chew. Start small and before you know it you will get into a good rhythm. Every so often dip the knife into the water to help keep it from sticking to the dough. With a slotted spoon, transfer the gnocchi as they are done to the prepared baking sheet.

5. Carefully remove the pheasant from the poaching liquid and let cool. Meanwhile, using a fine-mesh seive, strain the poaching liquid and discard the solids. (Though you will use some of the liquid below, you'll also have some left over. Use it to cook rice and you will have some of the most bad-ass tasting rice you have ever made.)

6. When the pheasant is cool enough to handle, carefully pick the skin and meat off the bones, shredding it with your fingers into small pieces. Reserve the meat and discard the skin and bones.

7. In a large sauté pan over medium heat, melt the pat of butter. Add the parsnips, garlic, and espelette pepper and sauté for about 2 minutes. Add the shredded pheasant and the gnocchi and continue to cook for 1 minute more. Add 1½ cups (375 ml) of the poaching liquid and continue cooking until reduced by three-quarters, about 3 minutes. Remove from the heat and stir in the parsnip pear butter. At this point, you might want to give it a squeeze of lemon. Finally, add the chives and give the pan a quick toss.

8. Divide the pheasant gnocchi between four bowls. Top with the sake pears and shiso leaves, drizzle with the shiso oil, and serve.

 THE PIGEON POUR: This dish was a tough one to pair with wine at first. We all loved the dish, but every wine we tried with it made us shrug our shoulders. It didn't add anything, and it didn't take anything away. So we gave up on a wine pairing and turned to beer. Baladin Nora, from Italy's Piedmont region, is this dish's long-lost love. The beer has mild notes of spice, ginger, orange, and flowers that play off the sweetness of the pear and parsnip and complement the shiso and sake delicately layered into the dish.

If you can't find Baladin Nora, look for a Belgian or Belgian-style ale with a light body and lightly spicy character. If you know of a local shop with a wide selection of beers, I bet there is someone who works there who would love to geek out about this and find you something cool.

This is a nice, simple, and rustic way to eat pigeon with pigeon. The real magic is the flavor-packed chopped liver mousse, a recipe inspired by Gabriel's good friend and old boss Tommy Habetz, i.e., Tommy from Bunk Bar (see page 192). This recipe sounds more challenging than it actually is. Simply put, it involves searing liver, sautéing goodies, and combining it all in a food processor. {SERVES 4}

PIGEON, LIVER CROSTINI, ANCHOVY

Red Wine Syrup
¼ cup (60 g) sugar
6 cloves garlic, sliced
4 anchovies
3 sprigs thyme
1 teaspoon black peppercorns
1 bottle (750 ml) red wine
⅓ cup (80 ml) red wine vinegar

Chopped Liver
Neutral oil for sautéing
8 ounces (250 g) duck livers
Livers from 2 pigeons
Kosher salt
2 tablespoons unsalted butter
1 large shallot, thinly sliced
2 cloves garlic, sliced
2 anchovies
2 teaspoons tomato paste
A pinch of red pepper flakes
2 tablespoons balsamic vinegar

Pigeon
Neutral oil for sautéing
Legs and breasts from 2 pigeons
Kosher salt and freshly ground pepper

4 thick slices rustic French bread, crust removed
1 tablespoon good-quality extra-virgin olive oil, plus more for brushing
½ cup (20 g) frisée
1 tablespoon coarsely chopped white anchovies (boquerones)
¼ cup (50 g) sliced green grapes
1 tablespoon tarragon leaves
1 tablespoon olive oil
A squeeze of fresh lemon juice

1. To make the syrup, in a medium saucepan over high heat, add the sugar and cook until it turns into a light amber caramel, about 4 minutes. Add the garlic, anchovies, thyme, and peppercorns and let them bloom in the sugar for a couple of seconds. Add the wine and vinegar. Cook until the mixture has a syrupy consistency, about 30 minutes. You will start to see big bubbles form as it is close to being done. (Keep in mind that it will be thinner when hot, and you're serving it at room temperature. If you reduce it too far, just add a splash of water.)

2. Let's make the chopped liver: First, in a 12-inch (30cm) sauté pan over high heat, heat a thin film of oil. Season the duck and pigeon livers with salt and sear them quickly, about 30 seconds per side. Be careful, as livers will sometimes pop and splatter oil. Remove the livers from the pan and reduce the heat to low, giving the pan a minute to cool down. Add the butter, shallot, garlic, anchovies, tomato paste, and red pepper flakes. Cook over low heat, stirring, for 5 minutes. Return the livers to the pan and toss well to combine. Transfer the liver mixture to a food processor and add the balsamic vinegar. Pulse to combine; you want a coarse, chunky puree. Season with salt to taste and set aside.

3. To make the pigeon, in a sauté pan over medium-high heat, heat a thin film of oil. Season the pigeon parts with salt and pepper and sear, skin side down, until golden and crispy, 3 to 4 minutes. Turn over and continue to cook for 2 minutes more. Remove the breasts from the pan and continue to cook the legs for 2 minutes more. Remove the legs from the pan and set aside.

GABRIEL'S NOTE ON BOQUERONES

Anchovies cured in salt and then marinated in vinegar: what could be better? Boquerones are brighter and less fishy than your everyday canned anchovy, so I strongly suggest you find a specialty store that carries them for the recipes in this book. Not only do I use them at work in many recipes, but I also keep them at home to eat them as a snack with a crusty baguette.

4. Preheat a gas grill or prepare a charcoal grill for cooking over medium heat. Brush the slices of bread with oil and grill (or toast) for 1 minute on each side, being careful not to burn it. Spread about 2 tablespoons of the chopped liver on each piece. Slice the pigeon breasts in half and place a half on top of each piece of toast.

5. In a bowl, toss the frisée, anchovies, grapes, and tarragon with the olive oil and lemon juice. Place a little of the salad next to the toast. Lean a pigeon leg against the toast, drizzle with the red wine syrup, and serve.

 THE PIGEON POUR: For a squab preparation like this one that revels in gamy fullness, Gevrey-Chambertin is where it's at. And for dark red fruit, earth, and iron blood—you can't go wrong with Domaine Maume.

Pheasant is a great bird to eat, lighter than pigeon or duck but gamier than chicken. It just tends to dry out very quickly. For this preparation, we poach it gently, pick the meat, and then rewarm it with butter and roasted shiitake mushrooms to create a warm pheasant salad perfect for a crisp fall day.

Note: The stems of the mushrooms are saved to make the dressing. {SERVES 6}

PHEASANT, SHIITAKE, UMAMI, MIZUNA

2 shallots, peeled and sliced
¼ cup (60 ml) sherry vinegar
Kosher salt
A pinch of red pepper flakes
1 medium bone-in pheasant, about 2 pounds (900 g), halved
1 yellow onion, diced
4 cloves elephant or regular garlic, coarsely chopped
1 teaspoon chopped fresh thyme
1½ cups (375 ml) dry white wine
½ cup (125 ml) extra-virgin olive oil
¼ cup (60 ml) plus 1 tablespoon soy sauce
4 ounces (125 g) shiitake mushrooms, stems removed (and reserved for making the Umami Bomb Dressing, opposite) and halved
¼ cup (60 g) unsalted butter, plus 1 tablespoon unsalted butter, melted
1 teaspoon Sriracha hot sauce
1 tablespoon chopped fresh flat-leaf parsley
3 cups (40 g) purple mizuna leaves
Umami Bomb Dressing (opposite)
A small chunk of San Andreas or other aged sheep's milk cheese
Garlic Chips for garnish (optional; page 323)

1.   First, we are going to macerate the shallots. In a small bowl combine the shallots, sherry vinegar, ¼ teaspoon salt, and the red pepper flakes. Let stand for at least 20 minutes or up to 1 hour. Drain the shallots and reserve, discarding the liquid.

2.   In a large saucepan over medium heat, combine the pheasant, onion, garlic, thyme, white wine, olive oil, ¼ cup (60 ml) of the soy sauce, and 1 tablespoon salt. Pour in just enough water to cover the pheasant, about 3 cups (750 ml). It may feel like you're carelessly bombing a slew of ingredients into a pot, but we promise you're on the right path. Bring the liquid to a gentle simmer and poach the pheasant until it is just cooked through, about 20 minutes. At this point, the bird will be slightly underdone. Remove the pheasant from the stove and let it cool completely in the poaching liquid. This will help the bird to retain its moisture.

3.   Preheat the oven to 425°F (220°C). Toss the mushrooms with the tablespoon of melted butter, the remaining 1 tablespoon soy sauce, and the Sriracha. Spread the mushrooms on a baking sheet and roast until all the liquid has evaporated, about 15 minutes.

4.   Remove the pheasant from the liquid and pick the meat off, discarding the bones. Strain the poaching liquid and reserve the liquid as well as the onions and garlic. Mix the onions and garlic with the pheasant meat and set aside.

5.   In a small sauté pan over medium heat, combine the pheasant, the macerated shallots, and the shiitake mushrooms. Add 1 cup (250 ml) of the reserved poaching liquid and the ¼ cup (60 g) butter. Cook until the liquid has reduced by three-quarters, 7 to 8 minutes. It will look slightly shredded, à la pulled pork. Stir in the parsley and season with salt.

6.   Toss the mizuna with 2 tablespoons of the umami dressing. Spoon the pheasant onto plates and top with the dressed mizuna. Drizzle each plate with the remaining dressing and grate the sheep's milk cheese over the top. Sprinkle the garlic chips on top and serve.

Umami Bomb Dressing

4 ounces (125 g) shiitake stems
    (reserved from making the
    mushrooms)
4 cloves garlic, chopped
½ cup (125 ml) soy sauce
¼ cup (60 ml) dry sherry
¼ cup (60 ml) plus 1 tablespoon sherry
    vinegar
1 tablespoon honey
1 teaspoon grated fresh ginger
1 teaspoon fish sauce
½ teaspoon Sriracha hot sauce
2 egg yolks
1 cup (250 ml) neutral oil

MAKES 1½ CUPS (375 ML)

In a medium saucepan, over medium heat, combine the shiitake stems, garlic, soy sauce, sherry, ¼ cup (60 ml) of the sherry vinegar, the honey, ginger, fish sauce, and Sriracha. Bring to a simmer and cook until reduced to ⅓ cup (80 ml), about 5 minutes. Strain, discarding the solids, and let cool to room temperature. In a blender, combine the strained liquid, the egg yolks, and the remaining 1 tablespoon sherry vinegar. Set the blender to puree and, with the motor running, add the oil in a thin, steady stream to create an emulsion. When the dressing is smooth, turn off the machine and set the dressing aside. It will keep in the refrigerator for up to 1 week.

This recipe is a great way to introduce your kids to duck. After they try these nuggets, they'll be on a one-way street to post-chickendom and will request this dish forevermore. {MAKES 25 NUGGETS*}

DUCK NUGGETS

Duck Mixture

1 pound (450 g) Duck Confit
   (page 322)
1 tablespoon sherry vinegar
1 tablespoon Dijon mustard
1 tablespoon olive oil
1 yellow onion, thinly sliced
6 cloves garlic, minced
½ teaspoon dried sage
½ teaspoon dried thyme
¼ teaspoon garlic powder
¼ teaspoon paprika
¼ teaspoon mustard powder

Dijon Dipping Sauce

1 cup (250 ml) prune juice
4 prunes (dried plums), finely chopped
¼ cup (60 ml) sherry vinegar
¼ cup (60 ml) Dijon mustard

Breading

4 eggs
½ cup (60 g) all-purpose flour
1 cup (75 g) fresh bread crumbs

Neutral oil for frying
A squeeze of fresh lemon juice
Kosher salt

1. To make the duck mixture, using a knife, finely shred and chop the meat and skin of the duck confit. In a medium bowl, stir together the shredded confit, sherry vinegar, and Dijon mustard and set aside. In a sauté pan over medium heat, heat the olive oil. When the oil is hot, add the onion, garlic, sage, thyme, garlic powder, paprika, and mustard powder and sauté until the onion is translucent, 3 to 4 minutes. Transfer the mixture to a bowl and let cool. When the mixture is just cool enough to handle, add the confit mixture and mix with your fingers. Let cool for another 20 minutes before forming the nuggets.

2. To make the dipping sauce, in a small saucepan over medium-low heat, combine the prune juice, prunes, and vinegar and bring to a simmer. Simmer until reduced to about 2 tablespoons of liquid, about 7 minutes. Transfer to a mixing bowl and let cool. Once cool, stir in the Dijon mustard. If the sauce seems too thick, add water to thin. Set aside.

3. To make the breading, lightly beat the eggs in a shallow dish. Place the flour and bread crumbs in separate shallow dishes next to the eggs. Scoop out a heaping tablespoon of the duck mixture and use your hands to form it into a nugget shape (we know you know what nuggets look like, don't pretend you don't!). Dip the nuggets into the flour first, then the egg, and finally into the bread crumbs. Set the nuggets aside on a platter.

4. Pour oil to a depth of ½ inch (12 mm) in a large skillet and heat over high heat. When the oil is hot but not smoking, carefully add the nuggets to the oil. Working in batches of about 8 nuggets, fry for 90 seconds, flip to the other side, and continue to fry for 90 seconds more. Transfer the nuggets to a plate lined with paper towels to drain.

5. Add a squeeze of lemon and a pinch of salt and serve with the dipping sauce.

*Are there ever enough nuggets?

This risotto gives you an excuse to use that dusty pressure cooker from the 1980s, the one your parents received as a wedding present and then happily passed down to you. In this recipe, we're cooking a risotto, but instead of using rice, we're using pine nuts. The key is to soak the pine nuts overnight so they already have a rice-like density before the pressure cooker comes into play. Topped with honey-glazed quail, this dish is made for those times when the Portland drizzle is bumming your pizzle. {SERVES 4}

QUAIL, PINE NUT RISOTTO, MARMALADE

Pine Nut Risotto
1 pound (450 g) pine nuts
4 cups (1 l) water
Kosher salt
1 cup (250 ml) chicken stock
1 teaspoon chopped fresh thyme
¼ cup (30 g) chopped prunes
  (dried plums)
2 tablespoons unsalted butter
¼ cup (20 g) grated Parmesan

Quail Glaze
½ cup (125 ml) honey
½ cup (125 g) sugar
3 small cloves garlic, crushed
1 teaspoon Chinese five-spice powder
½ teaspoon red pepper flakes

Port Syrup
1 cup (250 ml) ruby port
1 cup (250 ml) red wine vinegar

Onion Confit
1 yellow onion, thinly sliced
2 tablespoons water
1 tablespoon unsalted butter
¼ teaspoon kosher salt

Quail
4 semiboneless quail
Kosher salt
Neutral oil for sautéing

Blood Orange Marmalade (page 321)
¼ cup (6 g) green onions, sliced on
  the diagonal

1. To make the risotto, in a large bowl, soak the pine nuts, water, and 1 teaspoon salt overnight at room temperature.

2. To make the glaze, in a small saucepan over medium heat, combine the honey and sugar and cook until it has the consistency of maple syrup, about 5 minutes. Add the garlic, five-spice powder, and red pepper flakes and remove from the heat. Set aside and let cool to room temperature.

3. To make the syrup, in a small saucepan over medium heat, combine the port and red wine vinegar and cook until reduced to a thick syrup, about 10 minutes.

4. Preheat the oven to 450°F (230°C).

5. To make the confit, in a small saucepan over low heat, combine the onion, water, butter, and salt. Cook, stirring occasionally, until the onion is soft but has no color, about 30 minutes. Set aside. This can be made a day ahead, covered, and stored in the refrigerator.

6. Place the pine nuts along with their soaking water in the pressure cooker and cook according to the manufacturer's instructions for 15 minutes. Drain the pine nuts and discard the liquid. In a medium pot over medium heat, combine the pine nuts, chicken stock, thyme, prunes, and the onion confit. Cook until the liquid is reduced to about ¼ cup (60 ml). Stir in the butter and Parmesan. Season with salt and set aside, keeping warm.

7. To make the quail, season them all over with salt. In a small pan over medium heat, heat a thin film of oil. Add the quail to the pan and sear until browned on both sides, about 90 seconds per side. Remove from the pan and pour off the oil. Brush the quail liberally with the quail glaze and return them to the pan. Place the pan in the oven for about 4 minutes to finish. If you're nervous about the quail being done, a meat thermometer inserted into the birds should read 145°F (63°C).

8. Divide the risotto among four bowls and top with quail. Spoon a dollop of the marmalade and a drizzle of port syrup around the risotto. Garnish with the green onions and serve.

Whenever this dish is on the menu and a line is forming outside of LP, we start searing duck breasts in preparation for an order onslaught, and our caution is always warranted.

The duck is, of course, delicious, but the pierogies on their own are worth the effort. The recipe makes about sixteen pierogies, which can be frozen for up to 2 months. They make a great snack for a Sunday afternoon. {SERVES 4}

DUCK BREAST, GOAT CHEESE PIEROGIES

Pierogi Dough

2½ cups (310 g) all-purpose flour, plus more for kneading and rolling
1 teaspoon kosher salt
1 egg
2 tablespoons sour cream
½ cup (125 ml) water

Filling

12 ounces (375 g) russet potatoes, peeled
Kosher salt
¼ yellow onion, coarsely diced
1 clove garlic, finely minced
1 tablespoon unsalted butter
1 leg Duck Confit, shredded (page 322)
2 ounces (60 g) soft goat cheese
1 teaspoon Maldon flake salt
A dash of freshly ground black pepper

Duck Breasts

4 duck breasts, trimmed of any excess fat
Kosher salt

½ cup (80 g) Sweet and Sour Radishes (page 328)
A squeeze of fresh lemon juice

1. To make the dough, in a stand mixer fitted with a dough hook, combine the flour and salt and make a well in the bottom of the bowl. Carefully place the egg, sour cream, and water into the well and mix on medium speed until well combined.

2. Dust your work surface with flour and turn the dough out onto the surface. Knead it for 3 to 5 minutes to form a ball. Loosely wrap the dough ball with plastic wrap and refrigerate for 1 hour.

3. In the meantime, let's work on our filling: Put the potatoes into a saucepan of cold salted water over high heat. Bring the potatoes to a simmer and cook until tender, about 20 minutes. Drain the potatoes and set aside to cool. In a sauté pan over medium heat, combine the onion, garlic, and butter and sauté until the onion is translucent, 3 to 4 minutes. Remove from the heat and set aside to cool. In a large bowl and with a potato masher, combine the potatoes, the onion mixture, the duck confit, and goat cheese until well combined. Stir in the Maldon salt and pepper and set aside.

4. Now it's time to roll out the pierogi dough. If you have a pasta roller, this step will be made much easier; just put it through the rollers with the machine on the number one setting and you are good to go. If you're doing it by hand, sprinkle your work surface with flour and roll out the dough with a rolling pin until it is about the thickness of a nickel. Cut out 16 circles with a 3¼-inch (8cm) round biscuit or cookie cutter or a large glass.

5. Spoon a scant tablespoon of filling onto each circle slightly off-center. Rub the edge of half of each circle with a bit of water, just so the dough is wet enough to stick to itself. Fold the dough in half over the filling, press the edges together, and crimp with a fork. Lightly oil a baking sheet and set aside. In a large saucepan, bring about 6 cups (1.5 l) water to a boil over high heat. Gently transfer the pierogies to the water and cook for 5 minutes. Remove with a slotted spoon to the prepared baking sheet.

6.   Finally, the duck breasts. Season them on both sides with salt and score the skin so that the fat will render when you cook them. In a large sauté pan over medium-low heat, arrange the breasts, skin side down. Cook on the first side until the fat has rendered and looks golden brown and crispy, about 10 minutes. Flip the breasts and cook on the second side until golden brown and crispy, 3 to 4 minutes more. About halfway through the cooking time, pour off any excess duck fat and reserve; you'll cook the pierogies in the rendered fat. When the duck breasts are done, transfer them to a plate lined with paper towels.

7.   Add the reserved duck fat to a large sauté pan over medium-low heat. Add the pierogies, and cook until brown, basting constantly with the fat, about 2 minutes. Flip the pierogies and cook for 2 minutes more, continuing to baste until brown.

8.   To serve, put one pierogi on each of four plates and accompany each with a spoonful of the radishes. Slice the duck breast and arrange on top of the pierogies and radishes. Sprinkle with salt and a squeeze of lemon juice. Drizzle with a bit of syrup from the sweet and sour radishes and serve.

Yes, eating pigeon crudo sounds crazy and weird. And it is. But paired with the right ingredients, you've got something fun and delicious.

It all started when Andy came back from a trip to New York and shared with Gabriel his wildest and most delicious bite from the trip: chicken sashimi. That got Gabriel thinking. We could never serve chicken sashimi, as the health inspector would have an absolute shit fit and shut us down, but the idea was stuck in his head. Pigeon is a dark meat best served rare to medium-rare, so naturally it would lend itself to being eaten almost raw. We are also always on the hunt for fun and new ways to serve our namesake. Our first try at pigeon crudo combined the classic lemon juice and grappa. It was good but lacking something. Then somebody suggested bourbon and we were off to the races. {SERVES 4}

PIGEON CRUDO, FIGS, BOURBON

6 fresh black Mission figs
4 tablespoons (60 ml) Eagle Rare or other good-quality bourbon
1 tablespoon balsamic vinegar
1 tablespoon molasses
1 tablespoon freshly squeezed lemon juice
4 pigeon breasts, skin removed
Extra-virgin olive oil for drizzling
Maldon flake salt
2 tablespoons crumbled blue cheese
1 tablespoon chopped chives

1. In a blender, combine 2 of the figs, 2 tablespoons of the bourbon, the balsamic vinegar, and the molasses. Puree until as smooth as possible. Using a fine-mesh strainer, strain the puree, pushing on the solids with a spoon to extract as much liquid as possible. Discard the solids and put the strained liquid in a small saucepan over low heat. Bring to a gentle simmer and reduce until the liquid has a syrupy consistency, about 5 minutes. Remove from the heat and let cool to room temperature.

2. In a shallow bowl, combine the remaining 2 tablespoons bourbon with the lemon juice. Slice the pigeon breasts as thinly as possible and add the slices to the bowl with the bourbon mixture. Let marinate for 1 minute, but no longer. Any longer and the pigeon will become tough and chewy.

3. Divide the slices among four plates. Thinly slice the remaining 4 figs and fan one next to the pigeon on each plate. Top the pigeon with a drizzle of olive oil and a pinch of Maldon salt. Sprinkle with the blue cheese and chives. Drizzle each plate with fig and bourbon syrup and serve.

 THE PIGEON POUR: With pigeon crudo, I gravitate to a real floral, mineral-tinged Burgundy like a Savigny-lès-Beaune or Pernand-Vergelesses from Domaine Chandon de Briailles. The finesse of these wines is arguably due to the elegance of its winemaker. This estate (which goes back almost two hundred years) is in its second generation of female winemakers. Claude de Nicolay follows her mom in this role. She brings a soft touch and a bright laugh to the wine. Our wine lists almost always have her wines on them.

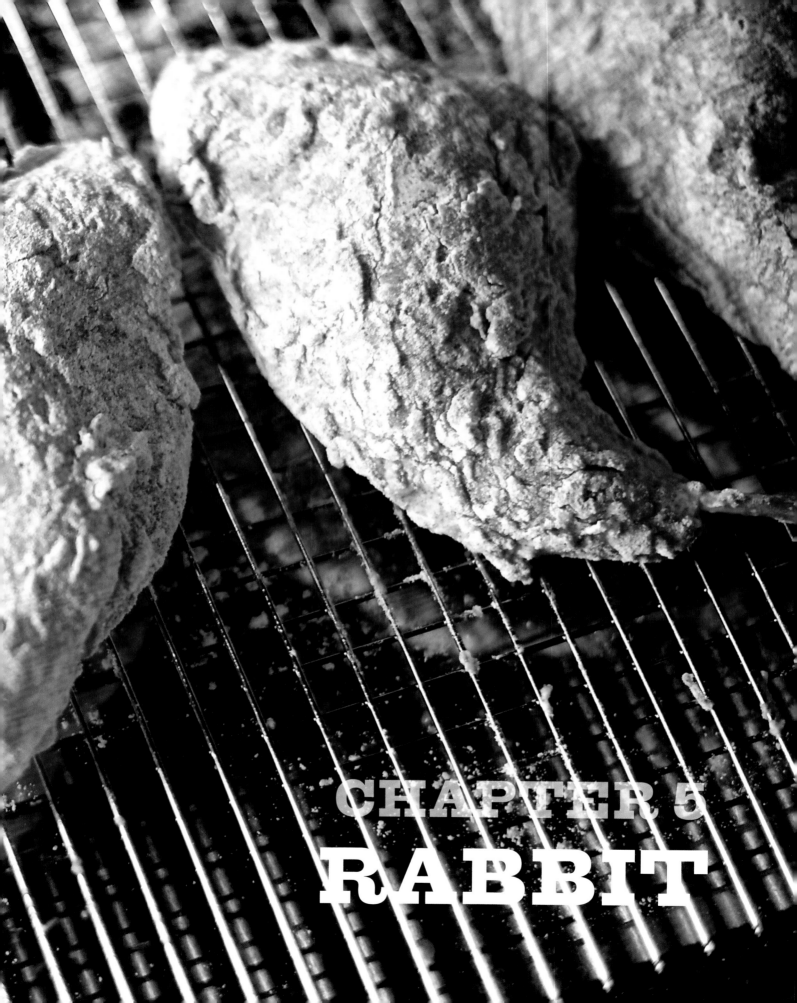

CHAPTER 5
RABBIT

Along with our Beef Cheeks Bourguignon (page 206), this is one of the dishes we're famous for, and it's the reason that Meredith wanted to work on this book with us.

This is not a difficult dish, but you will need a way to smoke the rabbit. We cold smoke with alder wood using a Little Chief Smoker, which you can find at almost any camping or sporting goods store, or, of course, online. If buying one is not in the cards for you, you can use a grill plus wood chips.

At the restaurant we serve the pie with Rabbit Hearts Chutney (page 104), Beecher's cheddar, and ice cream made from mustard produced by Beaver Brand, an Oregon company that makes mustard so good they dare you to make an ice cream of it.

You can either buy the individual piecrusts, or you can make them yourself using the quiche crust dough recipe on page 268. If using the quiche recipe, substitute aged cheddar for the Gruyère.

Note: It will take up to 4 hours to braise and smoke the rabbit. And since the smoked rabbit can be stored in the fridge for up to 5 days, we suggest preparing this dish the day before you want to serve it; that will allow you to freeze the ice cream and brine the rabbit hearts overnight, too. {SERVES 4}

SMOKED RABBIT PIE, CHEDDAR, MUSTARD ICE CREAM

Neutral oil for searing
1 whole rabbit, quartered
1 yellow onion, peeled
5 or 6 dried apricots, diced
4 cloves garlic, sliced
1 (12-ounce/375ml) bottle Miller High Life or other mildly flavored beer
¼ cup (60 ml) Moscatel vinegar
2 cups (500 ml) chicken stock
½ cup (125 g) plus 2 tablespoons Beaver Brand Sweet Hot Mustard or other hot mustard
½ teaspoon freshly ground black pepper
1 cup (250 ml) crème fraîche
¼ cup (50 g) minced bacon
4 (3-inch/7.5cm diameter) prebaked individual piecrusts, purchased or homemade (page 268)
1 cup (125 g) grated aged cheddar cheese, preferably Beecher's
2 tablespoons Herb Pistou (page 324)
Rabbit Hearts Chutney (page 104)
Mustard Ice Cream (page 105)

1. Preheat the oven to 400°F (200°C). In a large Dutch oven over high heat, heat a thin film of oil. Add the rabbit quarters and sear until browned all over. Remove from the pan and set aside. Add the onion, apricots, and garlic to the Dutch oven and sauté until the onion is slightly translucent, about 4 minutes. Return the rabbit to the Dutch oven. Add the beer and vinegar and deglaze the pan, scraping the bottom of the pan to release any browned bits. Stir in the chicken stock, 2 tablespoons of the mustard, and the pepper.

2. Place the Dutch oven in the oven to braise the rabbit. At around the 2-hour mark, start to check the rabbit every 15 minutes. It is ready to be pulled when the meat begins falling from the bone, which could take up to 3 hours but may happen sooner, so be on your toes.

3. Remove the rabbit mixture from the oven and let cool for 5 to 10 minutes. Taking care not to burn yourself, remove the rabbit pieces from the liquid. Set the rabbit on a plate and gently wipe the pieces dry to prepare them for the smoker. Reserve the braising liquid.

4.   If you're using a smoker, prepare it according to the manufacturer's instructions. Place the rabbit pieces in the smoker and smoke until the rabbit has a nice smoky aroma, 30 to 35 minutes. It should be pungent and sweet, with a little sour note to it. If you're using a charcoal grill, light a small fire in the corner of the grill and toss a handful of wood chips on the fire. Place the rabbit on the grill as far away from the fire as possible and close the lid. Smoke, checking every 10 minutes or so to make sure that there is plenty of smoke and to add more wood chips as needed, until the rabbit has a smoky aroma, about 30 minutes.

5.   Remove the rabbit from the smoker and *carefully* pick all the meat off the bones. Rabbits have many sharp little bones, so we suggest that you sit down, have a beer, and go through the meat two or three times. Return the meat to the Dutch oven and stir in the reserved braising liquid, ¾ cup (180 ml) of the crème fraîche, and the bacon. Cook the mixture over medium heat until almost all of the liquid has reduced (when you tilt the pan there should be about 2 tablespoons of juice visible). The meat should look like pulled pork. Check the seasoning and then let cool to room temperature. At this point, the braised rabbit can be stored in the refrigerator for up to 5 days.

{Continued}

6. Preheat the oven to 350°F (180°C). Fill each piecrust with about 4 ounces (125 g) of the rabbit braise, so that the filling just hits the lip. Bake for 12 minutes. Remove the pies and increase the heat to 450°F (230°C). Top the pies with the cheddar and bake until the pies are warmed through and the cheese is melted, 4 to 5 minutes.

7. While the pies are in the oven, make your mustard crème fraîche by mixing the remaining ¼ cup (60 g) of crème fraîche with the remaining ½ cup (125 g) of hot mustard.

8. Gingerly remove the pies from the oven and place one on each plate. Spoon the mustard crème fraîche around the plate. Do the same with the pistou. If you've made the rabbit hearts chutney (good for you), add a nice spoonful beside the pie. Top with a small spoonful of mustard ice cream and serve.

Rabbit Hearts Chutney

Rabbit Hearts

2 cups (500 ml) water
10 whole coriander seeds
6 white peppercorns
5 cloves garlic, crushed
1 bay leaf
1 tablespoon sugar
2 tablespoons kosher salt
¼ teaspoon pink curing salt
¼ teaspoon red pepper flakes
8 ounces (250 g) rabbit or chicken
    hearts

Apricot Chutney

½ cup (125 ml) Moscatel vinegar
½ cup (60 g) diced dried apricots
½ cup (75 g) finely diced red onions
1 tablespoon yellow mustard seeds
1 tablespoon poppy seeds
A dash of paprika
A dash of kosher salt

1 tablespoon good-quality olive oil
    (see sidebar, opposite)

SERVES 4

1. Let's brine the hearts first: In a medium saucepan over high heat, combine the water, coriander seeds, peppercorns, garlic, bay leaf, sugar, kosher and curing salts, and red pepper flakes and bring to a boil. Once the mixture boils, give it a good stir to make sure all of the salt and sugar is dissolved. Remove from the heat and add the hearts. Set aside and let cool to room temperature. Place the hearts with their brining liquid in a covered container and refrigerate for 24 hours.

2. The next day, transfer the hearts and their brining liquid to a small saucepan over medium heat and bring to a simmer. Simmer for 50 to 60 minutes, until the hearts have the texture of a steak cooked medium—not too soft, but not chewy either. They will have that meaty "iron" taste. Let the hearts cool in the liquid for about 20 minutes. Then, using a slotted spoon, remove the hearts from the pan and discard the brine. On the bottom of each heart will be a small ring of white fat (you can't miss it). Hold the heart in your hand and use a paring knife to trim the fat. Think about peeling an apple. Discard the fat and quarter the hearts lengthwise.

3. Now for the chutney: In a heavy saucepan over medium heat, combine the vinegar, apricots, red onions, mustard seeds, poppy seeds, paprika, and salt and cook until there is no liquid left and the apricots are plump, about 5 minutes. Remove from the heat and let cool to room temperature.

4. In a bowl, toss together the chutney, olive oil, and hearts and serve.

Mustard Ice Cream

1 cup (250 ml) whole milk
½ cup (125 ml) crème fraîche
½ cup (125 ml) heavy cream
¼ cup (60 ml) glucose syrup
1½ cups (375 ml) hot mustard
2 tablespoon Dijon mustard
2 tablespoons sugar
½ teaspoon kosher salt
5 egg yolks

MAKES 1 QUART (1 L)

In a large saucepan over medium-high heat, combine the milk, crème fraîche, cream, glucose syrup, ¾ cup (185 ml) of the hot mustard, the Dijon mustard, 1 tablespoon of the sugar, and the salt and heat until it registers 150°F (65°C) on a thermometer. Meanwhile, in a small bowl whisk together the remaining 1 tablespoon of sugar and the egg yolks. When the cream mixture reaches the proper heat, pour a small amount into the yolk mixture and whisk together. Whisking constantly, pour the yolk mixture back into the saucepan and continue to whisk until smooth. Heat the mixture to 180°F (80°C), constantly scraping the bottom of the pan with a rubber spatula. Using a fine-mesh sieve, strain the custard into a bowl and place over an ice water bath to chill. Freeze according to the instructions for your ice cream maker until it reaches the consistency of soft-serve ice cream. Swirl in the remaining ¾ cup (185 ml) of hot mustard for just a few seconds to leave a nice ribbon. Freeze overnight before serving.

A NOTE ON GOOD OLIVE OIL

Portland's indie olive oil purveyor is a gentleman (and writer) named Jim Dixon. We don't freak out about olive oil, but that's partly because Jim does that for us, and we usually just buy what he tells us to.

Always reserve your best olive oil like you save the aged balsamic vinegar for a special meal. Don't fry taco meat with it; use it for drizzling, marinating, and dressing super-simple greens.

Some of our favorite olive oils are Arbequina (which I love for its grassy and vegetal nature), Madre Terra (the candy cane of olive oil; it works with sweet flavors), and Olio Verde (the workhorse olive oil; it fits any dish).

We love the combination of rabbit and mustard, which is why we love to pair this dish with the Mustard Greens Quiche (page 268). The sharp, creamy sauce accented with vermouth is a perfect complement to the slightly gamy taste of a good farm-fresh rabbit. Be sure to choose your rabbit wisely. Mass-produced animals tend to be bland and way too lean, which leads to dry, flavorless meat. As in all of our rabbit recipes, we use rabbits from Nicky Farms. Rabbit was their first product, and I remember when Geoff, the owner, would drive around town delivering them to chefs out of the back of a red Ford Escort. {SERVES 4 TO 6}

RABBIT IN A PIG BLANKET

Rabbit
1 pound (450 g) ground rabbit meat
1 egg
¼ cup (60 ml) heavy cream
1 teaspoon mustard powder
A dash of onion powder
A dash of garlic powder
A dash of ground white pepper
1 tablespoon kosher salt
12 slices bacon, each ⅛ inch
    (3 mm) thick
1 tablespoon neutral oil

Sauce
1 tablespoon unsalted butter
½ yellow onion, thinly sliced
4 cloves garlic, crushed
2 bay leaves
1 teaspoon black peppercorns
A small pinch of red pepper flakes
2 cups (500 ml) dry vermouth
2 tablespoons vermouth vinegar
4 cups (1 l) chicken stock
¼ cup (60 ml) crème fraîche
1 tablespoon Dijon mustard
1 tablespoon whole-grain mustard
2 teaspoons chopped fresh flat-leaf
    parsley
Kosher salt

1 radish, thinly sliced
½ cup (7 g) purple mizuna leaves

1.   To make the rabbit, in stand mixer fitted with the paddle attachment, combine the rabbit, egg, cream, mustard powder, onion powder, garlic powder, white pepper, and salt. Mix for 2 minutes on medium speed. You will see the cream and eggs start to emulsify with the meat, and the mixture will take on a tacky, almost gummy texture. Cover and cool in the fridge for 1 hour.

2.   Lay out a large piece of plastic wrap on your work surface. Arrange the bacon slices on top of the plastic wrap, with the short ends of the bacon facing you and the slices overlapping slightly to create a large rectangle. Spoon the rabbit mixture on top of the bacon near the edge closest to you, forming the rabbit into a log shape all along the edge of the bacon. Using the plastic wrap, start rolling the rectangle of bacon tightly around the rabbit to form a bacon-wrapped rabbit cylinder. Twist the ends of the plastic wrap to form an even tighter cylinder.

3.   If you have the tools for sous-vide cooking, place the cylinder in a vacuum bag and vacuum pack using the medium setting. Place the bag in a water bath at 150°F (65°C) for 90 minutes. Remove from the water and chill in an ice bath. Once chilled, remove the cylinder from the bag and slice ¼ inch (6 mm) off each end, as it will most likely be all bacon.

4.   If you do not have the tools for sous-vide, wrap your rabbit cylinder tightly in aluminum foil and gently simmer completely submerged in water until an instant-read thermometer inserted into the middle of the cylinder reads 150°F (65°C), about 25 minutes. Let the rabbit cool before cutting ¼ inch (6 mm) off each end.

{Continued}

5.   Time to work on the sauce: In a large sauté pan over medium heat, melt the pat of butter. Add the onion, garlic, bay leaves, peppercorns, and red pepper flakes. Sauté until the onion is translucent, 3 to 4 minutes. Add the vermouth and vermouth vinegar and reduce by half, 8 to 10 minutes. Add the chicken stock and cook until the mixture is reduced to about 1 cup (250 ml) total, about 15 minutes. Using a fine-mesh sieve, strain the mixture, discard the solids, and return the liquid to the pan. Continue cooking until reduced to about ½ cup (125 ml), about 5 minutes. Stir in the crème fraîche and the Dijon and whole-grain mustards and reduce by half again, 3 to 4 minutes. Now you're there; no more reductions. Stir in the parsley and season with salt.

6.   Cut the rabbit cylinder into as many equal pieces as you have guests, each about the size of a hockey puck. In a sauté pan large enough to hold all the slices of rabbit in a single layer, heat the oil over medium-high heat. Add the rabbit and sauté until browned, about 4 minutes on each side.

7.   To serve, put a piece of rabbit on each of four plates. Top with the radish slices, mizuna leaves, and the sauce and enjoy.

RABBIT IN A PIG BLANKET

Grind up some fresh rabbit meat.

Get some fresh cut slices of bacon. Lay out plastic on work table.

Lay bacon slices overlapping vertically on top of plastic.

Form the rabbit into a log shape all along the edge of the bacon.

Using plastic wrap, roll bacon sheet tightly around the rabbit.

Pull and twist ends of plastic wrap to form a tight bacon-wrapped rabbit cylinder.

Wrap tightly in foil. Simmer in water fully submerged for 25 minutes.

Remove foil and plastic. Cut into equal cylinders about the size of a hockey puck. Heat oil and fry 4 minutes on each side.

Spoon rabbit sauce liberally atop and serve!

In this surf-and-turf terrine, the mild flavor of rabbit mixes perfectly with the rich, sweet unagi. This is a great warm-weather terrine. Light and bright, it's perfect for a late Sunday lunch with a glass of something nice. We know that ground rabbit is tough to find; you may have to buy a whole rabbit and have the meat ground for you. At the restaurant, we serve this with slices of ripe avocado tossed with a little yuzu and sesame seeds, but you can serve it with almost anything, including a fresh baguette.

Note: The terrine must be refrigerated for at least 1 day or up to 3 days before serving. {SERVES 8 TO 10}

RABBIT AND EEL TERRINE

1½ pounds (680 g) ground rabbit meat
⅓ cup (80 ml) heavy cream
1 egg
1 egg white
4 teaspoons kosher salt
2 teaspoons yuzu juice, or a mixture of lemon and lime juices
2 teaspoons soy sauce
2 teaspoons Sriracha hot sauce
2 teaspoons fish sauce
½ teaspoon ground ginger
¼ teaspoon ground cinnamon
⅛ teaspoon freshly grated nutmeg
2 fillets unagi (freshwater eel), each about 10 ounces (315 g)
5 ounces (150 g) foie gras, cut into bite-sized pieces (see page 51)
Maldon flake salt
2 avocados, peeled, pitted, and thinly sliced (optional)
1 tablespoon yuzu juice (optional)
1 teaspoon sesame seeds (optional)
Baguette slices for serving (optional)

1.   Place the rabbit, cream, egg, egg white, salt, juice, soy sauce, Sriracha, fish sauce, ginger, cinnamon, and nutmeg in a food processor and puree, scraping down the sides, until the mixture is fairly smooth and looks like uncooked Spam. Transfer the mixture to a bowl and refrigerate for 20 minutes.

2.   Line a 12 by 3 by 3-inch (30 by 7.5 by 7.5cm) terrine mold with plastic wrap, leaving enough so it overlaps 4 inches (10 cm) on each side. Using your hands, peel the skin off the unagi and discard. Set aside. With a rubber spatula, fold the foie gras pieces into the chilled rabbit mixture.

3.   Preheat the oven to 300°F (150°C). To assemble the terrine, spread one-third of the rabbit mixture on the bottom of the terrine mold and gently press so it fills all the corners. Lay an unagi fillet on top of the rabbit layer and press down. Spread another third of the rabbit on top, and top with the second unagi fillet. Top with the final third of the rabbit mixture and tap the terrine on the countertop to release any air pockets. Fold over the plastic wrap to cover the terrine tightly.

4.   Place the terrine in a roasting pan and add hot water to the pan to come halfway up the sides of the terrine. Cover the terrine mold with its lid and place in the oven. After 40 minutes, prepare an ice water bath that is large enough to hold the mold and start checking the temperature of the terrine. It is done when an instant-read thermometer reads 155°F (70°C), after 45 to 60 minutes. Carefully remove the terrine from the oven and place it in the ice water bath. The water should reach about three quarters of the way up the side of the mold. Let it sit for an hour in the ice water and then remove the mold, pat it dry, and refrigerate overnight or for up to 3 days.

5.   To serve, remove the terrine from the mold and unwrap it. With a damp towel, wipe away any gelée that collected on the surface during the cooking process. Cut ½-inch (12mm) slices and sprinkle with Maldon salt. In a small bowl, toss together the avocado, yuzu juice, and sesame seeds. Serve the terrine with the avocado and baguette slices.

We've served many variations of veal blanquette over the last five years, but you can find a recipe for that anywhere, so we decided to apply a similar technique to rabbit. Over many troubleshooting sessions, Gabriel realized that the traditional method of simmering meat in an aromatic broth and then thickening it with a mixture of egg yolk and cream yielded a slightly dry rabbit. So instead, he cut to the chase and cooked the rabbit and vegetables right in the cream, which produced this rich, moist, and deliciously deep-flavored rabbit stew. We serve this with our Crepe Lasagna (page 281), but you could just as easily serve it with white rice or plain egg noodles.

{SERVES 4}

RABBIT BLANQUETTE, PEARL ONIONS, MUSHROOMS

1 whole rabbit
2 cups (500 ml) chicken stock
1 cup (250 ml) white wine
1 cup (250 ml) heavy cream
1 cup (70 g) peeled pearl onions
1 cup (100 g) quartered button mushrooms
1 teaspoon kosher salt
A pinch of freshly grated nutmeg
A pinch of ground white pepper

1. Preheat the oven to 350°F (180°C). If the butcher hasn't already done it for you, break down the rabbit into hindquarters, forequarters, and saddle, and then split the saddle in two, giving you six pieces total.

2. In a Dutch oven or a flameproof braising dish with a lid, combine the rabbit, chicken stock, wine, cream, pearl onions, mushrooms, salt, nutmeg, and white pepper and mix well. Cover and braise for about 2½ hours, checking after 2 hours. When the hindquarters are tender and aromatic, remove the dish from the oven.

3. Put the braising dish on the stove top over medium heat and cook until the sauce is reduced to a stew-like consistency, about 5 minutes. Taste and adjust the seasoning, if necessary. Serve on top of a starch of your choice.

 THE PIGEON POUR: At the restaurant, we don't trump our guests' wine choices. If they want to drink Bordeaux with oysters, god bless. Dessert wine with their beef cheeks? Live and let live.

However, I cannot in good conscience suggest red wine with this dish. That actually makes it *less* good. The wine will taste sharp, the sauce will taste off. Try this with white Burgundy, a funky rich Savennières, or, if you can find it, Grange des Pères Blanc (a crazy white from the Languedoc region made from Roussane, Marsanne, and Chardonnay grapes). The dish together with this wine will make you cry.

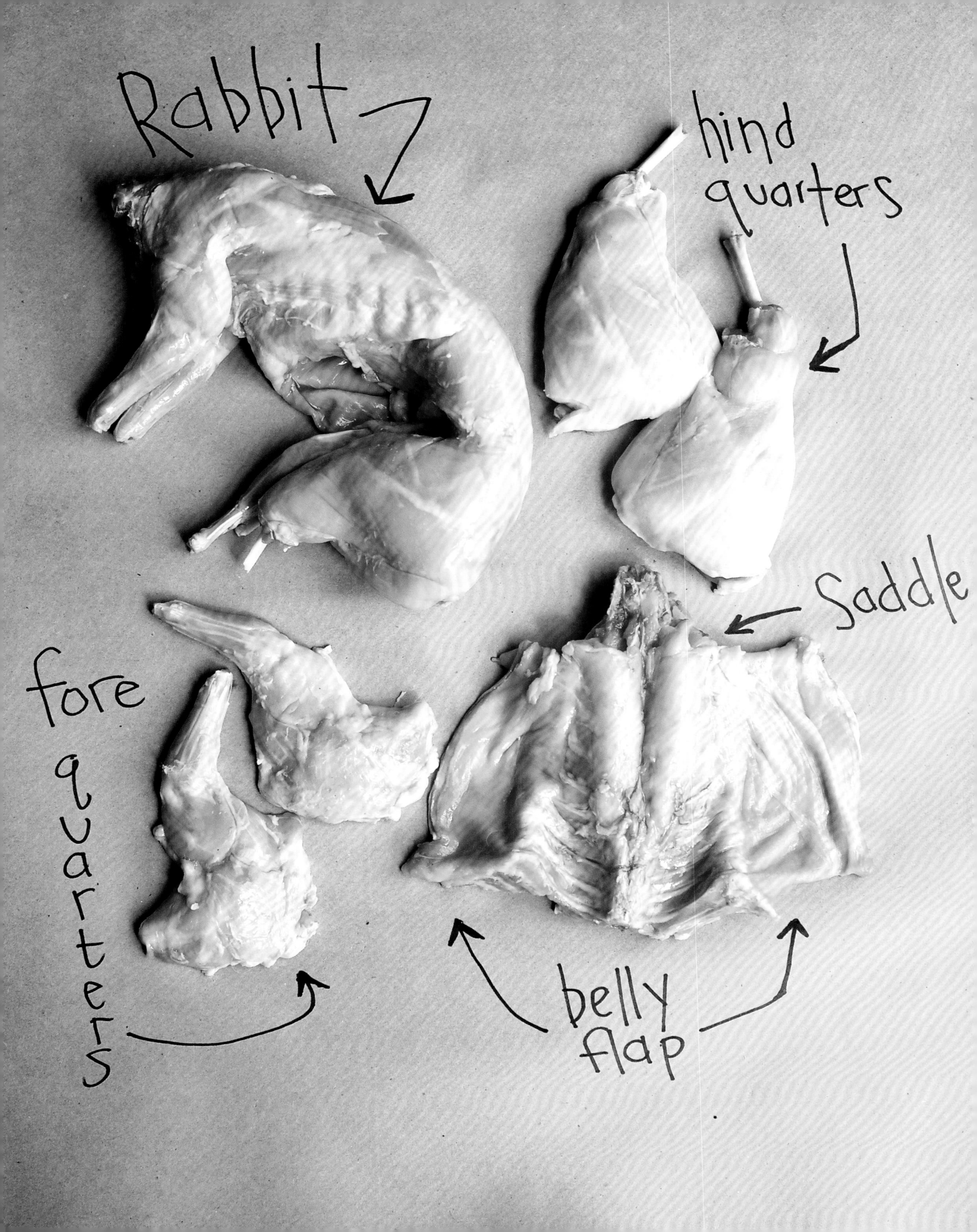

Rabbit

hind
quarters

Saddle

fore
quarters

belly
flap

Gabriel first encountered Oregon truffles while working at Paley's Place, the kind of kitchen where you're not only allowed but actually encouraged to play with black truffles, the holy grail of luxury ingredients. Oregon truffles come into season in October and last until spring, and though they aren't as mind-blowing as truffles from Alba or Périgord, they still take you where you want to go flavorwise. During a good year you can almost taste the roots of the trees where the foragers dug them up. Musty but with an almost sweet aroma, they are like nothing else in the world (see The Weird and Wonderful World of Lars Norgren, page 198). Oregons don't make it out of the state often, but if you know the right guy—and he actually has a phone that works—you might be able to get some shipped to you. {SERVES 4}

CREAMED RABBIT, POLENTA, BLACK TRUFFLES

Rabbit Braise
2 rabbit hindquarters
½ yellow onion, quartered
4 cloves garlic, crushed
1 cup (250 ml) water
1 cup (250 ml) dry sherry
1 cup (250 ml) heavy cream
⅓ cup (80 ml) soy sauce
¼ cup (60 ml) honey
1 tablespoon Worcestershire sauce
2 bay leaves
2 tablespoons kosher salt
½ teaspoon red pepper flakes
A pinch of freshly grated nutmeg
Neutral oil for sautéing
2 tablespoons very finely diced carrots
1 tablespoon chopped fresh flat-leaf
    parsley

Polenta
1 cup (250 ml) chicken stock
1 cup (250 ml) milk
1 teaspoon kosher salt
½ cup (105 g) instant polenta,
    preferably Golden Pheasant brand
1 tablespoon unsalted butter
2 tablespoons grated Parmesan
1 cup (125 g) all-purpose flour
Canola or rice oil for deep-frying

1. Preheat the oven to 350°F (180°C).

2. To make the rabbit braise, in a Dutch oven, snugly fit the rabbit, onion, garlic, water, sherry, cream, soy sauce, honey, Worcestershire sauce, bay leaves, salt, red pepper flakes, and nutmeg. Cover and braise in the oven until the meat is falling off the bone, about 2½ hours.

3. While the rabbit is cooking, let's make the polenta: Grease a 5 by 9 by 3-inch (13 by 23 by 7.5cm) loaf pan and set aside. In a medium pot over high heat, combine the stock, milk, and salt and bring to a boil. Once the stock mixture is boiling, slowly add the polenta in a steady stream, whisking constantly. Reduce the heat to medium-low and simmer, stirring frequently, until the polenta is rich and creamy, 15 to 20 minutes. Remove the pot from the heat and stir in the butter and cheese. Fill the prepared loaf pan with the cooked polenta and smooth out the top with a spatula. Chill the pan in the refrigerator for at least 1 hour. Once chilled, remove the pan from the refrigerator and run a knife between the polenta and the pan to loosen the polenta. Place a cutting board on top of the pan and carefully turn the pan over, tapping the bottom, to release the polenta onto the board. Cut four 1-inch-wide (2.5cm) slices of polenta; set aside. The leftover polenta can be stored in an airtight container in the refrigerator for 2 days. Use it as a base for Tripe (page 209) or serve it with Pork Shoulder Confit (page 186).

4. To make the truffle crème fraîche, in a small bowl, combine the crème fraîche with the truffles using a whisk. Cover and refrigerate until ready to use.

Truffle Crème Fraîche

½ cup (125 ml) crème fraîche
1 tablespoon chopped black truffle

½ cup (125 ml) Truffle Vinny (page 329)
Black truffle for shaving

5. When the rabbit is done braising, remove the rabbit pieces from the liquid. Let the rabbit cool until you can handle the pieces, and then carefully remove the rabbit meat, being cautious of the small, sharp bones. Finely shred the meat with your fingers, discarding the bones. Strain the braising liquid, discard the solids, and reserve the liquid gold.

6. In a large saucepan, heat a thin film of oil over high heat. Add the carrots and sauté until al dente, 4 to 5 minutes. Add the shredded rabbit and the strained braising liquid and simmer, stirring occasionally, until the liquid is reduced by half, 10 to 12 minutes. Add the truffle crème fraîche to the mixture and continue cooking until reduced by half again, 4 to 6 minutes. Stir in the parsley and place the saucepan in the oven, which is off but should still be warm, while you deep-fry the polenta.

7. Spread the flour in a shallow dish. Coat each piece of polenta in the flour, turning to coat it evenly. Pour oil to a depth of 2 inches (5 cm) in a sauté pan and heat over high heat. Add the polenta pieces and deep-fry until golden brown and very crispy, about 2 minutes on each side. Using a slotted spoon, carefully remove the polenta from the oil and drain on a plate lined with paper towels.

8. Place a piece of polenta on each of four plates and generously spoon the creamed rabbit on top. Drizzle the truffle vinny on top and garnish with additional shaved truffle.

When peach season arrives in Oregon, our favorite way to enjoy peaches is fresh with some salty slices of prosciutto. We wanted to serve something like this at the restaurant, but it was just too simple for what we do there, so Gabriel went to work finding the perfect way to jazz it up. The delicate crunch of phyllo with a creamy rabbit and goat cheese filling in this spanakopita provided a great bridge between sweet peach, salty prosciutto, and tangy goat cheese. {SERVES 6}

RABBIT SPANAKOPITA, PROSCIUTTO, TRUFFLES

Filling
2 rabbit hindquarters (from 1 rabbit)
Kosher salt
Neutral oil for searing
1 yellow onion, diced
4 cloves garlic, thinly sliced
1 peach, pitted and quartered
2 cups (500 ml) whole milk
1 cup (250 ml) white wine
1 cup (250 ml) water
1½ teaspoons truffle oil
1 bay leaf
8 ounces (250 g) spinach leaves
    (about 2 bunches)
8 ounces (250 g) goat cheese
A pinch of red pepper flakes

Spanakopita
6 sheets phyllo dough, each
    8 by 11 inches (20 by 28 cm)
½ cup (125 g) unsalted butter, melted

6 slices prosciutto
6 slices fresh peach
3 tablespoons Truffle Vinny (page 329)
12 to 18 fresh arugula leaves
12 slices fresh black truffle (optional)

1. Preheat the oven to 300°F (150°C).

2. To make the filling, season the rabbit well with salt. In a Dutch oven over medium-high heat, heat a thin film of oil. Sear the rabbit until golden brown, about 3 minutes on each side. Pour off the excess oil from the pan, leaving only a thin film, and then add the onion, garlic, peach, milk, wine, water, truffle oil, and bay leaf and season with 1 teaspoon salt. Bring to a boil, cover, and braise in the oven until the rabbit is falling off the bone, about 3 hours. Remove from the oven and let rest for 5 to 10 minutes. Gently remove the rabbit from the braising liquid. Carefully pick all the meat off the rabbit hindquarters, being very cautious of the small, sharp bones. Discard the bones and reserve the meat.

3. Return the meat to the liquid in the Dutch oven. Remove the bay leaf and cook over medium heat until reduced. You want it almost dry, with only enough liquid left so that you have to tilt the Dutch oven to find it. Remove from the heat. Stir in the spinach, goat cheese, and red pepper flakes. Taste, adjust the seasoning if necessary, and let cool to room temperature.

4. Turn the oven up to 400°F (200°C). To assemble the spanakopita, place a sheet of the phyllo dough on your work surface, covering the rest of the phyllo with a damp kitchen towel to keep it from drying out. Working carefully (the dough is very fragile), use a pastry brush to liberally brush the phyllo with melted butter. (If you get a little tear in the phyllo, don't worry about it too much.) Place a second sheet on top of the first and repeat with the butter. I know this sounds crazy, but you are going to do it again a third time. Trust me, it's good.

{Continued}

RABBIT SPANAKOPITA

Assemble necessary items—
sheets of phyllo dough, brush,
melted butter, and ingredients.

sheets of phyllo
dough are very thin
and fragile!

Lightly brush melted butter
across sheet of phyllo dough,
repeating the process for
three layers.

Once buttered, vertically
cut sheet into thirds.

Place ingredients into lower
third of a phyllo strip.

Fold lower right corner
up and over to the left,
covering the ingredients.

Fold lower left corner up
to the top left.

Fold left corner to meet the upper
right corner, creating a triangle.

Repeat.

5. Once you have your three layers, cut it in thirds, so you have three fat rectangles. In the lower third of each rectangle place ⅓ cup (85 g) of the rabbit filling. Now you are going to do something called the flag fold: bring the bottom right edge of the dough up diagonally toward the left edge to form a triangle. Fold upward, keeping that triangle shape in mind, and keep going till you run out of dough. Fold up the other pieces in the same manner, and then repeat the whole process with the three remaining sheets of phyllo, the remaining melted butter, and the remaining rabbit filling. You will now have six beautiful spanakopita triangles. Place them on a baking sheet and bake until golden brown, about 18 minutes.

6. Arrange a slice of prosciutto in the middle of each of six plates and top with a rabbit spanakopita. Arrange a slice of peach next to the spanakopita and drizzle with truffle vinny. Garnish with arugula and the truffle slices and serve.

Do you know that feeling when you open a cupboard and discover the land of misfit toys? Dusty bottles of booze, unwanted condiments, and random pantry items? That sums up Gabriel's experience at the restaurant-that-was-not-yet-Pigeon during the first few weeks before opening. Can you really do something with chestnuts, dried plums, and an old bottle of Cognac? May we present . . . our first rabbit dish. {SERVES 4}

COGNAC, BRAISED RABBIT, PRUNES, SWEET POTATO, CHESTNUT CREAM

Rabbit

4 rabbit hindquarters
Kosher salt
2 tablespoons neutral oil
2 yellow onions, coarsely chopped
4 cloves garlic, minced
1 cup (250 ml) Cognac
½ cup (60 g) chopped prunes (dried plums)
1 tablespoon chopped fresh sage
2 bay leaves
4 cups (1 l) chicken stock
Freshly ground black pepper

Chestnut Cream

½ cup (125 g) chopped roasted chestnuts
¼ cup (60 ml) Cognac (as cheap as you can buy)
½ cup (125 ml) crème fraîche
1 teaspoon chestnut honey (see headnote on page 165)

Potato

1 large sweet potato, peeled and cut into rounds ¼ inch (6 mm) thick
2 teaspoons olive oil
1 teaspoon kosher salt

1. Preheat the oven to 350°F (180°C).

2. To make the rabbit, rub the hindquarters generously with 2 tablespoons of salt. In a Dutch oven over medium-high heat, heat the oil and sear the rabbit until just colored, about 4 minutes on each side. Transfer the rabbit to a plate and lower the heat to medium. Add the onions and garlic to the Dutch oven and cook until soft and translucent, 3 to 4 minutes. Add the Cognac, prunes, sage, bay leaves, and chicken stock and bring to a boil. When it's nice and aromatic, after about 3 minutes, return the rabbit to the pan. Add a dash of salt and pepper, place the pan in the oven, and braise until the meat is tender but not falling off the bone, about 2 hours.

3. While the rabbit is cooking, work on the chestnut cream. Combine the chestnuts and Cognac in a food processor and process until it forms a paste. Add the crème fraîche and honey and process briefly; you don't want to buzz it for too long, or the crème fraîche will curdle. Set aside.

4. To make the potato, toss the sweet potato with the olive oil and salt. About 15 minutes before the rabbit is done, spread the sweet potato on a baking sheet and roast in the oven alongside the rabbit until tender, about 15 minutes.

5. Remove the rabbit from the oven and stir in the chestnut cream; the consistency will be creamy and rich, with a slightly funky aroma. Serve with the potato rounds alongside.

It seems to us that people who don't think they can stomach bunny are often surprised that they enjoy it, whereas those who say they "really love it" are often the ones who find something to complain about, calling it too lean or too gamy. Some say, "I don't know, I thought it would taste like chicken." We even had a guest tell us he thought it would be moister if we left the skin on. Think about that for a minute.

So here is something for the masses: rabbit poached in butter and flash fried. Rabbit 2.0. The flavor of the rabbit stays true. It's mild and delicate—a great foil for the rich mushroom flavor—but the preparation makes the meat itself rich and succulent. {SERVES 4}

CHICKEN-FRIED RABBIT, WILD MUSHROOM SALAD

4 rabbit hindquarters, each about 8 ounces (250 g)

Kosher salt

2 pounds (900 g) unsalted butter, melted

1 bunch plus 1 teaspoon chopped fresh thyme

1 head garlic, halved, plus 3 cloves garlic, minced

2 lemons

2 cups (500 ml) buttermilk

2 cups (250 g) all-purpose flour

1 teaspoon paprika

½ teaspoon mustard powder

½ teaspoon onion powder

½ teaspoon garlic powder

Neutral oil for frying

4 shallots, sliced

½ cup (50 g) cremini mushrooms, quartered

½ cup (50 g) oyster mushrooms

½ cup (50 g) shiitake mushrooms, sliced

½ cup (50 g) king oyster mushrooms, sliced ¼ inch (6 mm) thick

½ cup (50 g) shimeji (beech) mushrooms

¼ cup chives cut into 2-inch (5cm) lengths

¼ cup (35 g) thinly sliced red onion

½ cup (15 g) watercress leaves

3 tablespoons Herb Aioli (page 321)

1. Preheat the oven to 300°F (150°C).

2. Season the rabbit liberally with salt and nestle the pieces in a Dutch oven. Pour in the butter and add the 1 bunch of thyme, the halved head of garlic, and the juice of 1 lemon. The rabbit should be fully submerged under the butter. Cover with the lid and bake until the legs are tender but not falling apart, 1½ to 2 hours. A fork should pierce the flesh easily. Remove from the oven and let cool, with the rabbit submerged in the butter, until the rabbit is cool enough to handle. Using your trusty tongs, transfer the pieces to a plate lined with paper towels. Carefully strain the butter in the Dutch oven. Reserve the liquid—you're going to use this in the mushroom salad—and discard the solids.

3. Pour the buttermilk into a bowl big enough to hold all four pieces of rabbit. Soak the rabbit in the buttermilk for about 10 minutes. Yes, we know that at this point you're probably asking, "Why all the soaking?" You'll find out when you see how tender and juicy the rabbit turns out.

4. In a large bowl, combine the flour with the paprika and the mustard, onion, and garlic powders. Season with salt. Remove the rabbit from the buttermilk and give it a little shake to remove the excess. Toss the rabbit well in the seasoned flour, making sure to completely cover the meat.

5. Pour oil to a depth of 1 inch (2.5 cm) in a large sauté pan and heat to 350°F (180°C) over medium-high heat. We can't stress enough how useful a thermometer is here. However, if you don't have one, you can drop a pinch of flour into the oil; when it sizzles, you're good. Using tongs, carefully drop

the rabbit pieces into the oil. Fry until golden brown, about 3 minutes per side. Using a slotted spoon or tongs, transfer the rabbit from the pan to a plate lined with paper towels. Give the rabbit a nice squeeze of juice from the remaining lemon.

6. Heat a large sauté pan over high heat. Add ¼ cup (60 ml) of the reserved butter from poaching the rabbit. Quickly add the shallots, the remaining 3 cloves of minced garlic, and the remaining 1 teaspoon of chopped thyme. Sauté for about 1 minute. Add all five kinds of mushrooms. Sauté, stirring occasionally, until golden on the edges and cooked through, about 5 minutes. Remove from the heat.

7. In a bowl, combine the chives with the onion and watercress. Stir the chive mixture into the mushrooms. Give a nice squeeze of lemon juice.

8. Divide the salad among four plates. Place a piece of fried rabbit alongside the salad, drape a spoonful of aioli over the rabbit, and serve.

THE BASEMENT TAPES BY ANDREW FORTGANG

Our basement is our wine cellar. In a tiny restaurant, you have to be creative with storage, and we are that. Upstairs we keep our wines by the glass, beers, dessert wines, and such, but all our wines by the bottle and backups are stowed away in the basement. During service, we are constantly bounding up and down the stairs for wine.

What makes this interesting is that the building above Le Pigeon is a performance venue called the Bossanova Ballroom.

The green rooms where the performers prepare to go onstage are located in the basement as well. So on any given night we're sharing our space with musicians, sweaty (and bloody) mixed martial artists, hip-hop acts, metal heads, psychics, ninjas, exotic dancers, and performers from the annual kink ball.

We used to have a repurposed, glass-doored supermarket display case to hold whites, Champagne, and ciders. (It died while we were working on this book, but it was $500 well spent back in 2006). In my office is the majority of the wine. Beyond hoarding, there is a reason for this; our amazing refrigeration guy, Joel Adams, rigged it so that even on the hottest days the office temperature never rises above 65°F (18°C).

We have an additional wine storage area on the far side of the basement. Our landlord gave each storage room down there a name rather than a number; ours is called Elmo. Down a desolate hallway in a crowded storeroom sit five vintages of Raveneau Chablis, three vintages of Lafon Meursault, cabernet from Ramey and Araujo (we always keep some gems from Napa around to give props to Gabriel's hometown), Nigl grüner veltliner, Brezza and Conterno Barolo, Allemand Cornas, and a whole smattering of red Burgundy. I often buy odd things in bulk if I can get a deal, and, as I write this, I am probably the owner of more Xinomavro than anyone else in Oregon.[1] When Gabriel and I have dinner together, Elmo is our sommelier.

At Le Pigeon, we are big believers in things that taste good. It sounds obvious, but what I mean is that we really don't get too hung up on what's standard, traditional, or trendy. If soy sauce makes it into a pot-au-feu, so be it. If veal blanquette comes with ravioli, that's how it is. That is how Gabriel approaches food, and it's how I approach drinks, too. I look for tasty things.

I taste thousands of wines each year, but ultimately our list is whatever fits on two sides of a legal-sized page (admittedly, the type is small). My main goal is that we don't have anything in the restaurant that is undelicious. To that end, we aren't a slave to labels or buzzwords. The wine world is full of organic, sustainable,

---

1. Xinomavro is a Greek varietal that is very similar to Italy's nebbiolo. It ages incredibly well, and we will get to see that happen, as I bought so much.

biodynamic, LIVE (Low Impact Viticulture and Enology) certified, and "Salmon-Safe" wines. Yet I have never bought a wine because it was, or was not, one of those things. As it turns out, most of the wines on our list are made with organic grapes, and many of them are biodynamic, but that's just because they are good. To grow organically or biodynamically, the grape grower has to pay attention to the vineyard and take special care. When someone is in tune with growing good grapes, they make better wine, period.

The Le Pigeon wine list includes wines from every part of the world. Wines from France are at the heart of this list because they pair well with food (and because that is what I want to drink). The look and feel of Le Pigeon lends itself to a Francophile mindset as well. The big copper hood hanging over the kitchen line, iron chandeliers, exposed brick, heavy wooden tables, and flickering candles give the restaurant the feeling of a little bistro on a Parisian side street. The name sets the mood, too, even though we pronounce it like Americans, not like the French would.

Once you enter the restaurant and get settled at a table or counter, the mood takes on a decidedly Portland feel: the music is *not* gypsy jazz, the cooks are *not* wearing whites and toques, and the servers are *not* mustachioed men in uniforms—Portlandians do not like their servers in uniform! What makes Le Pigeon a Portland restaurant is that we don't revere everything, we just endeavor to do it right.

Proper service, on-point food, good wine choices (with very little "wine speak"), and a warm atmosphere. The whole Oregon experience is about genuineness, not a show.

There is one winery that always makes our list, and that is Belle Pente. In the interests of full disclosure, Brian and Jill O'Donnell, Belle Pente's proprietors and winemakers, are close friends of mine, but I have been a fan of Belle Pente wine since we lived in New York. After I moved to Oregon, my admiration

for their product only grew. In a way, Belle Pente is to Burgundy, what Le Pigeon is to a French bistro: they are the real deal, but with a unique Pacific Northwest sensibility.

Brian makes wines that have depth, brightness, and a strong sense of place and vintage. They are similar in nature yet different from the wines of Burgundy; his are more approachable and certainly more affordable (think double digits versus Burgundies that run hundreds or thousands of dollars). His home and winery

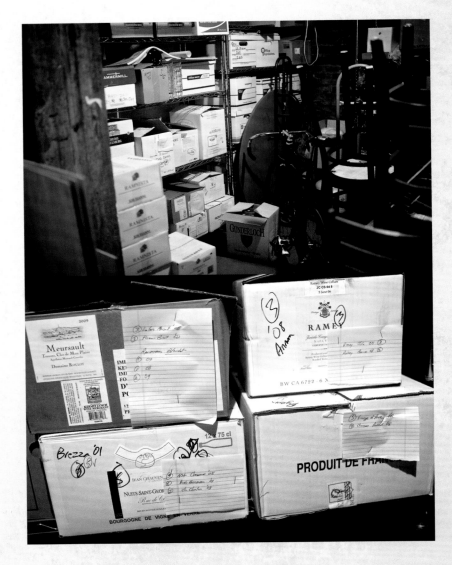

share the vineyard property with geese, chickens, goats, cows, and a couple of dogs, which conjures up the image of a traditional French *domaine*. However, on closer inspection, this is an Oregon place, with hazelnut and plum trees, blackberry bushes, and an Airstream trailer in the driveway.

In general terms, Oregon wines and Burgundies are relatives, but Oregon wine is a little less grown up. Our local wine-makers are focused on quality, but the whole experience of making and drinking wine here is not as reverential as it is in Burgundy.

We like to include some obscure wines from odd corners of the world on the list, like one from Oregon's Umpqua Valley, where Terry and Sue Brandborg make incredible Alsatian-style white varietals and pinot. Or Saperavi from Kondoli Vineyards

{Continued}

THE WINE-SHARING COMPROMISE

Here are ten wines that we often use to bridge the gap between dishes when a table of four or six wants a bottle to pair with all of their entrées:

1. Cerasuola di Vittoria, from COS. If there is a wine that can go with more dishes, I haven't found it yet.

2. Savigny-lès-Beaune, Les Lavières, from Domaine Chandon de Briailles. A red Burgundy with both power and lightness.

3. Mâcon-Cruzille, Les Perrières, from Domaine Guillot-Broux. An elegant, complex chardonnay.

4. Estate Vineyard Pinot Noir, from Belle Pente. Ripe with fruit, yet supple and balanced.

5. Saint-Joseph Rouge, from Domaine Faury. Earthy and spicy, but lively and fresh.

6. La Rioja Alta Viña Ardanza, from Rioja. Deeply satisfying, with persistent flavor.

7. Savennières, from Nicolas Joly, Domaine des Forges, Château d'Epiré, or Domaine du Closel. Powerful and gorgeous white wine that can take on lots of foods.

8. Chinon, from Jean-Maurice Raffault. Make sure it has a few years of age.

9. Saint-Joseph Blanc, Les Oliviers, from Pierre Gonon. Round, powerful, and complex.

10. Cantina del Pino Barbaresco, from Piedmont. If white fish isn't in the mix and we can decant it at appetizer time.

of Georgia (the Republic of, that is). We also try to find wines from the back alleys of the world's famous wine regions.

We believe Burgundy can be inexpensive, so in addition to Chambolle, Pommard, and Meursault, we seek out Fixin, Givry, Marsannay, and Monthelie. Our friend and wine importer, Scott Wright, helps us find some of these gems that are off Burgundy's beaten paths. Likewise, we love barbera and Langhe Nebbiolo from Piedmont. We also like to feature producers that make small quantities of cool juice, like Abe Schoener's Scholium Project wines from California, John Paul's Cameron nebbiolo from nearby, Thierry Germain's L'Insolite Saumur Blanc (one of the coolest chenin blancs around), or the Mâconnais wines from Domaine Guillot-Broux.

Before moving to Portland in 2007, I spent my entire life in New York City, the last few years of which I was working at Craft. I was very lucky to get the gig as the beverage director there. On paper, I was not qualified to be the buyer for a top restaurant. There were people with many more years of wine experience that would have killed for the job. However, I had worked for Tom Colicchio on and off since I was sixteen, and the general manager had known me for almost as long. So they gave me a shot.

In fact, in mid-2004 I had even gone in to give notice that I was leaving Craft, because I had been offered a job elsewhere, and Tom said, "Well, maybe you should stick around. There is an opening coming up." I knew a good

bit about wine, and I had worked with some great wine people, but I'd only been involved in the management of a wine program in a supporting role, and even then I had done it for only a few months. There was a lot of self-education that I had to do. However, I think that gave me great perspective. I bought what I liked, and I organized things in a way that was logical to me rather than following someone else's model. And I formed my opinions about wine by tasting, tasting, and more tasting.

During those years, I got to travel. In Germany, I learned that one *can* have too much riesling, especially if you need to wake up the next day and taste more, and that Germans make killer grappa (aka Tresterbrand). I bought a bottle at every winery that distilled, and I think most people were surprised by my

interest. In Australia, I saw what 150-year-old vines look like, and I learned how many people you can squeeze into the back of a Subaru Outback. In California, I came to understand how micro-climates can be so distinct—just drive down Highway 101 on the Central Coast—and how money can distort how wine is valued. In Oregon, I learned how a whole wine industry can work together and, more importantly, I found a new home.

The differences between wine drinkers in New York and Portland are the same as the differences between diners in these cities. New Yorkers like a bit more show, Portlandians can do without it. When restaurants try to get too fancy in Portland, they get called out on it. Sometimes you need to sneak fancy service into a casual groove, and that's what we do at Le Pigeon.

In general, there are four types of wine-buying guests at Le Pigeon. The first guest is the same on either coast: "I'll have the second least expensive wine, please." I really like these buyers and they should be applauded. They know that, at Le Pigeon, whatever they order they will still be getting a great wine. The second type of wine buyer knows a bit about wine and wants no help from me. In Portland, if this person doesn't like the wine they pick, they will probably let me know that they don't like it. In New York, they will probably tell me that the wine is off, because, *obviously, they aren't wrong.*

(Sorry, New Yorkers. Just calling it as I see it.) Either way, I always take the wine back. It is just silly to have someone sitting in our restaurant unhappy about their wine; it just clouds their whole experience. Also, life is too short for anyone to drink something they don't like. The third wine buyer wants us to help them find something they haven't had before. These are the best people . . . on either coast. The fourth group is the big spenders. In New York, the big spenders spend way bigger, but in Portland there is less status drinking.[2]

---

2. A bunch of years back, some guys came to Craft and started looking at a pricey cult Australian shiraz. I let the ringleader know that, in addition to the wine he was looking at, we had another wine by the same winery that was not on the list. After I left him to consider his choices, he did some searching on his Blackberry, and the following conversation took place:

Him (aggravated): Why did you offer me that other wine?
Me (a little confused): Well, sir, you seemed very interested in the winery, and they are all hard-to-get wines. I thought you would appreciate the additional option.
Him: But the wine you offered me is inferior.
Me: I don't follow.
Him: The wine on the list scored a 96; the other one you offered me scored a 94. You cannot deny that this is a quantitative measure of quality.
Me (absolutely flabbergasted): No, I guess not.

That conversation would never happen in Portland. Frankly, I can still hardly believe it ever took place at all.

In Portland, the people who spend a lot of money do it because they love the wine. We have a regular who comes to Le Pigeon a few times a year, usually with his wife but sometimes by himself. He always starts with a Meursault or a Condrieu, and he gets how cool Grange des Pères Blanc is. He orders wine at this level even if he is alone; it isn't about showing off.

Living in a small city with an informed market means that in Portland, compared to a city like San Francisco, it's easier to get your hands on rare allocated wines. It also means that distributors often hold onto vintages of some wines, so I can buy a ten-year-old Aldo Conterno Granbussia that is actually ready to drink, or a Chauvenet Nuits-St-Georges with eight years under its belt.

Portland wine shops like Great Wine Buys, Liner & Elsen, and my favorite, E&R Wine Shop, are staffed with passionate people picking cool wines. When I get stumped with my list and need some fresh ideas or reminders about wines that I may have forgotten about, I will often stop by E&R to get inspired. Ed Paladino and Richard Eldin always have special things hidden on the shelves. There's also a good barbecue place called Reo's Ribs right next door, so it's doubly worth the stop. (I've never told Ed and Richard that because their whole neighborhood has complained about Reo's strong smell of smoke. Oh well. The cat's out of that bag).

Gabriel's food can be challenging to pair wine with because so many of his dishes have multiple flavors and great balance. He loves to finish things off with a squeeze of lemon, which leaves me with a challenge. How do I add balance to something that is already balanced? Instead, I focus on texture. I ask myself how his food feels in the mouth, not just how it tastes. With pairings, I really look at the textures of a dish and the beverage. If a food is brothy, then you don't want a wine that is too crisp because the overall feel might be watery. If it's crispy, you might want the brightness and crispness of the wine to highlight the crunch. If the dish is creamy, I need to decide if I want to complement it with a round wine, or contrast it with a leaner one. If there's a runny egg, that changes everything. Likewise, how does the wine feel? Rich or crisp? Oily or creamy? Lush or dusty? At times, lining up the right textures can be more important than finding the right flavors. That is why I often serve sherry and Madeira, beer and cider, aperitifs, and the like. These really expand the options that I have when I put together pairings.

All this being said, the Pigeon Pours are simply my own thoughts and guidelines after fifteen years in the business. It is always better to have high-quality company than wine, and the ultimate is to experiment with wine (or booze) and food however you like.

MR. PICKLES'S CABINET OF CURIOSITIES

This is the wine (and some other goodies) that I keep on hand at home.

1. Chablis, from Raveneau. If Andy deserves a treat, this is it.

2. Scotch, most likely Laphroaig. Keeps things mellow.

3. McCarthy's Oregon Single Malt. A Scotch-style whiskey made by Steve McCarthy from Clear Creek. It goes to show that there is nothing we cannot do in Oregon.

4. Old Grand-Dad Bourbon. For the missus. We always have the fancy stuff, too, but this is her favorite.

5. Channing Daughters. A killer winery on Long Island. They send us a mixed case of wine every year, and we drink it when we miss the East Coast.

6. De Conciliis Fiano. I love this wine, and you can't buy it in Oregon, which probably makes me love it even more. Anytime I am in Washington or California, I have to pick some up.

7. Combier Crozes-Hermitage. The red equivalent to the Fiano. I cannot buy it in Oregon, so I always covet it.

8. Beefeater Gin. What summer smells like.

9. Good silver tequila. Tequila, lime, a splash of soda; there's nothing better.

10. Little bottles of tonic and club soda. You don't want to find that you've run out, and you really don't want to get a drink all made up, reach into the fridge, and pull out a 1-liter bottle of flat soda; that is just no good.

11. Grappa and eaux-de-vie. I love it at the end of the meal. The local stuff from Clear Creek Distillery is great. Best recipe for cleaning up a dinner party: a healthy glass of grappa, tunes, and you wake up the next day with no memory of doing the dishes!

12. Okay, beer snobs, I'm sorry: Bud Light Lime. I knocked it, and then I tried it. After working around the house or in the yard, it is super-refreshing. I think marathon runners drink it during the race.

13. Prager Riesling Wachstum Bodenstein '01. Well, until December 2017, anyway. My wife and I had this in 2005 when I proposed, so I bought a case and we drink one every year. It keeps getting better.

14. Half a dozen almost-empty bottles of vodka. Every year we have a latke and vodka party, where all the guests have to bring a bottle. Try as we might, they are never all polished off.

15. California wine. Really. It is never a big part of the restaurant list, so I crave it sometimes. Tensley and Peay syrah, Rockpile petite sirah, Littorai pinot, Arcadian chardonnay. I need to have these bottles close by to satisfy my cravings.

16. Saint-Joseph and Cornas. The elegant and gamey sides of northern Rhône syrah. Gonon, Cuilleron, Clape, Paris. These are wines I buy to age, but I keep drinking them.

17. A smattering of Burgundy. I don't keep too much at home because we have so much at the restaurant.

18. Savennières! If you do not know about it, go buy a bottle. We always have some Nicolas Joly at home. Joly is a polarizing producer; some wine people love his wines and some think they are, frankly, bad. But I love them, and, more importantly, so does my wife.

19. Dönnhoff riesling. My benchmark for riesling and balance in wine. When I look in my wine fridge and see this, it makes me smile.

20. Inexpensive white wine. The wife and I drink white wine like water. Touraine sauvignon blanc, verdicchio, grüner veltliner, Chablis, muscadet, Macon, Arneis. We always seem to be out, and I feel like I am always bringing cases of white wine home. If we run out of quaffing white in my house, it is akin to using the last of the milk and not putting it on the grocery list. A staple.

CHAPTER 6
LITTLE TERRY
(small fish dishes)

WHAT'S TERRY?

The *call* system—what the floor staff at Pigeon writes on their tickets to order—hit a snag one night when *steak* and *skate* were both on the menu. The dishes were being misread on the handwritten tickets and misheard in the loud, busy restaurant. So we renamed the skate *terry* (because that is the first name that came to mind) to avoid further confusion. When the skate dish was replaced with another fish the following week, we decided to keep the name.

If we're serving a fish appetizer, it's known as "little terry," and if there's a main fish dish it's referred to as "big terry." Calling a fish by its actual name would seem out of place. And in five years of business, only two guests have asked us why they were charged for terry.

A note from Gabriel: This dish reminds me of my first job, where once I had to quarter a 50-pound bag of macadamia nuts with a paring knife. I have since gotten over my fear of macadamias, as shown here, where we toast them in a rich, curry butter.

Note: The foie must cure for 2 days for this dish. {SERVES 4 AS AN APPETIZER}

HAMACHI, FOIE GRAS, TRUFFLES, MANDARINS

Cure
1 cup (250 g) sugar
1 cup (140 g) kosher salt
⅛ teaspoon pink curing salt
4 juniper berries, crushed

1. To make the foie cure, in a bowl combine the sugar, both salts, and the juniper berries and mix well. Transfer to an airtight container and bury the foie in the cure mixture. Make sure the foie is completely covered so it cures well. It should look like treasure buried in white sand. Refrigerate for 48 hours.

One 4-ounce (120 g) chunk foie gras (see page 51)

½ cup coarsely chopped macadamia nuts

1 tablespoon unsalted butter, melted

½ teaspoon curry powder

Kosher salt

8 ounces (250 g) hamachi, diced into ¼-inch (6mm) pieces

1 large shallot, thinly sliced

1 tablespoon chopped chives

Juice of 1 lemon

Juice of 1 orange

2 tablespoons Aioli (page 321)

Maldon flake salt

Segments from 2 mandarins

1 medium black truffle, preferably from Oregon, shaved into thin slices

½ cup (15 g) baby arugula leaves

Truffle Vinny (page 329)

2. Remove the foie from the container and carefully rinse under cold water. Gently pat it dry. If you're not using it right away, store it in an airtight container in the refrigerator for up to 1 week. Anything left over will freeze well.

3. Preheat the oven to 350°F (180°C). Toss the macadamia nuts with the butter and curry powder. Season with kosher salt and spread out evenly on a baking sheet. Bake the nuts until lightly toasted, 5 to 7 minutes.

4. In a bowl, combine the hamachi, shallot, chives, lemon and orange juices, aioli, and Maldon salt to taste. Mix gently with a spoon. Divide the hamachi among four plates. Sprinkle the hamachi with the macadamia nuts. Top each plate with four segments of mandarin.

5. Using a vegetable peeler, shave the foie gras; you want to make sure you have a sharp peeler and very cold foie gras. It seems super fancy, but you are just peeling thin pieces off the foie, as you would Parmesan cheese to top a salad. Top the hamachi with 4 or 5 shavings of foie. Arrange the slices of fresh truffle and the baby arugula leaves on top. Sprinkle with Maldon salt to taste. Drizzle the vinny around the plate like it's 1985 and serve.

 THE PIGEON POUR: Alsatian muscat is a funny wine. It doesn't really go with that many things. It's super-floral, with lots of orange peel and not really that bright with acidity. However, with this dish it sings. The texture of the wine makes a great match with the slick hamachi and the creamy foie. The truffle brings out the minerality of the Alsatian terroir, and the mandarins bring out the orangey muscat flavors. Slam dunk. The best one in my book is André Ostertag's Fronholz Muscat.

This dish—like so many LP hits—was inspired by a classic and then given a facelift. Radish, good butter, and Maldon flake salt is a perfect combination in the early spring, when radishes are at their freshest and sweetest. However, the compact menu at Le Pigeon doesn't lend itself to "snacks" (which is how *radis beurre* is usually served), so we had to turn this into a composed dish. The real fun here is the ocean butter; it's chock-full of caviar, decadently rich, and has a nice pop as you eat it. I've used tobiko (flying fish roe) and sevruga caviar here for their gorgeous colors and depth of flavor. {SERVES 4 AS AN APPETIZER}

RADIS BEURRE (OCEAN)

½ cup (125 g) good-quality unsalted butter, softened
1 teaspoon red tobiko
1 teaspoon green tobiko
1 teaspoon black tobiko
1 tablespoon sevruga caviar
1 bunch red radishes, quartered
20 mint leaves
Good-quality olive oil (see sidebar on page 105)
Maldon flake salt
Juice of ½ lemon

1. In a bowl, using a wooden spoon or even your hands, carefully combine the butter, all three tobikos, and the caviar. Mix well without bursting the caviar, and set aside.

2. In a small bowl, toss the radishes with the mint, a little drizzle of olive oil, Maldon salt to taste, and the lemon juice. Arrange the radishes on each plate. Using a tablespoon, make a delicate scoop of the butter and caviar mixture and place it alongside. Sprinkle the butter with more Maldon salt and serve.

We love clamming along the Oregon coast in May and June, as it's only a two-hour drive west from Portland. If you're in the Pacific Northwest during these months, it's definitely worth a day trip. We're not clamming champs, but luckily my brother-in-law Ben and his girlfriend, Jen, are clamming gurus and actually have clamming licenses. So we went camping over a weekend in June to clam, cook, and take in the Tillamook Forest.

FRIED RAZOR CLAMS, HABANERO BUTTERMILK

Here's how it went down: We gathered at Le Pigeon at 8:30 a.m. and started loading up the cars with provisions. We hit the road a bit after 9 and two hours later rendezvoused at Netarts Bay, which is just west of Tillamook. We parked on the side of the road next to a parking lot that was filled with people, all of whom were there to clam. The tide was out at this point, which meant you could walk almost half a mile out into the bay (later that afternoon, during high tide, the water was completely in and there was no access at all). There were hundreds of people out there clamming; some were real geared-up pros, but others looked more like us, meaning they had no idea what the hell they were doing.

To get into the thick of it, we had to trudge out into the bay. It was like quicksand; we were all getting stuck and sucked into the wet mud. A lot of our time was spent on our hands and knees, laughing hysterically, while we tried to retrieve our shoes from the depths.

Like fishing, digging for clams is mind-numbingly boring when you are not finding any but extremely satisfying when you are—and we experienced both. We found five kinds of clams: razors, quahogs, butters, cockles, and gapers. Of all the clams, we focused on collecting razors, as they're large, meaty, and perfect for breading and frying up. This is the recipe that we ended up making on the beach that day. A word from Jen about her delicious buttermilk habanero dipping sauce: "My inspiration for this dressing came from some of my favorite regulars at Sinnott's Lil Cooperstown, where I tend bar. The recipe makes more than you will need for four people, but surely you'll find other things in your fridge to dip into it." {SERVES 4 AS AN APPETIZER}

Rice oil or other neutral oil for deep-frying
4 eggs
¼ cup (60 ml) whole milk
1 cup (125 g) all-purpose flour
1 sleeve saltines, finely crumbled
3 teaspoons Old Bay Seasoning
Kosher salt
16 razor clams, cleaned and filleted (see sidebar on page 140)
Lemon wedges for serving
Habanero Buttermilk Dressing (see recipe below)

1. In a pot over medium-high heat, pour oil to a depth of 6 inches (15 cm). Heat until the oil reaches 350°F (180°C) on a thermometer, or it's hot enough so that a pinch of flour sizzles when dropped into the pot.

2. In a small, shallow bowl, whisk together the eggs and milk. Set up three bowls, the first containing the flour, the second the egg wash, and the final one the saltines. Season each bowl with a teaspoon of Old Bay Seasoning and a dash of salt. Dredge the clams in the flour, shake off any excess, then dip them in the egg wash. Shake off any excess egg wash and then dredge them carefully in the saltines.

3. In four batches, fry the clams until golden brown, about 2 minutes per batch. With a slotted spoon, remove the clams to a plate lined with paper towels. Serve with some lemon wedges and the buttermilk dressing.

Buttermilk Habanero Dressing

1 egg yolk
1 tablespoon freshly squeezed lemon juice
1 tablespoon red wine vinegar
2 teaspoons mustard powder
½ teaspoon sugar
1 clove garlic, thinly sliced
1 cup (250 ml) olive oil
½ cup (20 g) chopped fresh flat-leaf parsley
½ cup (20 g) chopped cilantro
3 habanero chiles, seeded and chopped
½ cup (80 g) chopped yellow bell pepper
1 teaspoon freshly ground black pepper
1½ cups (375 ml) buttermilk
Kosher salt

MAKES 3 CUPS (750 ML)

In a bowl, stir together the egg yolk, lemon juice, and vinegar and let sit for 10 minutes. Transfer the mixture to a food processor and process until thickened. Add the mustard powder, sugar, and garlic and process until well incorporated. With the motor running, add the olive oil in a thin, steady stream to create an emulsion. Next, add the parsley, cilantro, habaneros, bell pepper, and black pepper. Blend well. With the motor running, slowly pour in the buttermilk and process until smooth. Add salt to taste and serve. This dressing will keep for 1 week, covered, in the refrigerator.

HOW TO CLEAN AND FILLET RAZOR CLAMS

You're going to need a sharp pair of scissors and a paring knife.

Prepare an ice water bath. Bring a large pot of water to a rolling boil over high heat. Add the razor clams and blanch for 10 seconds. Transfer the clams to the ice water bath. Remove the shells from the clams and give them a good rinse under cold running water. This is a sink job, or in our case, the camp faucet.

Using your scissors, cut the black tip off the neck, or as it is technically called, the siphon. (A good rule of thumb when cleaning razors is: If it's not white, get rid of it!) Cut the body open, starting at the base and working your way up the siphon. The idea here is to kind of butterfly the clam open, exposing the insides that we want to dispose of. The brown bits found near the base, or digger, are the gills and palps; cut them off completely. Finally, gently snip the digger from the body. Snip through the opening to butterfly the digger open. Using your paring knife, gently scrape away any brown bits. Be careful to scrape lightly as you want that fatty white material—the "goods"—intact. Rinse both parts under cold water and pat dry on paper towels.

Razors are best when dug, cleaned, and fried right away, but they'll keep stored in a cooler or refrigerator overnight.

A note from Andy: One thing I love—and now that I have a baby daughter, one thing I never to get to do—is camp on the coast. Ah, to crawl into bed with a stomach full of steak and whiskey and wake up sandy-haired to a seafood feast. These are the mornings that I *don't* miss living in New York. Gabriel and I started on these clams at 11 a.m. on a hazy (referring to my mind, not the sky) morning. From the tent, I brought out a killer bottle of '02 Foreau sparkling Vouvray, an elegant start to the day (considering the inelegant previous night). A couple of minutes later, Gabriel was pouring crappy beer into a cast-iron pan of clams over the campfire, asking me, "How will this pair with the wine?"

We used manila clams from Taylor Shellfish. Yes, that's cheating, but there are no manilas at Tillamook, and any small clam could be used.

{SERVES 4 TO 6 AS AN APPETIZER}

CLAMS, KIELBASA, BEER

2 tablespoons olive oil
5 cloves garlic, coarsely chopped
1 kielbasa sausage, about 8 ounces
    (250 g), sliced ¼ inch (6 mm) thick
3 pounds (1.4 kg) manila clams, soaked
    in salt water and rinsed
1 can of cheap beer, such as Pabst Blue
    Ribbon or Budweiser
2 tablespoons chopped fresh flat-leaf
    parsley
Kosher salt

1. Get a hot campfire going and place your cast-iron pan above it. If you're in your kitchen and not at the beach, you want to be on medium heat on the stove top. Add the oil and garlic and sauté until fragrant, about 1 minute.

2. Add the kielbasa and clams and continue to cook for 1 minute more so the flavors can marry. Add the beer and cook until the clams have opened, 3 to 4 minutes, discarding any clams that don't open. Sprinkle with the parsley, season with salt to taste, and divide among bowls to serve.

CLEANING A DUNGENESS CRAB

Get a fresh Dungeness crab.

Steam or boil your crab for 7–8 minutes a pound.

Rinse and cool. Flip it over a couple of times to get both sides with the spray.

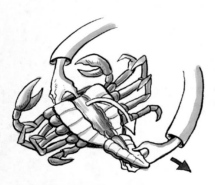

Flip over the apron and break it off from the back of the shell.

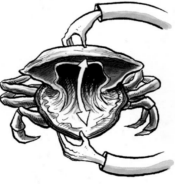

Remove the carapace.

Remove the gills and mandibles.

Rinse clean until there is just shell and tasty meat.

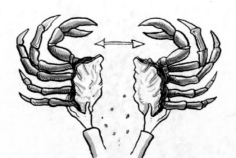

Break in half.

Serve and enjoy!

Living in Oregon definitely has its advantages, and one of those is our proximity to Dungeness crab, the sweetest and tastiest of crabs. Starting in early December and running all the way into August, the long and bountiful crab season has resulted in many dishes on the Le Pigeon menu. Oxtail Stew (page 210) and tomato soup with a crab melt sandwich (think the best tuna melt of your life) are a couple of those menu items, but the best way to enjoy Dungeness crab is to boil them live and whole and just dig in using your teeth and hands to get at all the tasty meat hidden in those claws and legs. Serve these whole, preferably at the beach with a beer. {SERVES 4 AS A LIGHT LUNCH, OR 2 FOR DINNER}

BOILED DUNGENESS CRAB

Crab

Kosher salt
2 live Dungeness crabs
2 lemons, cut into wedges

Cocktail Sauce

1 cup (250 ml) LP Ketchup (page 324)
    or purchased ketchup
1 tablespoon prepared horseradish
1 teaspoon Tabasco
Juice of 1 lemon
1 teaspoon Worcestershire sauce
1 teaspoon kosher salt

1.   To make the crab, bring a large pot of water to a boil and season it with salt so it tastes like the sea. I use ocean water when cooking crabs at the coast, and I think you should, too, if possible. Add your crabs and cook, covered, for 15 minutes.

2.   While the crabs are boiling, work on the cocktail sauce. In a large measuring cup or bowl, combine the ketchup, horseradish, Tabasco, lemon juice, Worcestershire sauce, and salt. Taste to check the seasoning; I like it with a good kick, but you can easily scale back on the horseradish and Tabasco if you prefer.

3.   Back to the crabs: Using tongs, remove the crabs from the pot and cool under cold running water. Turn your crab over and remove the little triangular belly flap, sometimes called the apron. Under running water, rip the top shell off and give it a good rinse to remove the gills. Remove the mandibles. Give your crab another good rinse and break it in half. Serve with lemon wedges, eat by the sea.

Geoduck (pronounced gooey-duck) is strictly a Pacific Northwest delicacy. It's found year-round at Puget Sound, where many folks go and pick it themselves in a geoduck free-for-all. We get ours from Taylor Shellfish (www.taylorshellfishfarms.com), where each geoduck weighs about 2 pounds. If you know me, or if you have ever worked in a kitchen, then you know that we've gone to great lengths here to restrain ourselves and talk about geoduck like adults. If you've ever seen a geoduck, you know how impossible this is.

Note: No salt is used in this recipe as geoduck is very salty on its own. Some chefs don't serve the geoduck mantle raw, but we feel the contrast in texture and flavor between softer mantle and the firmer siphon is what makes this dish truly rad. {SERVES 6 TO 10 AS AN APPETIZER}

GEODUCK, PORTOBELLO, YUZU

1 portobello mushroom, stemmed and gills removed with a spoon, finely diced

¼ cup (60 ml) plus 2 tablespoons white soy sauce

2 tablespoons yuzu juice, or a mixture of lemon and lime juices

1 teaspoon fish sauce

1 teaspoon Sriracha hot sauce

1 tablespoon brown sugar

1 geoduck

1 tablespoon minced chives

20 green shiso leaves, stems removed

¼ cup (60 ml) neutral oil

1. In a small saucepan over medium heat, combine the mushrooms, ¼ cup (60 ml) of the white soy sauce, 1 tablespoon of the yuzu juice, the fish sauce, Sriracha, and brown sugar. Simmer until the mushrooms are infused with the flavor of the liquid and the liquid has a syrupy consistency, about 45 minutes. Strain the mushrooms and reserve the mushrooms and the syrup separately. Let them come to room temperature.

2. Bring a large pot of water to boil over high heat and prepare two bowls of ice water. Blanch the geoduck in the boiling water for 12 seconds, then transfer it to one of the bowls of ice water to cool. Blanch the shiso leaves in the boiling water for 20 seconds, then transfer them to the second bowl of ice water to cool.

3. To prepare the geoduck, cut the siphon from the body. Using your hands, peel the thin membrane off. Now are you feeling perverted? Discard the membrane. Cut the siphon in half lengthwise and rinse under cold water. Now let's clean the body, which is known as the mantle. Split the shell and remove the meat in one piece; it should come out quite easily. In the center there will be a round ball of firm-looking flesh. Yep, this is the clam's gonads. Pull the gonads out of the mantle and discard. Rinse the mantle under cold water.

4. Make the geoduck marinade by combining the remaining 2 tablespoons white soy sauce, the remaining 1 tablespoon yuzu juice, and the chives. Now sharpen your knife! Slice both pieces of geoduck very thinly at a sharp diagonal, toss with the marinade, and let sit for 2 minutes.

5. Add the shiso and oil to a blender and puree until smooth. (The puree can be made up to 2 days in advance and kept, covered, in the refrigerator.)

6. Spoon a line of shiso puree down the middle of each plate and arrange the marinated geoduck on top. In front of the geoduck, make a line of the portobello mushrooms, and in the back, drizzle the syrup. If you want to serve it in a bowl, you can do that too; we just want it all presented as cleanly as possible, with the geoduck on its own and mushrooms and shiso as condiments of sorts.

Sweet nectarines and earthy porcini mushrooms might sound like an odd combination at first, but once you taste them together your mind will be spinning with ideas about what other fruit and mushroom pairings you can make. The slow-braised then flash-fried octopus provides a hot and crunchy contrast to this recipe. We get frozen octopuses from Spain that have a wonderful briny flavor and super-tender texture. Make sure that the octopus has been cleaned when you buy it, as you do not want to deal with the ink sac.

Note: You will have extra octopus left over. We like to fry it up and eat it like popcorn shrimp with Buttermilk Habanero Dressing (page 139). {SERVES 4 AS AN APPETIZER}

OCTOPUS, NECTARINES, PORCINIS

Octopus

1 small octopus, about 2 pounds (900 g), cleaned
1 bottle (750 ml) dry white wine
2 cups (500 ml) water
2 lemons, halved, plus a squeeze of fresh lemon juice
3 sprigs tarragon
½ teaspoon red pepper flakes
Kosher salt
¼ cup (60 ml) extra-virgin olive oil
1 cup (155 g) rice flour
1 cup (120 g) cornstarch
Neutral oil for frying

Porcini Puree

1 cup (250 ml) water
2 ounces (60 g) dried porcini mushrooms
1 tablespoon unsalted butter
½ cup (70 g) diced yellow onion
1 clove garlic, minced
⅓ cup (80 ml) heavy cream
1 tablespoon Katz honey-viognier vinegar (see sidebar on page 42) or Moscatel vinegar
¼ teaspoon truffle oil
Pinch of chopped fresh thyme
½ teaspoon kosher salt

1 nectarine, cut into various shapes and sizes
Orange Relish (page 324)
2 pieces canned hearts of palm, cut into various shapes and sizes

1. To make the octopus, in a large pot over medium heat, combine the octopus, wine, water, 2 lemons, tarragon, red pepper flakes, 2 tablespoons of salt, and the extra-virgin olive oil. Bring to a simmer and let simmer until the octopus is tender when pierced with a fork (it should feel soft but retain its texture), about 1 hour. Remove from the heat and let the octopus cool in the cooking liquid.

2. Remove the octopus from the liquid and, under running water, use a kitchen towel to wipe off any of the pink membrane that will come off. Don't wipe too hard, as you might damage the tentacles and the membrane isn't harmful; it just doesn't agree with the fryer. Cut the tentacles into 1-inch (2.5cm) pieces and slice the head into thin strips about the width of a pencil. In a bowl stir together the rice flour and cornstarch and set aside.

3. To make the porcini puree, in a deep saucepan over medium heat, combine the water, mushrooms, butter, onion, garlic, cream, vinegar, truffle oil, thyme, and salt. Bring to a simmer and simmer for 30 minutes. Transfer the contents of the pan to a blender and puree until smooth. Set aside. (The puree can be made up to 1 week in advance and kept, covered, in the refrigerator.)

4. On each of four plates place about 1 tablespoon of the porcini puree. In a bowl, toss the nectarine pieces with orange relish and arrange three or four nectarine pieces on top of the porcini puree. Now arrange about three pieces of the palm hearts on the porcini puree.

5. In a large sauté pan over medium-high heat, pour oil to a depth of 2 inches. Heat until the oil reaches 350°F (180°C) on a thermometer, or it's hot enough so that a pinch of rice flour sizzles when dropped into the pan. Dredge the octopus pieces in the rice flour mixture and fry them until golden brown, about 2 minutes. Transfer the octopus to a plate lined with paper towels and sprinkle with salt and lemon juice.

6. Arrange the octopus on top of the nectarines and palm hearts. Garnish with a little orange relish from the bowl that had the nectarines and serve.

THE PIGEON POUR: Drink riesling. The mellow oceanic tinge of the octopus, the sweetness of the nectarine, the petrol quality of the truffle . . . it sounds like a riesling already. A German Kabinett like Leitz's Rüdesheimer Klosterlay or the Meddersheimer Rheingrafenberg from Hexamer are good starts. Austrian riesling will serve you well here too. Be cautious of Alsatian rieslings with this dish. Many would overwhelm it with their fruit and weight.

Parisian gnocchi, which are made without potatoes, are more akin to the light pastry dough *pâte à choux* than their Italian cousins. Regardless of the type, however, gnocchi love butter, parsley, and Monica Bellucci. At the restaurant, we use bone marrow butter to give the gnocchi a deep, rich flavor. We always encourage decadence, but the dish would be delicious made with regular butter as well. {SERVES 4 AS LUNCH OR A LIGHT DINNER}

PARISIAN GNOCCHI, ESCARGOT, BONE MARROW

Marrow Butter

6 tablespoons (85 g) bone marrow, softened

6 tablespoons (90 g) unsalted butter, softened

Parisian Gnocchi

4 cups (160 g) loosely packed fresh flat-leaf parsley, plus 3 tablespoons chopped

6 eggs

Kosher salt and freshly ground black pepper

2 cups (250 g) all-purpose flour

¼ cup (60 g) unsalted butter

1 (12 ounce/375 g) can escargot (about 24 snails), drained

7 cloves garlic, chopped

Kosher salt

A squeeze of fresh lemon juice

Maldon flake salt

1.　To make the marrow butter, using a handheld mixer, whip the bone marrow and butter together until evenly incorporated. Set aside.

2.　To make the gnocchi, bring a large pot of water to a boil over high heat and prepare an ice water bath. Add the 4 cups (120 g) of parsley to the pot, cook for 10 seconds, and immediately transfer to the ice bath to cool. Once the parsley is cold, squeeze dry. Transfer the parsley to a blender, add the eggs, and puree until bright green.

3.　In a heavy saucepan over high heat, combine 1½ cups (375 ml) of water with the marrow butter, 1 teaspoon salt, and ¼ teaspoon ground pepper. Bring to a boil, then reduce the heat to medium. Add the flour all at once and stir rapidly with a wooden spoon until the dough pulls away from the sides of the pan. The bottom of the pan should be clean, with no dough sticking to it. Continue to stir for 1 to 2 minutes more. Transfer the dough to the bowl of a stand mixer fitted with the paddle attachment. Let cool for 5 minutes. Turn the mixer on low and slowly pour in the parsley and egg mixture in six additions. Allow the mixture to incorporate fully each time before adding the next.

4.　Bring a large pot of salted water to a boil over high heat. Meanwhile, lightly oil a baking sheet. Fill a pasty bag fitted with a medium (⅝-inch/1.5cm) tip with the dough. If you don't have a pastry bag, you can shape the gnocchi using two tablespoons instead. Turn the water down to a simmer. Hold the pastry bag over the pot with one hand and a small knife in the other, squeeze out 1-inch (2.5cm) segments and cut them off with the knife into the water. The gnocchi will sink to the bottom. When they rise to the top, they're done, after 1 to 2 minutes. You have to be quick here; work in batches and don't bite off more than you can chew. Start small and before you know it you will get into a good rhythm. Every so often dip the knife into the water to help keep it from sticking to the dough. With a slotted spoon, transfer the gnocchi as they are done to the prepared baking sheet.

{Continued}

5. When ready to serve, in a sauté pan over medium-high heat, melt the unsalted butter. When the butter is hot and frothy, add the gnocchi and swirl to warm for 1 to 2 minutes. Add the snails and garlic and season with a pinch of kosher salt. When the garlic has softened and is aromatic, add a squeeze of lemon juice to finish. Divide among four bowls, sprinkle with Maldon salt, and serve.

Gabriel has never been to one of Jean-Georges Vongerichten's restaurants, but he loves his books. *Simple to Spectacular* in particular is one of his go-tos. In this dish, we've taken Jean-George's lobster pappardelle recipe and Le Pigeonized it, so it comes out barely recognizable but still clearly influenced by the master.

Portland isn't really a lobster town, maybe because we have no shortage of crab and tiny pink shrimp. But we love the flavor of lobster, so over the years Gabriel has learned some ways to get great flavor without serving a $50 lobster tail. Using the roe is one of those ways, and this dish is one of our favorite ways to showcase it. The roe is a somewhat special and sought-after ingredient. We suggest you call the folks at www.seafoods.com and order some. This is a great way to make stunning red noodles with a vibrant lobster flavor.

{SERVES 4 AS AN APPETIZER}

LOBSTER ROE PAPPARDELLE, CRAB, LEMON, CRÈME FRAÎCHE

Pasta Dough

2¼ cups (280 g) all-purpose flour, plus more for dusting
6 egg yolks
1 teaspoon olive oil
2 tablespoons lobster roe
Semolina flour for dusting

Kosher salt
1 cup (250 ml) Shellfish Crème Fraîche (page 328)
2 tablespoons minced Preserved Lemons (page 326)
1 pound (450 g) Dungeness crabmeat (see page 143)
1 teaspoon chopped chives
1 teaspoon chopped fresh flat-leaf parsley
½ teaspoon chopped fresh chervil
½ teaspoon chopped fresh tarragon

1. To make the pasta dough, in a food processor combine the all-purpose flour, egg yolks, olive oil, and lobster roe. Pulse a couple of times to combine; it will look slightly crumbly. Dust your work surface with all-purpose flour and empty the contents of the food processor onto it. Knead the dough for about 5 minutes to form a shiny elastic ball. Wrap the pasta in plastic wrap and refrigerate for 1 hour.

2. Once the pasta has rested, cut the ball into quarters. Set a pasta machine to the number one setting. Dust your work surface and rolling pin with all-purpose flour. Roll a piece of the dough into a thin rectangle. Pass it through your pasta machine, fold it over on itself, and repeat two more times. Set the machine to the number two setting and pass the dough through the machine once. Continue the process, increasing the setting by one each time and passing the dough through the machine once, until the pasta is thin but not transparent. Pasta machines vary, but on our Kitchen-Aid machine we go to number four. Repeat with remaining pieces of dough. Once all the dough is rolled out, gently roll the sheets into loose logs and cut the pasta into noodles ½ inch (12 mm) wide. At this point, they can be stored in an airtight container for up to a month in the freezer. If you are using them right away, then store them on a baking sheet dusted with a little semolina flour in the fridge while you put everything else together.

{Continued}

3.   Bring a large pot of heavily salted water to a boil. Meanwhile, in a large sauté pan over medium heat, combine the crème fraîche with the preserved lemon and crabmeat and sauté to reduce the sauce and thicken slightly. Drop the pasta in the boiling water and cook until al dente, 3 to 4 minutes. Drain the noodles and add them to the sauté pan with the sauce. Cook for 30 seconds, just long enough to marry the flavors. Stir in the chives, parsley, chervil, and tarragon and taste for seasoning. The mixture should be saucy but not runny.

4.   Divide the pasta among four bowls, making sure you get all of that crab and sauce out of the pan, and serve.

Sometimes a dish is born out of pure fun. When cooked, these scallops look almost identical to pieces of charcoal. When you slice into the scallop, however, you get that bright white flesh contrasting with the black ink. (At the restaurant, we sous-vide the scallops with the ink at 122°F / 50°C for 30 minutes to get the color to stick, but at home you can just marinate them.) If the ink is too difficult to procure, the dish will still work, though it won't have the fun of the optical illusion. Paired with sweet Oregon Dungeness crab, spicy paprika-spiked ketchup, and a rich egg yolk that has been torched on top, this is a great Spanish-style brunch dish. {SERVES 4}

BLACK SCALLOPS, CRAB SALAD

4 large scallops, each 2 to 3 ounces (60 to 90 g), adductor muscles removed

1 tablespoon squid ink

3 tablespoons kosher salt

1½ cups (340 g) Yukon gold potatoes, peeled and finely diced

2 cups (500 ml) neutral oil plus more for searing

½ cup (100 g) Dungeness crabmeat (see page 143)

1 teaspoon chopped fresh flat-leaf parsley

2 tablespoons Aioli (page 321)

1 tablespoon unsalted butter for basting

Maldon flake salt

A squeeze of fresh lemon juice

¼ cup (60 ml) Spanish Ketchup (page 324)

4 eggs yolks

Oregano Salsa Verde

1 tablespoon chopped fresh oregano

1 tablespoon chopped fresh flat-leaf parsley

¼ cup (60 ml) good-quality olive oil (see sidebar on page 105)

A pinch of kosher salt

A squeeze of fresh lemon juice

1. In a bowl, toss together the scallops, squid ink, and 1 tablespoon of the kosher salt and let marinate in the refrigerator while you cook the potatoes.

2. In a bowl, toss the potatoes with 1 tablespoon of the kosher salt. Let sit for 20 minutes; they will release some of their liquid.

3. Preheat the oven to 350°F (180°C). Pat the potatoes dry and transfer to a baking dish. Pour the oil over the potatoes just to cover (you may not use the entire 2 cups) and bake until tender when pierced with a fork, 8 to 10 minutes. Remove from the oven and transfer the potatoes to a plate lined with paper towels, reserving the cooking oil.

4. To make the salsa verde, in a small mixing bowl, combine the oregano, parsley, olive oil, salt, and lemon juice and set aside. (Use within a couple of hours as the lemon juice will cause the herbs to brown.)

5. In a heavy saucepan over medium-high heat, heat the reserved potato oil to 350°F (180°C) and fry the potatoes until golden brown, about 2 minutes. Using a slotted spoon, transfer the potatoes to a bowl. Toss with the remaining 1 tablespoon of kosher salt and stir in the crab, parsley, and aioli.

6. In a separate sauté pan over high heat, heat a thin film of oil until just smoking. Add the scallops and sear for about a minute, flip, and continue to sear for 30 seconds more. Add the butter to the pan, let it melt, and baste the scallops for 1 minute. Transfer the scallops to a plate lined with paper towels and sprinkle with Maldon salt and a squeeze of lemon juice.

7. Place a scallop on each of four plates and arrange a spoonful of the potatoes next to it. Place a spoonful of ketchup right where the scallop and the potatoes meet, make a little well in each mound of potatoes, and fill each with an egg yolk. Using a kitchen torch, brulée the top of each yolk. Drizzle each plate with the salsa verde and serve.

CHAPTER 7

BIG TERRY

(large fish dishes)

A lot of people like to crust sea bass with potato, and there are many top-tier chefs who have been doing it for ages. That being said, it's tricky: you have to get the potatoes to stick to the fish just right, and then you have to cook the potatoes until they're crispy without over-cooking the fish. If you can pull it off, it's delicious, but it's also a pain in the ass. Here is an easier way to get similar results with a high success rate: by using instant mashed potatoes as the breading. Instant mashed potatoes are just freeze-dried potatoes, and when fried in butter and oil, the flavor is out of this world. {SERVES 4}

POTATO-CRUSTED SEA BASS, LEEKS, BOTTARGA

Bottarga Vinaigrette
4 ounces (110 g) Yukon gold potatoes, peeled and finely diced
1 cup (250 ml) heavy cream
A pinch of kosher salt
½ cup (125 ml) Katz sauvignon blanc vinegar or other white wine vinegar (see sidebar on page 42)
½ cup (125 ml) potato vodka
2 tablespoons grated mullet bottarga

Leeks
Kosher salt
1 pound (450 g) leeks, white and light green parts only, cut into ½-inch (12mm) rounds
1 tablespoon unsalted butter
1 clove garlic, minced
½ cup (125 ml) dry white wine
A squeeze of fresh lemon juice
2 tablespoons chopped chives

Sea Bass
4 skinless sea bass fillets, each about 6 ounces (170 g)
Kosher salt and freshly ground black pepper
2 eggs
1 tablespoon whole milk
1 cup (100 g) instant mashed potatoes
Neutral oil for sautéing
2 tablespoons unsalted butter, melted

Grated mullet bottarga to finish
A squeeze of fresh lemon juice
Maldon flake salt

1. We're going to make the bottarga vinaigrette first. In a small stainless steel or copper saucepan over low heat, combine the potatoes, cream, and salt and cook until the potatoes are very soft, about 15 minutes. Transfer to a blender. Add the vinegar, vodka, and bottarga. Puree until smooth and fairly loose. Taste and adjust for salt and acid. Keep warm in a small saucepan over very low heat.

2. To make the leeks, bring a pot of salted water to a boil and prepare an ice water bath. Blanch the leeks in the boiling water for 30 seconds, then immediately transfer to the ice water bath to cool. Remove and pat dry. In a small saucepan over medium heat, melt the butter. Add the garlic and sauté until aromatic, 2 to 3 minutes. Add the white wine and leeks and cook until the leeks are soft and the wine has evaporated, about 2 minutes. Season with salt and lemon juice, stir in the chives, and keep warm.

3. To make the sea bass, preheat the oven to 450°F (230°C). Season the fish fillets with salt and pepper. In a shallow bowl, whisk together the eggs and milk until thoroughly combined. Spread the instant mashed potatoes in a separate bowl. Working carefully (sea bass can be flaky), dip the top part of each fillet in the egg wash and then into the mashed potatoes to create a crust.

4. In large, heavy sauté pan over medium-high heat, pour oil to a depth of ⅛ inch (3 mm). When the oil begins smoking, add the fish, potato side down, and cook until golden brown on the bottom, about 4 minutes. Carefully flip the fish with a slotted spatula and baste with the melted butter. Transfer to the oven and continue cooking until there is no resistance when the flesh is pierced with a fork, about 2 minutes more. Transfer the fish to a plate lined with paper towels.

5. To serve, spoon a nice pile of leeks onto the center of each of four plates. Top with a piece of fish and spoon the vinaigrette around to your liking, using at least a couple spoonfuls. Give a nice grate of bottarga, sprinkle with lemon juice and Maldon salt.

 THE PIGEON POUR: Saint-Joseph Blancs are wines from the northern Rhône Valley made of marsanne or roussanne grapes or a combination. Cuilleron, Gonon, Coursodon, Gripa, Faury, and Perret are all great producers. None are cheap, but they won't set you back like Burgundy. The northern Rhône Valley is the cooler yin to the southern Rhône's yang. The wines you find in the north almost seem schizophrenic. They share the warm south's grape varieties, but they have the finesse of France's cooler northern regions.

Made from varying amounts of roussanne and marsanne, these wines have killer texture, almost a beeswax quality, but are balanced by fruit and just enough acidity. This dish has great crunchy, creamy, and chewy textures, with deep but not electric flavors. So a texture-driven wine, with complex but mellow flavors, is a great complement. They won't be cheap, but remember that a $50 wine in a wine shop would cost you $100 in most restaurants, which should soften the sticker shock.

One of Gabriel's favorite things to do in the kitchen is combine land and sea on one plate. The rich flavors of cow or pig offset by the bright saltiness of seafood: this is what he wants to eat almost all of the time. Here we combine melt-in-your-mouth short ribs with seared scallops. To add contrasting textures, we serve these with a sweet-hot succotash and some blistered padrón peppers from Viridian Farms.

Manuel and Lesley of Viridian have been bringing the produce and flavors of Spain to Oregon for the last few years, both by taking yearly seed-buying trips to Spain and by growing a variety of heirloom peppers and beans, among other things. This recipe highlights the bounty of their farm. You can order from Viridian at www.viridianfarms.com. {SERVES 4}

SHORT RIB, SCALLOPS, SUCCOTASH

Short Rib

6 heads garlic, peeled
¼ cup (60 ml) plus 1 tablespoon soy sauce
1 tablespoon dried porcini powder
2 tablespoons kosher salt
1 piece bone-in short rib, about 3 pounds (1.4 kg)
¼ cup (60 ml) water

Succotash

¼ cup (60 g) plus 1 tablespoon unsalted butter
4 ounces (125 g) pancetta, cut into small batons
1 cup (150 g) corn kernels
½ cup (70 g) sliced red onions
½ cup (42 g) piparra vasca peppers or sweet banana peppers, cut into ¼-inch (6mm) rings
½ cup (50 g) sliced red bell peppers
Kosher salt
1 cup (160 g) fresh pocha beans or other shelling beans
3 cups (750 ml) Corn Stock (page 322); double the recipe and freeze any leftovers
1 cup (250 ml) chicken stock
2 tablespoons minced chives

1. Work on the short rib first, as roasting it overnight gives the best results. In a small food processor, combine the garlic, 1 tablespoon of the soy sauce, the porcini powder, and salt and puree until it forms a paste. Rub the rib well with the paste and let sit, refrigerated, for 2 to 24 hours.

2. Preheat the oven to 225°F (110°C).

3. Place the rib in a small baking dish and add the water and the remaining ¼ cup (60 ml) soy sauce. Cover and roast for a minimum of 6 hours and up to 8 hours. When done, it will be the softest piece of meat you have ever witnessed. If you look at it wrong, it will fall apart on you. Gently remove the rib from the baking dish, reserving the baking dish and roasting liquid, and slide the bones out and discard. Let the rib cool to room temperature on a cooling rack. Once it is firm enough to handle, cut into quarters and return the meat to the baking dish.

4. To make the succotash, in a heavy saucepan over medium heat, melt the ¼ cup (60 g) of butter. Add the pancetta and cook, stirring, until the fat is rendered, about 4 minutes. Add the corn, onions, and both of the peppers and continue to cook until the onion is translucent, 3 to 4 minutes more. Season with a couple pinches of salt and add the pocha beans and corn and chicken stocks. Bring the mixture to a simmer and cook until the beans are tender, about 30 minutes. Once the beans are tender, increase the heat to high and reduce the remaining liquid to about ½ cup (125 ml). Remove from the heat and quickly stir in the remaining 1 tablespoon of butter. Stir in the chives and add more salt if necessary. Keep warm.

{Continued}

Short Rib, Scallops, Succotash, *continued*

Scallops

Neutral oil for sautéing

4 large sea scallops, each about
3 ounces (90 g), adductor muscles
removed

Kosher salt

¼ cup (60 ml) extra-virgin olive oil

12 padrón peppers

Maldon flake salt

¼ cup (100 g) Tomato Jam (page 272),
at room temperature

A squeeze of fresh lemon juice

5. Preheat the oven to 400°F (200°C). Place the pan of ribs in the oven, uncovered, until just heated through, about 10 minutes. While the ribs are reheating, cook the scallops.

6. In a medium sauté pan over high heat, heat a thin film of oil. Season the scallops with kosher salt and sear for about 2 minutes on the first side, flip, and sear 1 minute more. Remove from the pan, discard the searing oil, and add the extra-virgin olive oil. When the oil is hot, add the padrón peppers to the pan, and cook, shaking occasionally, until the skin is blistered and charred, about 2 minutes. Remove from the pan and sprinkle with Maldon salt.

7. Now let's put it together. Spoon a scoop of succotash in the bottom of a bowl, making sure to get some of the nice juices at the bottom. Place a piece of short rib on top of the succotash. Top with a dollop of tomato jam, three of the padrón peppers, and a scallop. Sprinkle with Maldon salt and a squeeze of lemon juice and serve.

This is not a recipe from the Pigeon lexicon, but rather a nostalgic re-creation of the cover of *American Cooking: The Northwest* from Time-Life's Foods of the World series. The scene is simple: rainbow trout on the rocks, lemon, bacon sizzling in a cast-iron pan, and some local flora thrown in for good measure. It's the perfect lakeside lunch. We've left out the bacon but added sage leaves to really bump up the flavor. If you want to serve bacon, by all means do. In the spirit of this homage, we're going to assume that you're cooking on an open fire, so please don't disappoint. Also, big props if you catch the trout yourself. {SERVES 4}

CAMPFIRE TROUT

4 whole rainbow trout, cleaned
    and gutted
Kosher salt
2 lemons, halved
Neutral oil for cooking
4 sprigs sage
2 tablespoons unsalted butter

1.   Season the trout inside and out with salt. Carefully place a large cast-iron pan on a grill above an open fire. Rub the lemon halves with a little oil and place them cut side down on the grill. Cook until you have a nice set of grill marks, about 3 minutes. Set aside.

2.   Pour oil into the hot pan to a depth of about ¼ inch (6mm). In batches if necessary, place the trout in the pan and cook for about 3 minutes. Flip the trout, add the sage to the pan, and cook for another 3 minutes. Remove the pan from the heat. Add the butter to the pan and let it melt. Squeeze the grilled lemon into the pan. Grab some forks or use your fingers and dig in.

Fall is a magical time at Le Pigeon. The candlelight is bouncing off the exposed brick wall and the days are growing shorter, making the heat that comes off our open kitchen even more inviting. The fishermen on the Columbia River are pulling out 20- to 30-pound king salmon that have a deep red flesh and a great store of rich fat, making them our favorite to cook with. At the same time, Lars (see page 198) is bringing big fat Oregon porcinis through the back door.

For this recipe, you'll need an untreated cedar plank measuring about 5 by 10 inches (13 by 25 cm), which can be found easily at any lumberyard or fine food store.

Note: We get chestnut honey from Pastaworks (www.pastaworks.com) in Portland. Almost any high-end grocer or cheese shop should carry it as well. {SERVES 4}

SEARED OREGON KING SALMON, CEDAR-PLANKED PORCINI

¼ cup (60 ml) extra-virgin olive oil
12 ounces (375 g) porcini or king oyster mushrooms, gills removed, cut into wedges
1 tablespoon chopped fresh sage
1 teaspoon chopped garlic, plus 3 cloves garlic, sliced
3 tablespoons balsamic vinegar
Kosher salt
2 tablespoons unsalted butter
3 Walla Walla or other sweet onions, sliced
1 cup (250 ml) chicken stock
4 ounces (125 g) peeled roasted chestnuts
1 teaspoon chestnut honey (see Note above)
2 tablespoons crème fraîche
Neutral oil for sautéing
4 skin-on king salmon fillets, each 5 ounces (155 g)
Aged balsamic vingear for drizzling

1. Preheat the oven to 450°F (230°C). Rub a cedar plank (see headnote) with the olive oil and place on a baking sheet. Heat the plank in the oven for 20 minutes. Meanwhile, in a bowl toss the mushrooms with the sage, the chopped garlic, and the balsamic vinegar. Season with salt to taste. Arrange the mushrooms on the cedar plank and roast until just tender, about 20 minutes. You still want them to have a little texture.

2. In a large sauté pan over low heat, melt the butter. Add the onions and sliced garlic and season with salt. Increase the heat to medium-low and cook, stirring occasionally, until the onions are very soft, about 15 minutes. Add the stock, chestnuts, and honey. Continue to cook until the liquid has reduced by three-quarters. Stir in the crème fraîche, then transfer the contents of the pan to a blender and puree. Season to taste with salt.

3. In a large sauté pan over high heat, heat a thin film of oil. Season the salmon with salt and place in the pan skin side down. Reduce the heat to medium and, using a spatula, press down on the top of each fillet to keep the skin in contact with the oil. Cook for 2 to 3 minutes, turn the salmon over, and continue to cook for 3 minutes more for medium-rare (the sides of the fillet should be slightly soft when squeezed). Remove the salmon from the pan and set aside.

4. Spoon a circle of the onion chestnut puree in the center of each of four plates. Lay the salmon on top of the puree, skin side up. Place the mushrooms on top of the salmon, letting some fall off to the sides. Drizzle a touch of aged balsamic vinegar around each plate, and serve.

A turn-of-the-century technique from France, larding meat is usually done with a lean piece of pork or beef, which is strung through with strips of fat using a larding needle. Traditionally, it was used to get fat into lean cuts of meat, but in this instance it's to inject a bit of flavor into a fish that could use a little excitement.

Swordfish tastes best when it's not cooked all the way through, and these steaks will cook quicker than usual because the pockets of anchovies allow the heat in. {SERVES 4}

ANCHOVY-LARDED SWORDFISH, FINGERLING POTATOES, ROSEMARY AIOLI

1 pound (450 g) fingerling potatoes
Kosher salt
¼ cup (60 ml) extra-virgin olive oil, plus more for rubbing
7 cloves garlic, peeled
4 swordfish steaks, each about 7 ounces (220 g) and ½ inch (12 mm) thick
12 anchovy fillets, preferably white anchovies (boquerones)
Neutral oil for sautéing
¼ teaspoon chopped fresh rosemary
½ cup (125 ml) Aioli (page 321)
Freshly squeezed lemon juice
¼ cup (30 g) Seasoned Bread Crumbs (page 327)

1. Preheat the oven to 425°F (220°C).

2. In a bowl, toss the potatoes with 1 teaspoon of salt and the olive oil. Using the side of a knife, crush the cloves of garlic and add to the potatoes. Spread on a baking sheet and roast in the oven until the potatoes are fork-tender, about 20 minutes, depending on their size. Remove from the oven but leave the potatoes on the baking sheet while you finish the recipe.

3. Using a paring knife, cut three little pockets into the side of each swordfish steak. Using a bamboo skewer, carefully stuff each pocket with an anchovy fillet; you want to fill the pocket as much as possible without tearing the fish. As our sous-chef Connor Sims would say, "You really want to romance it in there." Season the fish with salt, but go a little lighter than normal, as anchovies are quite salty. Rub with some olive oil.

4. In a heavy cast-iron pot, heat a thin film of neutral oil over high heat. When the oil just starts to smoke, add the swordfish and sauté for 3 to 4 minutes, until a golden brown crust forms. Flip and cook until the fish has only a slight give when pressed with a finger (for medium), 2 to 3 minutes more.

5. While the fish is sauteing, stir the rosemary into the aioli, combining them well. Remove the fish from the pot and give each steak an assertive squeeze of lemon juice. Top each piece of fish with bread crumbs and a dollop of the aioli and serve alongside the potatoes.

There's nothing unusual to an Oregonian about getting up early to fish for sturgeon before heading to work. The sun rises early in May, and it's only necessary to get up a little sooner than is customary on a weekday to take advantage of the plentiful fish. The adventure takes place in downtown Portland in the river beneath the US Bank Tower and Standard Plaza.

White sturgeons are always there, down on the bottom, out of sight and certainly out of everyone's mind. A constant concern for the sturgeon fisherman is the size of the catch. Any fish over 56 inches (142 cm) long must be returned to the water unharmed because only mature sturgeon lay eggs. And unlike salmon, sturgeon can live for centuries. The largest freshwater fish ever caught was a white sturgeon from the Columbia River. As our friend Lars tells it, "It weighed 1,000 pounds and was hauled from the water by a team of oxen."

Sturgeon is commonly called the "steak fish" because of its dense, meaty texture. Don't try this crust with a delicate fish. {SERVES 4}

STURGEON AU POIVRE

3 teaspoons crushed black peppercorns
3 teaspoons crushed pink peppercorns
3 teaspoons crushed white
    peppercorns
4 sturgeon fillets, each 6 ounces (185 g)
Kosher salt
4 ounces (125 g) bacon, cut into thin
    batons
1 pound (450 g) cipollini onions, peeled
1 tablespoon sherry vinegar
Neutral oil for searing
1 clove garlic, minced
1 shallot, minced
¼ cup (60 ml) brandy
1 cup (250 ml) Veal Stock (page 329)
1 tablespoon Dijon mustard
2 tablespoons unsalted butter
Juice of ¼ lemon quarter
1 teaspoon minced fresh flat-leaf
    parsley

1. Preheat the oven to 400°F (200°C).

2. Spread all the peppercorns evenly on a plate. Season the fish with salt and lay one side of each fillet in the peppercorn mixture. Press down to form a nice even crust.

3. Add the bacon to a baking dish and place it in the oven until the fat has rendered and the bacon is crispy, 10 to 12 minutes. Remove the bacon from the dish and set aside. Toss the onions in the rendered fat. Add the vinegar to the dish, deglaze the pan, and transfer to the oven. Roast the onions until just fork-tender and slightly glazed with the bacon fat, about 10 minutes. Remove from the oven and return the bacon to the dish.

4. In a large sauté pan over medium-high heat, heat a thin film of oil. Sear the fish on the crusted side for 2 minutes. Flip over and add the garlic and shallot to the pan. Cook for about 30 seconds. Remove the pan from the heat, and very carefully add the brandy, just to let it flame. Pour in the veal stock, reduce the heat to medium, cover the pan, and cook for 3 minutes. Remove the fish from the pan with a slotted spatula, but continue cooking the sauce until it's reduced to about ¼ cup (60 ml), another 5 to 6 minutes. Stir in the Dijon about a minute before the sauce is finished.

5. Turn off the heat and quickly stir in the butter to create a silky sauce. Stir in the lemon juice, parsley, and salt to taste. Generously spoon the sauce over the fillets and serve with the cipollinis and bacon alongside.

One of our first (and most successful) fish items was halibut poached in carrot butter. We really wanted to include that recipe in this book, but we couldn't remember what we originally served it with. So we experimented, and fennel came up the winner. After all of our experimentation, we decided we loved this new recipe so much that we ran it on the menu for a week and it has become a new staple. {SERVES 4}

CARROT BUTTER–POACHED HALIBUT, ANCHOVY-ROASTED CARROTS, FENNEL

2 pounds (900 g) small carrots, with tops
3½ cups (875 g) unsalted butter
3 anchovy fillets, minced
3 lemons
Kosher salt
2 cups (500 ml) fresh carrot juice
3 cloves garlic, crushed, plus 1 whole clove garlic
1 bay leaf
Zest of 1 orange
¼ cup (60 ml) extra-virgin olive oil
4 halibut fillets, each about 6 ounces (185 g)
Maldon flake salt

Fennel Salad

1 fennel bulb, sliced ⅛ inch (3 mm) thick using a mandoline
2 tablespoons extra-virgin olive oil
2 tablespoons chopped chives
1 tablespoon chopped white anchovies (boquerones)
Kosher salt and freshly ground black pepper

1. Preheat the oven to 350°F (180°C).

2. Remove the carrot tops, wash, and set aside. Peel the carrots and halve them lengthwise. In a sauté pan over medium heat, melt ½ cup (125 g) of the butter with the anchovies and the grated zest from two of the lemons. Add the carrots and season with kosher salt. Transfer to a baking sheet, spread in a single layer, and roast in the oven until slightly softened but still a little crunchy, about 12 minutes. Remove from oven and toss with the juice of one lemon.

3. In a shallow sauté pan over medium heat, combine the carrot juice, the crushed garlic, bay leaf, and orange zest. Cook until reduced by three-quarters, about 10 minutes. Add the remaining 3 cups (750 g) butter and stir until melted, then reduce the heat to very low and keep warm.

4. Next we're going to buzz our carrot top pesto. Simply combine the carrot tops, the whole clove garlic, the olive oil, the juice of one lemon, and a pinch of kosher salt in a blender and blend until you have a fine pesto consistency. Set aside.

5. To make the fennel salad, in a bowl combine the fennel, olive oil, chives, and anchovies and season to taste with salt and pepper. Set aside.

6. Now, to poach the fish. Heat the carrot butter to 130°F (55°C) over low heat. Season the halibut with kosher salt and add the fish to the butter. Keeping the butter at 130°F (55°C), poach the halibut until you can press down on the fish with a fork and don't feel a pop (that pop is connective tissue that hasn't yet broken down), about 10 minutes. Using a slotted spatula, transfer the halibut to a plate lined with paper towels. Squeeze the juice of the third lemon over the fish and sprinkle with Maldon salt.

7. To serve, place roasted carrots in the center of four shallow bowls and top each with a halibut fillet. Top each halibut fillet with the fennel salad. Drizzle the pesto around the fish, spoon a tablespoon of carrot butter over each plate, and serve.

By spreading a shrimp and egg puree over halibut fillets and frying them in hot oil, you get a sweet puffed shrimp crust over moist flaky halibut. To really nail the sweet rich shrimp flavor, we make shellfish stock, using heavy cream rather than water. This is a really impressive dish for dinner guests (unless your guests are cardiologists).

{SERVES 4}

SHRIMP-CRUSTED HALIBUT, CHERVIL

6 ounces (185 g) medium shrimp, peeled and deveined, shells reserved
1 egg yolk
¾ teaspoon chopped fresh tarragon
A dash of Tabasco
Zest and juice of 1 lemon
Kosher salt
Freshly ground white pepper
2 tablespoons unsalted butter, cut into small chunks
Neutral oil for cooking
1 teaspoon tomato paste
½ cup (125 ml) white wine
1½ cups (375 ml) heavy cream
1 teaspoon white peppercorns
Freshly ground white pepper
4 halibut or cod fillets, each about 5 ounces (155 g)
3 tablespoons Herb Pistou (page 324)
Fresh chervil sprigs for garnish

1. In a food processor, combine the shrimp, egg yolk, ¼ teaspoon of the tarragon, the Tabasco, lemon zest, ¼ teaspoon salt, and a pinch of white pepper. Puree for 30 seconds. Add the butter and pulse to combine. It's okay if there are some little chunks of butter left. Refrigerate the puree until ready to use. It will last up to 3 days.

2. In a heavy saucepan over high heat, heat a thin film of oil. Once the oil is very hot, add the reserved shrimp shells and tomato paste. Cook, stirring frequently, until the shells have turned bright red and the paste smells caramelized and is rust-colored, about 2 minutes. Add the wine and reduce the heat to medium. Continue to cook until the wine has reduced by half, about 4 minutes. Add the cream, white peppercorns, and lemon juice. Cook until reduced by half again, about 10 minutes. Season with salt and strain, discarding the solids. Stir in the remaining ½ teaspoon chopped tarragon and set aside.

3. Preheat the oven to 400°F (200°C).

4. Season the halibut with salt and white pepper. Using a small spatula, spread the shrimp puree evenly on top of each fillet, like you would butter toast, but with a lot more puree than you would put butter on your toast. There should be about a ¼ inch (6 mm) on each fillet. Don't worry about making it look perfect.

5. In a sauté pan over medium-high heat, heat a good ⅛ inch (3 mm) of oil. When the oil is hot, add the halibut, puree side down. Cook for about 2 minutes; the puree should be puffed and golden. Flip, and, using your spatula to hold the fish in place, tilt the pan and drain the oil. Add the shrimp and cream mixture to the pan. It will bubble up and hiss; this is a good thing. Place the pan in the oven and bake until the fish is crispy on the outside, moist on the inside, about 5 minutes, depending on the thickness of the fish.

6. Remove the fish from the pan and place the fillets in the center of a shallow serving dish. Spoon the reduced cream around the halibut and dot with the pistou. Garnish with the chervil and serve.

A note from Gabriel: I was first introduced to tripe by eating pho up the street from my first house in Portland. (It was a pretty wild and crazy place where I hosted many drunken industry parties. We—a bunch of fellow Portland cooks and Lyle Railsback, the former wine guy at Paley's Place and now a Kermit Lynch employee—would do "offal" Mondays and cook up whatever was leftover from service that was going to go to waste.) Pho Hung is still my favorite place to get pho in Portland. I can't encourage you enough to check this place out. Go for the "Super Bowl," which is a soup with beef, tripe, knuckle, and some kind of meatball (fish and pork?) that I still can't figure out.

Note: The tripe has to soak in the fridge for 24 hours and the white beans must soak overnight. The pork belly has to bake for at least 3 hours. {SERVES 4}

PORK BELLY, TRIPE, FENNEL JAM

Fennel Jam and Fronds

1 fennel bulb, fronds removed and reserved and bulb cored and thinly sliced
1 clove garlic, thinly sliced
½ yellow onion, sliced
1 teaspoon grated orange zest
1 cup (250 ml) good-quality sweet wine, such as Sauternes
2 tablespoons Moscatel vinegar
2 tablespoons honey
½ teaspoon kosher salt
Neutral oil for frying

Pork Belly

1 tablespoon kosher salt
2 teaspoons brown sugar
½ teaspoon fennel pollen
½ teaspoon ground fennel seeds
1 pound (450 g) meaty skin-on pork belly
1 cup (250 ml) dry white wine
A squeeze of fresh lemon juice
Maldon flake salt

1. To make the fennel jam, in a saucepan over medium heat, combine the fennel bulb, garlic, onion, orange zest, Sauternes, vinegar, honey, and salt. Simmer, stirring occasionally, until the onions and fennel are very soft, 45 to 55 minutes. Once the fennel is soft and delicious, mash everything up using the back of a fork. We want some texture left, not a smooth puree. This will keep for up to 2 weeks in the refrigerator.

2. Preheat the oven to 350°F (180°C).

3. To make the pork belly, in a bowl stir together the salt, brown sugar, fennel pollen, and fennel seeds. Score the skin on the belly, cutting through the skin about ⅛ inch (3 mm), and rub the seasoning mixture in well, really getting into those nooks and crannies. Nestle the belly into a baking dish, and add the white wine. Cover and bake for about 3 hours; it's done when a meat fork goes in with very little resistance (kind of like poking soft butter). Remove the belly from the pan and refrigerate, covered, for at least an hour. Cut the belly into four pieces of equal size.

4. Now we are going to cook our tripe beans: In a medium pot over medium heat, combine the tripe, sherries, stock, onion, garlic, bay leaves, pepper, water, and salt. Bring to a simmer and simmer for about 1½ hours. Test your tripe by cutting off a little slice and trying it; it should taste pungent and gamy, with some sweet notes, and have a slightly chewy texture. At this point add your beans and continue to cook for 1 hour more. Remove the tripe from the pot, slice into pencil-thin strips, and return to the pot. Continue cooking until the liquid is reduced to about 1 cup (250 ml), about 10 minutes. Right before serving, remove the pot from the heat and stir in

Tripe Beans

8 ounces (250 g) honeycomb tripe, soaked for 24 hours in water in the refrigerator

1 cup (250 ml) cream sherry

1 cup (250 ml) dry sherry

2 cups (500 ml) chicken stock

1 yellow onion, thinly sliced

5 cloves garlic, thinly sliced

2 bay leaves

1 teaspoon freshly ground black pepper

2 cups (500 ml) water

2 teaspoons kosher salt

2 cups (14 ounces/400 g) dried small white beans, soaked overnight

¼ cup (60 ml) Aioli (page 321)

¼ cup (10 g) chopped fresh flat-leaf parsley

Oregano Salsa Verde (optional; page 154)

the aioli and parsley. (It's important to not stir the aioli in until right before serving or it will separate.) Check the seasoning.

5. About 10 minutes before the beans are done, in a large, heavy pot over high heat, pour oil to a depth of 2 inches (5 cm). When the oil is hot, add the reserved fennel fronds and fry for 10 seconds. Using a slotted spoon, transfer the fronds to a plate lined with paper towels; set aside. Add the pieces of pork belly to the pot with the oil and fry until golden, about 3 minutes. Transfer to a plate lined with paper towels. Sprinkle with lemon juice and Maldon salt.

6. Divide the beans and tripe among four bowls and top each with a piece of pork belly. Top the pork belly with a dollop of fennel jam and spoon a little salsa verde around the beans. Top with the fried fennel fronds and serve.

When spring arrives in the Pacific Northwest, nettles are a huge thing, with enormous bags being harvested by the same people who forage for mushrooms. Yes, these are stinging nettles, the same plant most people try to avoid when hiking. The flavor is kind of like tangy spinach with a little earthy broccoli note. If you can't get your hands on nettles, you can substitute spinach. When harvesting or cleaning nettles, be sure to wear gloves, as they will sting you. However, once they have been blanched in water, they are perfectly safe. The pork croutons here are our version of oyster crackers. {SERVES 6}

POTATO AND NETTLE SOUP, CRISPY PORK

Kosher salt
1 pound (450 g) nettles, cleaned
2 tablespoons unsalted butter
1 yellow onion, thinly sliced
5 cloves garlic, thinly sliced
1½ pounds (675 g) Yukon gold potatoes, peeled and diced
1 tablespoon champagne vinegar
6 cups (1.5 l) chicken stock
½ cup (125 ml) heavy cream
Neutral oil for frying
8 ounces (250 g) Pork Shoulder Confit (page 186)

1.　Prepare an ice water bath. Bring a large pot of heavily salted water to boil over high heat. Wearing rubber gloves, add the nettles to the pot and blanch for 30 seconds. Using a spider or large slotted spoon, transfer the nettles to the ice water bath and cool for 2 minutes. Remove the nettles from the ice water, pat dry, and set aside.

2.　In a large pot over medium heat, melt the butter. Add the onion and garlic and sauté until translucent, about 4 minutes. Season with 1 tablespoon salt. Add the potatoes, vinegar, and stock. Bring to a boil and then reduce to a simmer. Cook over medium heat until the potatoes are very tender, about 40 minutes. Add the blanched nettles and stir to combine.

3.　Working in batches as necessary, carefully puree the soup, starting your blender at low speed. Return the puree to the pot over very low heat, stir in the cream, and check for seasoning.

4.　In a heavy pot over high heat, warm ½ inch (12 mm) of oil. Tear or shred the pork into ½-inch (12mm) cubes. Fry the pork in the oil, turning the pieces as you cook them, until crisp on all sides, 2 to 3 minutes.

5.　Ladle the soup into bowls, divide the pork croutons among the bowls to garnish, and serve.

We braise these pork cheeks in ouzo and kalamata olives, and then puree the braising liquid to make an olive barbecue sauce of sorts. Served with a quick Greek salad, this dish combines a couple of our favorite things: rich and tangy feta cheese and potent anise-flavored ouzo. {SERVES 4 AS A SIDE, 2 AS A STARTER}

PORK CHEEK, OUZO, FETA

4 pork cheeks, about 1½ pounds (680 g) total
Kosher salt
½ yellow onion, thinly sliced
4 cloves garlic, thinly sliced
A small pinch of red pepper flakes
1 cup (250 ml) ouzo
¼ cup (40 g) kalamata olives
1 cup (250 ml) chicken stock
Quick Greek Salad (see recipe below)

1. Preheat the oven to 350°F (180°C).

2. Season the pork cheeks well with salt. In a small Dutch oven over medium-high heat, sear the pork cheeks until brown on all sides, about 3 minutes per side. Add the onion, garlic, and red pepper flakes and continue to cook for 2 minutes. Add the ouzo, olives, and stock. Cover and braise in the oven until the cheeks are knife-tender, about 3 hours. Once the cheeks are done, remove them from the pan with tongs or a slotted spoon and keep warm.

3. Carefully—you're working with searing hot liquid here—pour the braising liquid, including the solids, into a blender or food processor. Puree until smooth. Return the mixture to the Dutch oven, turn the heat to medium, and reduce to about ½ cup (125 ml) liquid; it should have the consistency of a nice glaze. Return the cheeks to the pan and toss to coat.

4. Serve the pork cheeks warm with the salad alongside.

Quick Greek Salad

Vinaigrette
1 shallot, minced
¼ cup (60 ml) red wine vinegar
1 teaspoon dried oregano
½ teaspoon freshly ground black pepper
½ cup (125 ml) extra-virgin olive oil
½ cup (75 g) crumbled feta
Kosher salt

¼ cup (40 g) sliced cherry tomatoes
2 tablespoons sliced kalamata olives
1 cucumber, peeled, seeded, and cut into half moons (about ½ cup/110 g)
¼ cup (35 g) thinly sliced red onion
¼ cup (40 g) crumbled feta
1 tablespoon fresh oregano leaves
1 tablespoon ouzo

SERVES 4 AS A SIDE, 2 AS A STARTER

To make the vinaigrette, in a small bowl combine the shallot and vinegar and let stand for 5 minutes. Stir in the oregano, pepper, olive oil, and feta. Taste and add salt, if necessary. In a large bowl, toss together the tomatoes, olives, cucumber, red onion, feta, and oregano. Add the vinaigrette and ouzo, toss to coat, and serve.

To make pretzels, you traditionally make the dough, proof it, blanch it in water and baking soda, and bake it. The baking soda gives it that salty/airy flavor that makes pretzels taste like pretzels. We did the same thing here with spaetzle, hoping to evoke a little more Oktoberfest, a little more *brotzeit,* if you will, in this already Bavarian-themed dish. You can buy spaetzle makers, and some people use potato ricers to make spaetzle, but we make ours using only a pot and a perforated hotel pan or an industrial-sized colander. A normal-sized colander will not work here. {SERVES 4}

PORK, PRETZEL SPAETZLE, KRAUT SLAW

Pork
1.5 pounds (680 g) pork tenderloin
1 tablespoon kosher salt
1 tablespoon mustard powder
2 tablespoons unsalted butter
2 tablespoons neutral oil
1 cup (140 g) No-Frills Sausage (page 185)
Crumbled honey and Dijon potato chips, for garnish (optional)

Pretzel Spaetzle
1¾ cups (220 g) all-purpose flour
3 eggs
½ cup (125 ml) whole milk
1 tablespoon active dry yeast
1 teaspoon kosher salt
1 teaspoon baking soda

Slaw
1 tablespoon brown mustard seeds
1 tablespoon yellow mustard seeds
1 tablespoon white wine vinegar
1 teaspoon malt vinegar
1 tablespoon sweet mustard
1½ teaspoons Tabasco
1½ teaspoons honey
½ cup (125 ml) neutral oil
Kosher salt
¾ cup (90 g) good-quality sauerkraut
½ cup (70 g) thinly sliced red onions
2 tablespoons chopped chives

Mustard Crème Fraîche
½ cup (125 ml) crème fraîche
3 tablespoons sweet mustard
2 teaspoons mustard powder

1. Let the pork sit at room temperature for 1 hour before cooking.

2. To make the spaetzle, butter or oil a baking sheet and set aside. In a stand mixer fitted with the paddle attachment, combine the flour, eggs, milk, yeast, and salt and blend on the second-lowest setting for 15 minutes. It will start off as a wet batter, but you want to work it until it starts to look and feel gluey. This is important, because if it isn't gluey, it will just fall apart when it hits the water.

3. If you have a spaetzle maker, use it now. If not, set up a large pot with a separate large colander; we use a 6-inch (15cm) hotel pan with a 2-inch (5cm) perforated hotel pan set inside of it. In the large pot, bring 4 quarts (4 l) of water to a boil. As it begins to boil, add the baking powder. Set up the colander or perforated pan over the boiling water, with your gluey batter in one hand and a nonstick spatula in another. Slowly pour the batter into the colander, using your spatula to push it through the holes. You want the holes to be larger than a normal colander, or else you'll be pushing it through for-ever and the heat will mess with the texture of the dough. Cook the spaetzle for 45 seconds, stirring it around with a skimmer. Be on your toes, because if you leave it in too long, it will start tearing apart and exploding to bits. Using a slotted spoon or sieve, transfer the spaetzle to the prepared baking sheet. Set the spaetzle aside until you're ready to use it; you can make this up to a day in advance.

4. To make the slaw, in a small mixing bowl, combine the brown and yellow mustard seeds, white wine vinegar, ¼ cup (60 ml) of water, the malt vinegar, sweet mustard, Tabasco, honey, and oil. Whisk thoroughly to combine and season to taste with salt. In a separate small bowl, combine the sauerkraut, red onions, and chives. Dress the sauerkraut mixture with 2 or 3 tablespoons of the vinegar mixture and reserve at room temperature.

{Continued}

5. To make the mustard crème fraîche, in a small bowl whisk together the crème fraîche, sweet mustard, and the mustard powder. Set aside.

6. To make the pork, trim the silver skin from the pork and season with the salt and mustard powder. Divide the tenderloin into four equal portions. In a cast-iron pan over high heat, add 1 tablespoon of the butter and sear the pork on one side until golden brown, about 2 minutes. Turn the heat down to medium and continue to cook the pork, basting occasionally, for 3 to 4 minutes. We like to serve pork medium, but if you like it cooked through, give it 2 more minutes. As with all things, the size and thickness of your pieces will affect the cooking time, so have a meat thermometer handy to check the temperature. Remove from the heat when a thermometer inserted into the middle of the pork registers 145°F (62°C). Let rest for 5 minutes.

7. While the pork is resting, in a large sauté pan over medium-high heat, heat the oil. Add the remaining 1 tablespoon of butter and throw in 2 cups of the cooked spaetzle. When the spaetzle starts to brown, add the sausage pieces and continue cooking until heated through, about 3 minutes. Drain off any excess fat and add around ½ cup of the mustard crème fraîche.

8. On each of four plates, spoon a nice helping of spaetzle. Slice each portion of pork on the diagonal into four pieces and arrange next to the spaetzle. Spoon the slaw on top of the pork, garnish the spaetzle with potato chips, drizzle some mustard crème fraîche on the plate, and serve.

 THE PIGEON POUR: This dish wants an Alsatian riesling, and if you are eating it, you do, too. Alsatian riesling is about elegance and power, but it has the acidity to balance everything out. Think about gymnasts. If German riesling is a tall, skinny girl doing rhythmic gymnastics with ribbons, Alsatian riesling is a 4-foot, 6-inch muscular powerhouse that swings on the parallel bars. The Alsatian rieslings we often have on hand are from Jean Sipp, Andre Ostertag, and Trimbach. The first two are not as widely available, but Trimbach is easy to find. Cuvée Frédéric Emile is one of their top wines and rocks with this dish, but one of their less expensive cuvées would work just fine, too.

No-Frills Sausage

12 ounces (375 g) ground pork
4 ounces (125 g) pork fatback
½ cup (70 g) diced yellow onion
2 cloves garlic, minced
1 tablespoon mustard powder
2 tablespoons whole-grain mustard
1 tablespoon kosher salt
Neutral oil for sautéing

MAKES 1 POUND (450 G)

In a medium bowl, stir together the ground pork, fatback, onion, garlic, mustard power, whole-grain mustard, and salt. In a large sauté pan over high heat, heat a nice film of oil. Add a very small piece of the sausage mixture and brown for about 2 minutes. Taste the sausage and add a little salt if it needs it. If not, you did well. Add the rest of the sausage to the pan and cook, scraping the bottom of the pan with a wooden spoon, until browned and cooked through, about 5 minutes. Remove the sausage from the pan and drain on a plate lined with paper towels.

This workhorse pork dish is easy to prepare yet stunning: moist, crisp, and delicious. Pork shoulder is a great cut; when seasoned and cooked slowly, it falls apart when you point your fork at it. We love to use Tails & Trotters (www.tailsandtrotters.com) pork. This local company mixes three breeds and feeds its pigs Oregon hazelnuts for the last 90 days before the slaughter. This gives them deliciously rich, flavorful fat. Ask your butcher for a high-quality boneless pork shoulder, also known as Boston butt, and to tie it up for you to ensure even cooking.

I always make extra pork when preparing this recipe, as the left-overs make the best *carnitas* (see Pork Tacos, opposite). So good that might there be a taco stand in our future? You'll just have to wait and see.

Note: The pork is seasoned and placed in the fridge for up to 24 hours, so plan ahead. {SERVES 6, WITH LEFTOVERS}

PORK SHOULDER CONFIT

3 tablespoons kosher salt
1 tablespoon freshly ground black pepper
1 teaspoon paprika
¼ teaspoon garlic powder
1 boneless pork shoulder, about 4 pounds (1.8 kg), tied by your butcher
1 cup (250 ml) neutral oil, plus more for panfrying
2 heads garlic, halved
A squeeze of fresh lemon juice
Maldon flake salt

1. In a small bowl, stir together the salt, pepper, paprika, and garlic powder. Rub the seasoning mixture all over the pork and refrigerate anywhere from 4 to 24 hours. The longer, the better.

2. Preheat the oven to 300°F (150°C). In a Dutch oven, combine the pork, oil, and garlic. Cover with aluminum foil and cook about 4 hours, checking after 3 hours. It is done when it is the most fork-tender meat you have ever poked. Remove from the oven and remove the foil. Let the meat sit in the fat for about 1 hour to cool.

3. Using two spatulas, gently lift the pork out of the oil and place on a cooling rack set over a baking sheet. At this point you won't be able to resist, so go ahead and pull a little piece off and give it a try. Okay, satisfied? Well, too bad; you'll have to wait a bit more. Refrigerate the pork until chilled and firm, about 2 hours.

4. Remove the pork from the refrigerator and transfer to a cutting board. Using a small pair of scissors, snip the butcher's twine from the pork and carefully remove it. Then, using a sharp knife, cut the pork into 2-inch (5cm) slices (saving any pieces that fall off for those tacos). You should be able to get six nice slices with plenty left over.

5. In a large cast-iron or other heavy sauté pan over medium-high heat, heat ¼ inch (6 mm) of oil. When the oil is hot, carefully add the slices of pork. Fry until well browned and crispy, about 2 minutes on each side. Using a slotted spatula, remove the pork from the oil and give a squeeze of lemon and a sprinkle of Maldon salt before serving.

A note from Gabriel: I'll admit I'm no taco purist; I like flour rather than corn for my tortillas, I put shredded lettuce and cheddar cheese in my tacos, and I season my meat with packets of dry seasoning bought at the store. Why would I try and re-create the real deal when I can just go to Lindo Michoacan on Division Street? These guys will make it better than I ever will.

When it's taco night at the Ruckers, all my family and friends want to come over (with the required six-pack), which means I'm slinging tacos for lots of folks and will end up with lots of leftover Tectate in the fridge. It's not a bad tradeoff.

Note: The pork for this recipe is the Pork Shoulder Confit (opposite). Rather than frying it as directed in that recipe, you'll pull the cooked pork confit into small pieces and fry it just before adding the taco seasoning, as described below. {MAKES 8 TACOS}

PORK TACOS, CONDIMENTS

Neutral oil for frying
1 pound (450 g) Pork Shoulder Confit (opposite), pulled into small pieces
1 package taco seasoning
8 small flour tortillas, warmed
1 cup (125 g) grated cheddar cheese
2 cups (90 g) shredded iceberg lettuce
Avocado Salsa (see recipe below)
Titular Sour Cream (see recipe below)

1. In a large cast-iron pan over medium-high heat, heat ½ inch (12 mm) of oil. When the oil is very hot, carefully add the pork confit and fry until browned and crispy, about 2 minutes per side. Remove from the oil with a slotted spoon and transfer to a bowl. Add the taco seasoning and stir to combine.

2. Place about ¼ cup (25 g) of the crispy pork in each tortilla. Top with the cheese, lettuce, salsa, and sour cream. Serve with additional salsa and sour cream on the side.

Avocado Salsa (No, This Is Not Guacamole)

2 large avocados, peeled, pitted, and finely diced
¼ cup (35 g) minced red onion
2 cloves garlic, minced
1 small Roma tomato, seeded and finely diced
1 tablespoon chopped cilantro

1 teaspoon seeded and finely minced jalapeño
2 tablespoons fresh lime juice
3 tablespoon extra-virgin olive oil
¼ teaspoon ground cumin
Kosher salt

MAKES 2 CUPS (280 G)

In a bowl, gently stir together all the ingredients.

Titular Sour Cream

¾ cup (180 ml) sour cream
1 tablespoon fresh lime juice
2 tablespoons chopped cilantro

MAKES ¾ CUP (180 ML)

In a bowl, stir together all the ingredients. Let sit for 10 minutes before serving.

This Erik Van Kley special is hands down the best pork chop I've ever tasted. Although it's a 2-day recipe, it's completely worth the effort. The foundation is curds and whey: the pork is brined in the whey and the curd becomes the cheese that's added to the green bean salad. Brining the pork in the whey pumps up the pork with a really strong, out-of-this-world flavor, hence the term *jacked*. {SERVES 4}

JACKED PORK CHOPS

2 quarts (2 l) whole milk
¼ cup (35 g) kosher salt
1 cup (250 ml) freshly squeezed
    lemon juice
1 teaspoon white vinegar
4-bone rack of pork loin, frenched by
    the butcher
Extra-virgin olive oil for rubbing
4 ounces (125 g) thinly sliced prosciutto

Hazelnut Pesto

½ cup (75 g) whole hazelnuts, toasted
    and skins removed
½ cup (75 g) sun-dried tomatoes
1 cup (40 g) chopped fresh flat-leaf
    parsley
2 cloves garlic
1 tablespoon hazelnut oil
1½ cups (375 ml) neutral oil
Kosher salt

Green Bean Salad

Kosher salt
4 cups (315 g) fresh green beans
1 cup (150 g) whole hazelnuts, toasted
    and skins removed
5 Calabrian chiles, seeded
A squeeze of fresh lemon juice

1. We're going to make the brine and the cheese simultaneously here: In a heavy pot over high heat, bring the milk to 175°F (80°C), just under a boil. Add the salt, lemon juice, and vinegar. Turn the heat off and let sit for 30 minutes. The curd and whey will naturally separate.

2. Line a colander with cheesecloth and place over a bowl. Pour the contents of the pot into the colander and wait for the curds (the solids in the colander) to drain completely, about 5 minutes. Transfer the whey (the liquid in the bowl) to the fridge for 20 minutes, and then add the pork to the bowl. Cover and brine the pork in the refrigerator for 24 hours.

3. Put the colander with the curds over another bowl, then fold the cheesecloth tightly around the curds and press. The easiest way to do this is to put a bowl with some sort of heavy weight in it on top of the curds and place in fridge for 24 hours. Add any whey that you squeezed out of the curds to the bowl with the pork.

4. The next day, remove the pork from the whey and pat dry. Rub the pork with a little olive oil so the prosciutto will adhere. Wrap the pork with the prosciutto all along the top edge. Slice into four chops and set aside.

5. To make the pesto, in a blender or food processor, puree the hazelnuts, sun-dried tomatoes, parsley, garlic, and the hazelnut oil. With the motor running, drizzle in the neutral oil until you have the right pesto consistency. Season with salt to taste.

6. To make the green bean salad, prepare an ice water bath. Bring a large pot of heavily salted water to a boil over high heat. Add the green beans and blanch for 2 minutes. Taste one of the beans; if it's not cooked enough for you, blanch for 1 minute more. When the beans are ready, using a spider or a large slotted spoon, transfer the beans to the ice water bath to cool for 5 minutes. Remove the beans from the water and pat dry; set aside.

{Continued}

Jacked Pork Chops, *continued*

7.   Remove the curds from the cheesecloth. They will be crumbly and soft; that's just how you want them. (Note: You will have leftover curds. We like to mix them into salads, omelets, kimchi, or French fries.) In a salad bowl, toss together the green beans, hazelnuts, Calabrian chiles, and crumbled curds. Season with salt to taste, a squeeze of lemon, and ⅓ cup (70 g) of the hazelnut pesto.

8.   To grill the pork chops, preheat a gas grill or prepare a charcoal grill for cooking over very high heat. Grill the pork chops for 5 minutes on the first side, flip, and then grill to medium doneness, 4 minutes more.

9.   Drizzle some of the hazelnut pesto over the pork chops and serve with green bean salad alongside.

Pig's feet, aka trotters, are a great addition to any stock or soup. Their rich pork flavor and thick gelatin gives an added kick to any winter stew. In this dish, we serve the meat as a spicy salad along-side late-summer watermelon and salty, tangy feta yogurt. Pig's feet should be easy to find at any Asian or Mexican market. Make sure to buy the feet with the shank attached, as that is where the majority of the meat comes from. {SERVES 4}

PIG'S FOOT, WATERMELON, FETA

Braise

2 pig's feet, shank attached, about 8 pounds (3.5 kg) total
1 cup (250 ml) balsamic vinegar
1 cup (250 ml) dry white wine
4 quarts (4 l) water
1 yellow onion, quartered
½ teaspoon red pepper flakes
½ teaspoon sambal chile paste
4 cloves garlic, crushed
2 bay leaves
2 tablespoons kosher salt
½ teaspoon freshly grated nutmeg

Marinade

1 tablespoon balsamic vinegar
1 tablespoon extra-virgin olive oil
1 teaspoon sambal chile paste
¼ teaspoon dry oregano
A pinch of freshly grated nutmeg
½ teaspoon grated orange zest
Kosher salt

Feta Yogurt

¼ cup (40 g) crumbled feta
¼ cup (40 g) plain yogurt

¼ cup (35 g) thinly sliced red onion
¼ cup (10 g) fresh flat-leaf parsley
Segments from 1 orange
1 cup (130 g) diced watermelon
2 tablespoons crumbled feta
A squeeze of fresh lemon juice

1.   To make the braise, in a large pot over medium-high heat, combine the pig's feet, balsamic vinegar, white wine, water, onion, red pepper flakes, sambal chile paste, garlic, bay leaves, salt, and nutmeg. Bring to a boil, and then turn down to a low simmer. Cover the pot and simmer until the meat is falling off the bone, about 2½ hours. Using a large slotted spoon, transfer the feet from the pot to a baking sheet. (Strain the liquid and reserve it for another use. You will have a nice, richly flavored stock. We don't need it for this recipe, but it's worth holding onto for cooking more trotters or making soup or drizzling on rice.)

2.   Let the pig's feet cool for about 30 minutes, then pick them apart. (Now, there is not a lot of meat on pigs' feet, so don't be surprised when your yield is small. Most of the meat is going to come from the shank portion. This is a dirty job but well worth it, so just dig in. There is lots of fat, skin, and bones, but you should have no trouble detecting the meat. It will be fairly dark.) Once all the meat has been picked, you can discard the skin and bones.

3.   Now we're going to make a marinade for the meat. In a bowl, stir together the balsamic vinegar, olive oil, chile paste, oregano, nutmeg, and orange zest. Add the picked meat to the bowl and toss gently to combine, so as not to mash the meat. Add salt to taste and set aside.

4.   To make the feta yogurt, in a blender, combine ¼ cup of the feta and the yogurt. Puree until smooth and set aside.

5.   In a bowl, toss the meat with the onion, parsley, and orange segments. You can get as creative as you want with the plating. At the restaurant, we arrange the diced watermelon on plates, about three large pieces per plate. Then we arrange the meat next to the watermelon to make a composed salad of sorts. Top with the feta and drizzle with the feta yogurt. Finish, as always, with a squeeze of lemon juice and serve.

Tommy Habetz, owner of Bunk Sandwiches, is a very mellow dude. He worked for some pretty heavy hitters (Batali!, Flay!) before settling in Portland. Tommy's nicknames range from "the flavor beast" to "the main event;" he's the guy who will laugh at *all* of your jokes— just not as much as he laughs at his own. He loves rock 'n' roll: LPs cover the walls at Bunk Bar and he'll force you to sit in his car listening to the latest Lil Wayne jam until the song is over. Tommy is an amazing dad and is loved by all. I mean, how can you *not* love a guy who names his sandwich shop after the character Bunk from the television show *The Wire*?

THE "LE BUNK" SANDWICH

Tommy opened the first Bunk Sandwiches on the east side of Portland in 2008. It has a diner vibe with a Pacific Northwest grunge element (the aesthetics, not the cleanliness!). The place is long and skinny with very little room; there is no fan or air conditioning, which means when you stop by for a meal, you will smell like pork belly for the day. On one wall is a gigantic chalkboard with an ever-rotating list of sandos and sides. Bunk was a huge hit right out of the gate. The lines would wrap around the block, causing the neighbor, an old-school electronics dealer and repairman whose shop entrance was blocked by Bunk patrons, to be furious! Today, Tommy and his business partner, Nick Wood, have two Bunk Sandwich locations (lucky for us, the second one is right next to Little Bird) and Bunk Bar (a restaurant and music venue that brings in great acts).

I have known Tommy since before the opening of Le Pigeon and wanted an excuse to cook with him again. And so we present to you: Le Bunk, a sandwich that will fill you up but is not a marathon prep project. Tommy and I were on a rare health kick while coming up with this, hence we decided to dress the sandwich with a cavolo nero slaw. We love Crystal Hot Sauce from Louisiana, but if it's impossible to get your hands on it, Tabasco will do. {SERVES 4}

4 bone-in pork chops, each about
    6 ounces (185 g)

1½ cups (25 g) shredded cavolo nero
    (Tuscan kale)

¼ cup (25 g) sliced red onions

2 tablespoons chopped cilantro

1 jalapeño, seeded and sliced into very
    thin rings

¼ cup (60 ml) mayonnaise

Juice of 1 lime

Kosher salt and freshly ground black
    pepper

Neutral oil for sautéing

1 tablespoon unsalted butter

1½ teaspoons hot sauce, plus more
    for garnish

4 kaiser rolls

1.   Place the pork chops on a wooden cutting board and, using a meat mallet or the back of a small sauté pan, gently pound each chop to about half its original thickness.

2.   Now let's make the slaw so it has time to soften and get *titular* (see sidebar on page 14) while we cook our chops. In a bowl, toss together the cavolo nero with the onions, cilantro, jalapeño, mayo, and the lime juice. Season to taste with salt and pepper. Set aside.

3.   In a large cast-iron pan over high heat, heat a thin film of oil. Season the pork chops with salt and pepper. When the oil is smoking, add the chops to the pan and cook for 2 minutes. Flip the chops, add the butter to the pan, and cook 2 minutes longer. Finally, add the hot sauce to the pan and toss the chops around to coat. Transfer the chops to a cutting board and carefully cut away the bone and discard. Transfer the chops to a plate to rest.

4.   Turn the heat down to medium and add the rolls to the pan, cut side down, to toast in the pork-flavored fatty goodness. Once browned and mouthwatering, remove from the pan.

5.   Place a chop on the bottom of the bun. Top with a nice pile of the slaw, about 2 heaping spoonfuls. Garnish with additional hot sauce, top with the other half of the bun, and serve.

Pork loin makes a great roast; it's cheap, easy, and goes with almost anything. Be sure to buy quality heritage pork as the flavor will be much deeper and the fat marbling akin to that of a nice cut of beef.

The sweetness of fennel pairs very well with the flavor of crispy pork fat, so I mixed fennel seeds and pollen with a little paprika for this dish. Serve this roast with Tomatoes, Plums, Watercress (page 21).

{SERVES 4}

SIMPLE ROAST PORK LOIN

1 tablespoon fennel pollen
1 tablespoon ground fennel seeds
2 teaspoons paprika
Kosher salt
2 tablespoons Pernod
1 boneless pork loin, about 2 pounds (900 g)
2 fennel bulbs, with fronds attached

1. Preheat the oven to 450°F (230°C).

2. In a small bowl, stir together the fennel pollen, fennel seeds, paprika, 2 tablespoons of salt, and Pernod to form a paste. Generously rub the pork with the spice paste and let sit for 1 hour at room temperature.

3. Pick the fronds from the fennel and chop coarsely. Core the fennel bulbs and cut into slices ¼ inch (6 mm) thick. Season with salt. Place the fennel and the fronds in the bottom of a roasting pan. Place the seasoned pork on top, fat side up. Roast until a nice brown crust forms, about 15 minutes. Turn the temperature down to 300°F (150°C) and continue roasting until a thermometer inserted into the pork reads 145°F (62°C), about 20 minutes more. Remove from the oven and let rest for 10 minutes.

4. With a slotted spoon, transfer the fennel to a serving platter. Slice the pork and serve the slices on top of the fennel.

THE WEIRD AND WONDERFUL WORLD OF LARS NORGREN

The first time Meredith met Lars Norgren, they were at the worst farmers' market of all time. It was twenty minutes outside the city, just off the highway, and they knew as soon as they drove up that this would be a get-what-we-came-for hit-and-run. There were two guys (both in Pantera T-shirts) playing post-rock apocalyptic drone noise, while the majority of stalls sold T-shirts from Walmart, handmade flutes, and store-bought jam.

Lars, a man so well known among restaurant owners in Portland that he needs no last name, has a full head of gray hair,

a focused gaze, and the requisite dirty fingernails of a woodsman. He has owned and operated Peak Forest Fruit, a distributor of wild Oregonian products, for nearly thirty years. Peak Forest services the greater Portland area with huckleberries, mushrooms, truffles, nettles, wood sorrel, fiddleheads, watercress, and anything else that grows in the Oregon forest. He has an "office" at milepost 47 of Highway 47, right next to a Dairy Queen. You'll know it by the eight-foot mountain quail painted on the front wall.

His office, which is actually an abandoned gas station, is not

simply that of an absent-minded distributor, but rather, according to Lars, "purposely disheveled" to appear deserted to passing methamphetamine addicts. But more on that later.

If you peer inside the dusty windows, you'll see stacks of

guidebooks, bikes, maps, ency-clopedias, random boxes, and general picking gear. Though his home (and surrounding forty acres) is only two miles away, this office acts as a buffer between his family life and the vagaries of "mycopecuniary malfeasance." For all intents and purposes, how-ever, Lars's business is run out of his van, a 2008 pine green Toyota Sienna.[1]

On this particular day, we had come to talk mushrooms and nettles, as Gabriel wanted to make a pickup for the week and introduce Meredith to a part of Le Pigeon that she couldn't experience in the restaurant. This

was vitally important, as Lars and Gabriel have worked together from the beginning; Gabriel loves Lars's aptitude for good quality, and Lars loves Gabriel's aptitude for quantity. And so what started as a meet and greet with Lars and a few questions about the bounty of Oregon became a seven-month discourse between Lars and Meredith on mushrooms, truffles, salmon, Oregonian forestry, Oakies and Arkies, the edibility of road kill, and why real men hunt elk.

There is a lot of talk about Portland's food scene, the trends, the people, the coffee, and the restaurants. To talk to Lars is to get a *real* sense of Portland's wild

frontier and what's available out-side the city's limits. If you're really interested in understanding the landscape of the Pacific North-west, then it's important to delve deeper, maybe by visiting the Til-lamook coast, maybe by reading H. L. Davis,[2] or maybe just by visit-ing an abandoned gas station.

What follows is an edited and very, very condensed take on what makes the forest of Oregon such a uniquely wild place. And it is told by the one-and-only Lars Norgren himself.

THE SURROUNDING FOREST

What was the first wild food I really collected? A pigeon! Not a city pigeon, but a band-tailed pigeon. A subtropical bird that visits Oregon in the summer and eats elderberries. I shot it with my

---

1. When I asked, "Why not a pickup?" Lars answered, "My son, the economics major, went to considerable lengths to show on paper that I should drive an F-150 like every other real man in Banks, Oregon. Well, minivans hold *more* product than a pickup (2,000 pounds of cherries, 1,000 pounds of mushrooms) but drive like a car. For those that deride minivans for not being sexy, it's a simple matter to remove or fold down the seats and have a great bedroom at the mountains or the beach. It'll be a cold day in a hot place before I attempt a ménage à trois in a Jetta."

2. A wild fiction writer, the first Oregonian to win a Pulitzer Prize.

mother's shotgun on September 1, 1969. I was ten years old.

It is true that all manner of natural landscapes in the developing world are under serious assault. But in wealthy countries that trend has been in reverse for nearly a century. If you were to take a walk in the neighborhood of Le Pigeon in daylight on a daily basis, you would see bald eagles several times a year. The peregrine falcon was even rarer than the bald eagle forty years ago, but it, too, can be seen without a dedicated effort on a monthly basis in the aforementioned neighborhood. These falcons nest on bridges and high-rise buildings, subsisting on . . . take a guess. Pigeons!

So we have two formerly endangered species frequenting the center of a metropolitan area. I'm not denying threats to the environment on a global level, nor advocating paving the remaining wildernesses. Far from it. But the prospect of an ecological apocalypse has been waning in Portland for quite awhile. Simply put, the abundance of wild foods in private homes and restaurants alike is due to the omnipresence of the wild in our everyday lives.

When I was a teenager, I would head to the Tillamook State Forest to find chanterelles. Someone told me to look under hemlock and maple. I didn't find anything. Why? Because chanterelles grow under Douglas fir here!

The dominant tree in the state and (rightfully) the state tree of Oregon, it can grow six feet a year and live for a thousand years. It is king where the summers are hot and dry, but the winters mild and wet. The tallest tree ever recorded on the planet is not a redwood in California, but a Douglas fir near Astoria at the mouth of the Columbia River. When it was toppled by a hurricane in 1964 it stood 375 feet above the soil that spawned it.

A chanterelle cannot live on its own. In Oregon, it is attached to the roots of Douglas fir by an organism known as ectomycorrhizae. The ultimate symbol of symbiosis in the mind of food folk is the truffles of Alba and Périgord, which grow on the roots of oak trees.[3] This is why people are invariably amazed to learn that Oregon truffles grow on the roots of the Douglas fir. It makes sense, however, as 99 percent of Oregon's forests are coniferous, and Douglas fir dominates the mix. The mild climate of Oregon means that Douglas firs are always producing a copious supply of carbohydrates for truffles and chanterelles. If you like to hunt for either of them, it's a long season. The first chanterelles fruit in the fog zone at the beach in early July. The last ones may be on the banks of the Columbia River in February.

When someone with a predilection for picking mushrooms

wakes up in Portland, they are usually faced with some agonizing choices: Do they drive west to the coast and pick porcini (but they can't stop along the way, as there are thousands of pounds of chanterelles, and they'll never make it to the spruce forest on the dunes where their spouse picked porcini two days ago)? Do they drive east to Mount Hood and pick matsutakes (but they can't stop along the way, as there are thousands of pounds of chanterelles and they'll never . . .)? Do they drive north to Mount Saint Helens and pick lobster mushrooms? Now just a darn minute! Why would anyone in his or her right mind make a dedicated foray for lobster mushrooms when porcini and matsutakes are readily available for the same effort? Both of them taste better and are more valuable. But there is no accounting for taste, or price.

What if there are porcini fruiting in the Cascades as well as the coast? Because there are. And there are porcini fruiting on the south coast as well as the north coast. No one wants to buy porcini in wholesale quantities today, and matsutakes are averaging two bucks a pound to the picker at the forest gate. But at the tail end of lobster mushroom season, any dealer will pay three or four dollars a pound for all you can pick. When the woods are white

---

3. If this meta-mycology is whetting your whistle, you should check out *Mushrooms Demystified* by David Arora. Besides being a friend of Lars's, David is best described as the leading mushroom writer in the English language. *Demystified* is a 500-page reference book that has an edibility section with lines like "Better trampled than sampled" and "Better kicked than licked." David compares himself to a black trumpet, "small, dark, and largely unappreciated." Also, we realize that Arora is published by the same publishing house as this book is. Do not charge us with nepotism; this is merely a coincidence.

with unpicked, now rotting matsutakes, it looks like the first snow of winter. The landscape of southwest Washington and almost all of Oregon is public property, open to all the year 'round.

The climate and plant communities of the Pacific Northwest are best described as a mosaic. Very diverse conditions exist in close proximity. A resident of most cities in the industrial world would have to drive a day or more to get to one interesting habitat. A resident of Portland can visit

almost all potentially good forests in the same day and still be home for a late supper. This makes hunting mushrooms affordable for the poorest residents, and accessible to the busiest. A doctor, lawyer, or executive chef can spend the first or last few hours of daylight hunting mushrooms and still put in a full day at a "real" job. Turkey

probably most resembles Oregon with its mosaic of climates and plant communities. But Turkey's soil, even though it defies the imagination, cannot live up to ours.[4] The Pacific Ocean drives the climate of Oregon with all the force of a nuclear power plant. The Mediterranean is more of a candelabra.

4. Our state soil, called "Jory," is the product of the prolonged weathering of basalt. Millionaires and paupers pour their passion into this soil by planting pinot noir grapes with plans of making the state's official wine. Farmers in much of the world wouldn't hesitate to sign a contract with Satan if it meant they could exchange their ground for Jory. Five feet or more to bedrock, Jory makes the fields of Brie and Normandy seem shallow and poor by comparison. It is a rich and wonderful red, the devil's food cake of dirt.

THE TRUFFLED AND THE DAMNED

The story you are about to read is true. The names have been changed to protect the innocent.

Whites truffles fruit quite close to the surface, sometimes immediately below the moss or duff, on top of mineral earth, rarely deeper than 6 inches (15 cm). Black truffles are typically 12 inches (30 cm) deep and are much less abundant. Thus they require considerably more work to harvest. All species require enormous amounts of grunt work, hence the prevalence of amphetamine addicts among the talent pool of truffle hunters.

A winter with a copious black truffle harvest may deliver a mediocre white truffle harvest and vice versa. Some winters yield no truffles at all. In some seasons, a professional harvester can dig 11 pounds (5 kg) a day of blacks and can't sell them for any price. Whites flood the market even more often. Both pickers and buyers freeze truffles in times of plenty, often waiting many years to get rid of them. Contrary to what you read, the number one problem in the domestic truffle industry is oversupply.

Hype about truffles began in France in the 1840s, I believe. As in Oregon, European truffles grow in forests regenerating on previously cultivated ground. Throughout the nineteenth century, marginal lands employed for subsistence agriculture were being abandoned. A few decades later, when passively established forests were sapling sized, truffle harvests would peak. There are

constant rumors of "cultivated" truffles, that is, seedlings of a host tree inoculated with some species of truffle, which when planted will eventually produce truffles. I have read such stories for three decades but never encountered evidence of consistent results, let alone any stellar success. Similarly, some hucksters will train your dog to find truffles (it may cost thousands of dollars, easily enough to fund a lifetime of ready-picked fungus) or sell you a dog alleged to be a dedicated breed of truffle hunter. In truth, any mixed-breed mutt has potential, but I've never met a truffle hunter that took their dog with them to work. I think the best outcome of all this hyperbole and obfuscation would be a Disney movie in which hillbilly kids in Tuscany are trying to fund

an operation for their terminally ill grandma by hunting truffles, only to have their trusty truffle dog (an adorable little Benji-like mutt, of course) kidnapped by urban thugs and held for ransom.

No dealer wants to hold too big a truffle inventory. At Peak Forest, truffles are typically a sideline for us. We are trying to serve cooks like Gabriel, whose everyday reality is frantic and grueling. For them, too, truffles are a sideline to the five-gallon jugs of cooking oil and fifty-pound boxes of potatoes they need.

Whenever a new truffle hunter comes out of the woodwork, someone who promises to lead a boring existence and deliver reliably, we buy his product and start to foster a relationship. The hope is always implicit that *this one* will prove to be an anomaly, to lead a life with some semblance of rhythm, and hence dependability. As you can imagine, this rarely happens.

Such is the case with Alvin and Simon, two truffle hunters who make the case against hunting truffles as a livelihood. When Alvin and Simon met, Simon was beside the road with a broken axle. He had always operated a car, but he hadn't held a valid driver's license in a decade and a half. No insurance, of course. Broken down beside the road, he was a sitting duck for the next peace officer to come along. He had possessed some cash at daybreak, but it all went into the gas tank. The gasoline had largely been converted to fresh truffles, which are usually a fungible commodity in northwest Oregon between October and April. If there was anything lucky about the day, it was that this breakdown occurred on Simon's way back out of the woods.

Alvin—a lovable bastard with a special aptitude for keeping the best of us from saying "no" when we totally know we should— picked Simon up that day. He drove Simon to the truffle buyer, the auto parts store, and back to the debilitated vehicle. As you can see, Alvin's heart is as big as his body. And since he's a former collegiate football player, that's saying something.

I had met Simon two years earlier, when he drove his peeling hardtop to my shop the day before Christmas Eve. I had bought his white truffles "field run," that is, ungraded by size. I paid less than the competitors for

the large ones, but I also bought the small ones. For the most part, dealers refuse small white truffles. This was a watershed moment for Simon.

It was a time of easy credit. American Express gave Simon a card, which he used to hire helicopters and float planes in Alaska. Large forest fires yielded morel crops the following summer, and Simon hoped to get in far from roads and competing pickers. His cost-to-benefit ratio was only off by an order of magnitude. Or two. Then a fire straddled the international border in northeastern Washington. Although he held no driver's license or insurance, let alone a passport, Simon somehow crossed the border in both directions. While leaving a similar burned forest near Kettle Falls, he chose a fallen old-growth ponderosa pine as a path. The bark had fallen off the aging log, and many of its branches had broken off, leaving sharp stubs. Simon slipped, falling hard onto one of the stubs. It missed an artery by an inch, and luckily Simon had held his breath, avoiding a collapsed lung. He somehow made it to Highway 395 and flagged a car. The Good Samaritans drove him to Republic, west over a 6,000-foot pass. He was flown by helicopter to Spokane, and after three days in a hospital bed he was back to picking morels.

Throughout all this, he continued to find more truffles than his peers. And he recognized multiple species of truffles where 90 percent of other harvesters, buyers, and chefs thought there was only one. Science has vindicated his taxonomy, I might add.

I have bought tons of porcini, chanterelles, and matsutakes from political refugees, largely Guatemaltecos, Cambodians, and Laotians who escaped their homelands with their lives, suffering unimaginable indignities before and after. They call the night before they go out to make sure we need the mushrooms. They verify the price and grading. They show up under their own power at the appointed hour of delivery and are in a multitude of ways delightful company.

I read about truffle harvests in Europe. It is a topic that magazine editors never tire of. These articles are almost boilerplate, describing nighttime forays with pigs or dogs, open-air markets where the trunks of cars hold manyfold the value of the vehicles, and a visit to some storied trattoria where diners arrive in cars that exceed the value of a truffle hunter's home. I'm confident the writers of every one of these stories has missed the real story. Whether it is in Piedmont or Slovenia, Périgord or Navarro, the life of a truffle hunter is characterized by chronic turbulence and uncertainty.

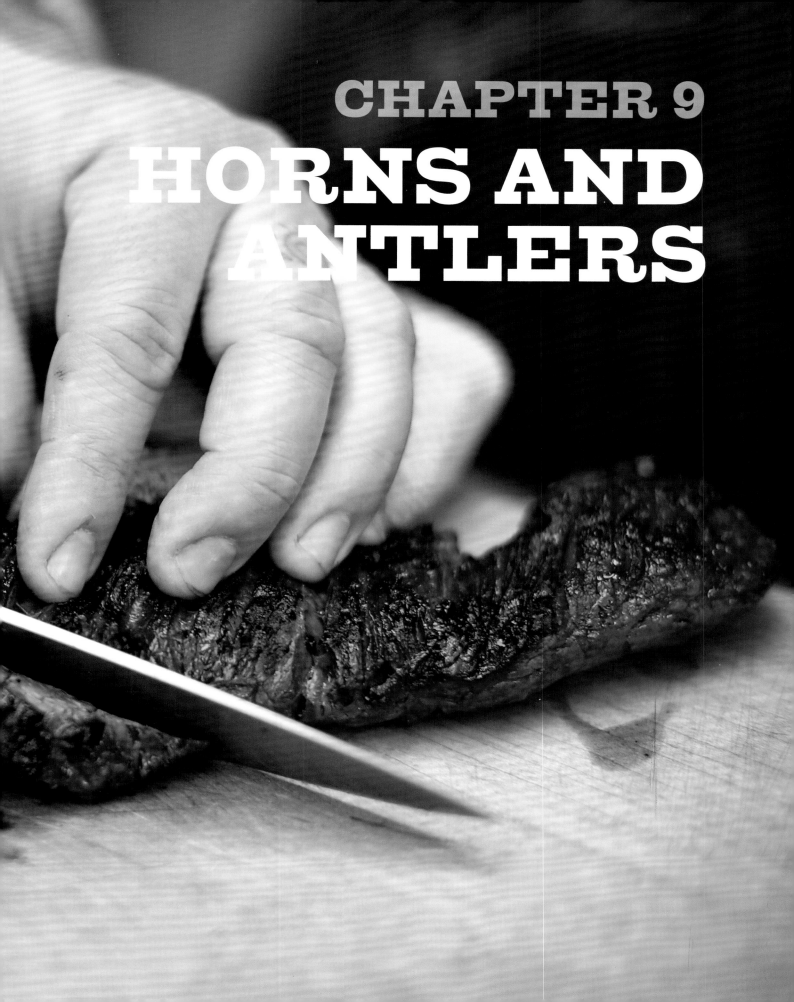

CHAPTER 9
HORNS AND ANTLERS

Back in 2006, Eric Van Kley (the old sous-chef at Pigeon and the present chef de cuisine at Little Bird) and Gabriel started making bourguignon using beef cheeks rather than chuck. This was also the first time we started doing overnight cooking. We cook the cheeks overnight at 200°F (95°C) for about 12 hours. This is the way you should go, but if cooking overnight gives you the heebie-jeebies, then cook the beef cheeks for 4 hours at 325°F (165°C). This is one of the only dishes that never leaves the menu (but it does get the occasional makeover; see Beef Cheeks 2012, page 208). {SERVES 6}

BEEF CHEEKS BOURGUIGNON

Beef Cheeks

6 beef cheek medallions, each 8 to 9 ounces (250 to 280 g)
Kosher salt and freshly ground black pepper
Neutral oil for searing
2 carrots, peeled and cut into 1-inch (2.5cm) pieces
2 celery stalks, cut into 1-inch (2.5cm) pieces
1 large yellow onion, peeled and cut into slices 1 inch (2.5 cm) thick
2 tablespoons tomato paste
1 bottle (750 ml) pinot noir or other light red wine
4 cups (1 l) veal or beef stock
3 cloves garlic
3 sprigs thyme
2 bay leaves
1 tablespoon black peppercorns

Glazed Onions

3 red onions, peeled and cut into slices 1 inch (2.5 cm) thick
2 tablespoons sugar
1 teaspoon kosher salt
1 tablespoon unsalted butter
1½ cups (375 ml) light red wine

Glazed Carrots

1 pound (450 g) baby carrots, peeled and halved lengthwise
1 tablespoon brown sugar
1 tablespoon unsalted butter
½ teaspoon kosher salt
1 bay leaf

1. Preheat the oven to 325°F (165°C) or 200°F (95°C), according to the method you prefer (see headnote).

2. To make the beef cheeks, season them liberally with salt and pepper. In a deep sauté pan over high heat, heat a thin film of oil. Add the beef cheeks and sear until browned on both sides, about 2 minutes per side. Transfer the cheeks to a roasting pan. Reduce the heat to medium, add the carrots, celery, and onion to the sauté pan, and then add the tomato paste. Cook, stirring with a wooden spoon and making sure to scrape up the brown bits from the bottom of the pan, until carmelized, about 5 minutes. Add half of the wine to the sauté pan and deglaze. Transfer the vegetables to the roasting pan and add the remaining half of the wine. Add the stock, garlic, thyme, bay leaves, and peppercorns to the roasting pan. Cover the pan tightly with foil and cook in the oven at 325°F (165°C) for about 4 hours or 200°F (95°C) for 12 hours, until very tender. We recommend the longer cooking time, if possible. When cooked, let cool in the liquid. Remove the beef cheeks with a slotted spoon and set aside while you reduce the sauce. Strain the liquid from the roasting pan and discard the solids. Place the liquid in a saucepan over medium-high heat and cook until the liquid is reduced by half, 35 to 40 minutes. Remove from the heat and set aside.

3. To make the glazed onions, in a heavy saucepan over medium heat, combine the red onions, sugar, salt, butter, and wine. Cook until the liquid has evaporated and the onions are glazed, about 20 minutes. Set aside.

4. To make the glazed carrots, place the carrots in a single layer in a saucepan over high heat. Add the brown sugar, butter, salt, bay leaf, and enough water to come three-quarters of the way up the side of the carrots. Cook until the water has evaporated and the carrots are cooked through and glazed, 3 to 4 minutes. Set aside.

5. To make the potatoes, fill a large pot with cold water and add the potatoes, garlic, bay leaf, and salt. Bring to a boil over high heat. Once the water

Potatoes

2 russet potatoes, peeled and cut into rounds ½ inch (12 mm) thick
1 clove garlic
1 bay leaf
1 tablespoon kosher salt
2 tablespoons unsalted butter

comes to a boil, turn off the heat and let sit for 4 minutes. Remove the potatoes with a slotted spoon and let cool to room temperature on a baking sheet. Discard the cooking liquid.

6.   Preheat the oven to 350°F (180°C). Stir together the glazed onions and carrots in a baking dish and bake for 15 minutes. Return the beef cheeks to the sauce and bring to a simmer over medium-high heat to warm through.

7.   Back to the potatoes: in a separate sauté pan over high heat, heat the butter until hot and frothy. Fry the potatoes in the butter until golden brown on the bottom, about 2 minutes; turn them with a spatula, and cook for 2 minutes more. Transfer the potatoes to a plate lined with paper towels and discard the butter.

8.   Now (finally) we're going to plate the dish. In each of six large, shallow bowls, place two potato slices and arrange the carrots and onions next to the potatoes. Top with a beef cheek, spoon the sauce over the entire dish to your liking, and serve.

THE PIGEON POUR: One would think that with a dish that never comes off the menu, we would have the perfect wine match. Nope. This dish loves all big red wines. Every single one. Really. I mean it.

This variation of Beef Cheeks Bourguignon (page 206) is prepared in the same way, but includes a gratin of onions, Gruyère, and potatoes served in a little baking dish and browned to perfection under the broiler. The carrots are still there, but they're roasted rather than glazed and served with their green tops in a pungent black garlic vinaigrette. Prepare the cheeks and the glazed onions as described on page 206 and then serve with this gratin in place of the glazed carrots and potatoes. {SERVES 6}

BEEF CHEEKS 2012 (AN ADDENDUM)

2 pounds (900 g) medium Yukon gold potatoes, peeled
Kosher salt
1 cup (250 g) unsalted butter, softened
1½ pounds (680 g) grated Gruyère cheese
½ cup (125 ml) heavy cream, warmed
1 bunch carrots with their tops
2 tablespoons extra-virgin olive oil
Freshly ground black pepper
Glazed Onions (page 206)
Beef Cheeks (page 206)
Black Garlic Vinny (page 321)

1. Put the potatoes in large pot filled with generously salted cold water. Bring the potatoes to a boil over high heat and then immediately reduce the heat to a simmer. Cook until potatoes are tender and easily pierced with a knife, about 20 minutes. Using a colander, drain the potatoes. Add the butter, cheese, and cream to the warm pot off the stove. If you have a ricer, push the potatoes through the ricer into the pot. If not, return the potatoes to the pot and mash them with the butter, cheese, and cream using a potato masher. Season with 1 tablespoon salt and stir to combine.

2. Preheat the oven to 400°F (200°C). Cut the tops off of the carrots and pick off about 1 cup (25 g) of the nicest fronds. Wash and dry them and set aside. Peel the carrots and cut them into ½-inch (12mm) rounds. In a bowl, toss the carrots with the oil and salt and pepper to taste. Spread the carrots on a baking sheet and roast until they are fairly tender but still have a little resistance when poked with a fork, about 20 minutes. Remove from oven and let cool to room temperature.

3. If you have six individual ramekins, you can serve the dish as we do at the restaurant. If not, serving it family-style using a single large baking dish works fine. Preheat the broiler. Spread the glazed onions in a layer on the bottom of your baking dish or dishes. Using a spatula, spread the mashed potatoes over the onions; they should reach about 1½ inches (4 cm) from the top of the dish. Place the ramekins or baking dish under the broiler until the potatoes are well browned, about 5 minutes.

4. In a saucepan over medium heat, reheat the beef cheeks in the sauce. In a bowl, toss the roasted carrots with the reserved tops and the black garlic vinny. Serve the cheeks with the gratin and carrot salad alongside.

This is a versatile stew with brightly flavored chorizo and tender pieces of tripe. You can serve this with almost anything, including plain noodles, a plate of crispy polenta, or slathered on top of a nice thick piece of grilled bread. {SERVES 4}

TRIPE, CHORIZO STEW

2 tablespoons extra-virgin olive oil
¾ cup (170 g) crumbled chorizo, as spicy as you can handle
1 yellow onion, sliced
6 cloves garlic, thinly sliced
¼ teaspoon red pepper flakes
¼ teaspoon dried oregano
¼ teaspoon pimentón paprika
Kosher salt
1 cup (250 ml) dry sherry
1 tablespoon sherry vinegar
1 pound (450 g) honeycomb tripe, soaked overnight in water and cut into strips ¼ inch (6 mm) wide
3 cups (550 g) crushed good-quality canned tomatoes, such as Pomi

1. In a large, heavy sauté pan over medium-high heat, heat the olive oil. Add the chorizo and cook, stirring occasionally, until browned and aromatic, about 5 minutes. Add the onion, garlic, red pepper flakes, oregano, and pimentón paprika and cook for another 5 minutes. Season with salt, add the sherry and sherry vinegar, and cook for 5 minutes more.

2. Add the tripe and tomatoes to the pan, reduce the heat to low, and cook, stirring every so often, until the tripe is tender, about 2 hours. When it's done, it should still have a little bite to it, but it shouldn't be chewy.

3. Divide among four bowls and serve warm with the starch of your choice.

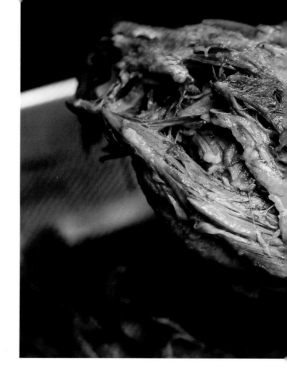

Tough and unyielding until it is simmered slowly for hours, oxtail is a great cut of meat for braising. For this dish, we chose to pair a creamy oxtail stew with deviled crab, adding paprika and spice to bring out the warm, sweet flavors of the crab. The key here is a favorite LP technique: stirring aioli into the stew at the last minute to make it thick and creamy. This trick is a great way to thicken a sauce or stew and also to make it creamy without adding any dairy. When I hand this across the bar, people who are lactose intolerant always look at me suspiciously, doubting that there is really no cream in it. Though the braise is somewhat laborious (you can make it a day ahead), the rest of this recipe comes together fairly quickly. Similar to veal blanquette, it's a beautiful dish for late summer or early fall.

Note: When cleaning oxtail, keep in mind that there is a lot of waste; be selective and make sure you use only the good stuff. Here are a couple of things you'll want to discard: Bones, that's an easy one. The cartilage, which is slightly translucent and will feel like rubber in your hand. The part that might throw you is the fat. You want a little in the dish, but get rid of any large chunks you come across.

{SERVES 4}

OXTAIL STEW, DEVILED CRAB

Oxtail Seasoning
3 tablespoons kosher salt
2 teaspoons pimentón paprika
1 teaspoon sweet paprika
1 teaspoon chili powder
1 teaspoon garlic powder
1 teaspoon onion powder
1 teaspoon freshly ground black pepper

Oxtail
5 pounds (2.25 kg) oxtail
¼ cup (60 ml) neutral oil
1 yellow onion, sliced
1 bottle (750 ml) dry white wine
2 cups (375 g) canned chopped tomatoes
2 bay leaves
1 tablespoon unsalted butter
1 cup (90 g) red onion, sliced into rings ¼ inch (6 mm) thick
¼ cup (50 ml) Deviled Aioli (page 321)
A squeeze of fresh lemon juice
Kosher salt and freshly ground black pepper
Oregano sprigs for garnish (optional)

1. Preheat the oven to 350°F (180°C).

2. To make the oxtail seasoning, in a small bowl stir together the salt, pimentón paprika, sweet paprika, chili powder, garlic powder, onion powder, and black pepper. Set aside.

3. Now let's make the oxtail. Hopefully your butcher has been nice enough to cut the oxtail into manageable pieces for you. If not, find where the vertebrae are and, using a heavy cleaver, cut through the joints. You might not find the sweet spot right away, but that's okay; just give it a couple tries. Now that you have roughly 2-inch (5cm) pieces of oxtail, you want to trim some of the fat from the outside. It isn't necessary to remove it all, but if you don't trim it your stew will be greasy.

4. Season the trimmed oxtail with the seasoning mixture. In a large sauté pan over medium-high heat, heat the oil. Sear the oxtail until browned on all sides, about 2 minutes per side. Transfer the oxtail to a plate and pour off the oil in the pan. Turn the heat down to medium, add the yellow onion, and sauté until translucent. Add the wine and tomatoes and deglaze the pan, scraping all the browned bits off the bottom of the pan. Transfer the contents of the sauté pan to a baking dish and add the oxtail, bay leaves, and 6 cups (1.5 l) of water. Cover and braise in the oven until the meat is falling off the bone, about 3½ hours. Remove the oxtail from the baking dish and reserve the braising liquid. Let the oxtail cool slightly. When it is cool enough to handle, pick the meat off the bones and discard the bones.

5. To make the crab, increase the oven to 375°F (190°C). In a small bowl, mix the crabmeat, aioli, lemon juice, oregano, parsley, and chives. Taste and adjust the seasoning with salt and pepper, if necessary. Brush the bread with the butter and sprinkle with the pimentón paprika. Toast in the oven until browned and toasted all the way through, about 7 minutes. Remove from the oven.

6. Increase the oven again to 400°F (200°C). Spread the crab mixture on top of the toasts, arrange them on a baking sheet, and bake until the crab is warmed through and slightly brown on top, about 4 minutes.

7. Meanwhile, return to the oxtail. In a medium saucepan over medium heat, melt the pat of butter. Add the red onion and sauté until softened, about 4 minutes. Add the oxtail meat and 2 cups (500 ml) of the reserved braising liquid to the saucepan. You will still have about 2 cups of braising liquid left; save it for making soups or pasta sauces. It's essentially a jacked-up beef stock. Turn the heat to high and reduce to about ½ cup (125 ml) liquid.

8. While the oxtail liquid is reducing, grill the eggs. Preheat a gas grill or prepare a charcoal grill for cooking over medium-high heat, or heat a grill pan on the stove top. Brush the cut side of your eggs with a little oil and grill for about a minute; we are just looking to give it a little char.

9. Remove the oxtail stew from the heat and immediately stir in the aioli until well combined. Add the lemon juice and check the seasoning.

10. To put it all together, divide the oxtail stew between four bowls and top with deviled crab toast. Place a grilled pickled egg next to it, garnish with a sprig of oregano, and serve.

Crab

8 ounces (250 g) Dungeness crabmeat
2 tablespoons Deviled Aioli (page 321)
A squeeze of fresh lemon juice
2 teaspoons minced fresh oregano
2 teaspoons minced fresh flat-leaf parsley
2 teaspoons minced chives
Kosher salt and freshly ground black pepper
4 slices white bread, each cut into a 3-inch (7.5cm) circle
3 tablespoons unsalted butter, melted
2 teaspoons pimento paprika

Grilled Eggs

2 Bacon Pickled Eggs (page 43), halved
Neutral oil for brushing

This is the first time that Connor Sims, sous-chef and resident cook-book nerd, showed his true genius in the kitchen. Connor started working as a cook at Pigeon in 2008. At first, he worked for free every Monday, and then when a full-time job opened up doing cold prep and desserts in the pantry, we hired him. Eventually, he worked his way up to sous-chef. He pinched this oyster mayo idea from René Redzepi, at Copenhagen's Noma, and pimped it to fit LP's needs. Hopefully some of the recipes in this book will be catalysts for your own creations, too. {SERVES 4}

HANGER, BROCCOLINI, OYSTER MAYO

½ cup (125 ml) soy sauce
1½ teaspoons fish sauce
1½ teaspoons Sriracha hot sauce
1 tablespoon grated fresh ginger
6 cloves garlic, grated
4 hanger steaks, about 6 ounces (185 g) each, trimmed
1 large shallot, thinly sliced
Juice of 2 lemons
2½ teaspoons espelette pepper
Kosher salt
2 bunches broccolini, ends trimmed
¼ cup (60 g) olive oil
Neutral oil for frying
⅔ cup (100 g) rice flour
⅔ cup (85 g) all-purpose flour
2 teaspoons mustard powder
1 teaspoon paprika
A pinch of freshly ground black pepper
8 medium oysters, shucked and drained
¼ cup (60 ml) Oyster Mayonnaise (page 324)
Sesame Oil Vinny (page 327)

1. In a large bowl, stir together the soy sauce, fish sauce, Sriracha, ginger, and garlic. Add the steaks, turn to coat, and marinate in the refrigerator for at least 2 hours and preferably overnight. In a small bowl, combine the shallot, juice of 1 of the lemons, the espelette pepper, and a pinch of salt. Refrigerate for a minimum of 1 hour.

2. Preheat the oven to 350°F (180°C). In a bowl, toss the broccolini with the olive oil and salt to taste. Spread on a baking sheet and roast in the oven for 10 minutes. Remove from the oven and keep warm.

3. Remove the steaks from the marinade and pat dry. In a cast-iron pan over very high heat, heat a thin film of oil. Cook the steaks, turning once, until medium-rare, about 4 minutes on the first side and 3 minutes on the second. Remove from the heat and set aside to let rest for about 5 minutes.

4. In a large bowl, combine the rice and all-purpose flours, mustard powder, paprika, and pepper. In a large sauté pan over high heat, pour oil to a depth of 1 inch (2.5 cm). Heat until the oil reaches 350°F (180°C) on a thermometer, or it's hot enough so that a pinch of flour sizzles when dropped into the pan. While the oil is heating, dredge the oysters in the flour mixture. Carefully drop the oysters in the oil and fry for 30 seconds. Remove with a slotted spoon and drain on a plate lined with paper towels.

5. Divide the broccolini among four plates and give a nice squeeze of juice from the remaining lemon. Slice the hanger steak against the grain. Arrange the steak on top of the broccolini and top each with two fried oysters and a dollop of oyster mayo. Finish with a drizzle of sesame oil vinny and the marinated shallots and serve.

 THE PIGEON POUR: This is a dish that really sings with the right wine. And in this case, the right wine is a bright, lively syrah from the northern Rhône. But it can't be just any syrah. It has to be on the leaner side, with good minerality to play with the oysters. You don't want a wine that is too big and intense, as it will clash with the oysters. Look for a less expensive wine, as many of the more expensive wines from the northern Rhône will be too powerful for the dish. I recommend Vin de Pays des Collines Rhodaniennes; these are syrahs made in the northern Rhône from vines grown outside the Côte Rôtie and Condrieu appellations in the very north of the valley. They tend to be lighter than a Côte Rôtie or Saint-Joseph, but they have the floral, peppery, mineral, tart berry quality of their big brothers, the aforementioned Côte Rôtie and Saint-Joseph. Many of the top producers of the northern Rhône area produce these kinds of syrahs, so shop by name. Some to look for are Bonnefond, Jasmin, Vernay, Faury, or Cuilleron.

Similar to romancing a beautiful lady, this terrine takes time and finesse to make properly. If you play your cards right, the result is worth every minute. A word about procuring a calf's (or any other animal's head): most are readily available, but you should give your butcher time to order it. Calves' heads are offensively cheap in price. The cost of this dish is solely your time.

Note that the terrine needs to refrigerate for at least 6 hours, so unless you're okay with shredding calf's head with your morning coffee, this is really a two-day process. Because this is such a laborious recipe, we encourage artistic license when it comes to plating. This is as much an art project as it is a dish. {SERVES 4}

TÊTE DE VEAU (CALF'S HEAD TERRINE), GRIBICHE, EGG

Calf's Head Terrine

1 calf's head
1 yellow onion, coarsely chopped
4 celery stalks, chopped, plus 1 stalk, diced
1 lemon, quartered
1 head garlic, halved
2¼ cups (560 ml) dry white wine
2 bay leaves
4 sprigs thyme
2 tablespoon white peppercorns
Kosher salt
2 quarts (2 l) water
½ cup (125 ml) heavy cream
2 tablespoons unsalted butter
⅓ cup (50 g) diced carrots
⅓ cup (50 g) diced red onion
A squeeze of fresh lemon juice
2 eggs
1 cup (125 g) all-purpose flour
1 cup panko
Neutral oil for frying

1. Preheat the oven to 325°F (165°C).

2. To make the terrine, in a large roasting pan, combine the calf's head, yellow onion, the chopped celery, the lemon quarters, garlic, 2 cups (500 ml) of the wine, the bay leaves, thyme, peppercorns, ¼ cup (35 g) salt, and water and place in the oven. After 2 hours, flip the head. Cook for 1 more hour, flip again, and cook for another 30 minutes. Remove from the oven and let rest until cool enough to handle. Strain and reserve the liquid.

3. Pick the meat from the head in pieces as large as you can and finely shred with your fingers. We know this feels weird. We find the weirdness goes away if you ask your friends to help and have a couple of drinks. Remove the tongue from the skull and peel (see sidebar on page 34). Coarsely chop the tongue into small pieces, about the size of marbles. In a large pot over medium heat, combine the meat and tongue with the reserved liquid, cream, the remaining ¼ cup (60 ml) of wine, the butter, carrots, red onion, the diced celery, and 1 teaspoon salt. Cook, stirring occasionally with a wooden spoon, until fully reduced, about 50 minutes. Taste and adjust the salt and acidity.

4. Line a 12 by 4 by 2¾-inch (30 by 10 by 7cm) terrine mold with plastic wrap. With a wooden spoon, transfer the calf's head mixture to the terrine. Tamp down the mixture well; the terrine should be about half full. Cover the mold and refrigerate for 6 hours. Clean up and take a break.

5. At about the 5½-hour mark, start the gribiche. In a small mixing bowl, combine the raw egg yolk, garlic, shallot, mustard, vinegar, parsley, chives, tarragon, lemon juice, and salt. Using a whisk, whisk in the oil in a thin, steady stream to create an emulsion. Chop the hard-boiled egg yolks and fold them into the gribiche. Set aside.

Gribiche

1 raw egg yolk

2 cloves garlic, chopped

½ shallot, minced

½ tablespoon Dijon mustard

1 teaspoon white wine vinegar

1 teaspoon chopped fresh flat-leaf parsley

1 teaspoon minced chives

1 teaspoon chopped fresh tarragon

Juice of 1 lemon

½ teaspoon kosher salt

⅓ cup (80 ml) neutral oil

2 hard-boiled eggs, carefully halved lengthwise, whites and yolks reserved separately

Sweetbreads

4 (3-ounce/90g) portions of sweetbreads

Kosher salt

Neutral oil for brushing

A squeeze of fresh lemon juice

Salad

½ cup (20 g) frisée

1 tablespoon capers

1 tablespoon cornichon, sliced thinly lengthwise

½ Roma tomato, seeded and cut into thin strips

1 tablespoon fresh flat-leaf parsley

1 tablespoon fresh tarragon leaves

A squeeze of fresh lemon juice

Bruléed Eggs

4 hard-boiled egg whites (reserved from making the gribiche)

4 egg yolks

¼ cup (60 ml) Herb Pistou (page 324)

6. To unmold the terrine, grab a little bit of the plastic and gently wiggle it out of the mold. Start at one corner; once you release that corner, the rest should come fairly easily. Cut four slices from the terrine, each 1 inch (2.5 cm) thick.

7. To fry the terrine, set up a breading assembly line. First make the egg wash by whisking together the eggs and ¼ cup (60 ml) water. Arrange three bowls on your work surface, the first with the flour, the second with the egg wash, and the third with the panko. Toss the terrine slices in the flour and gently shake off any excess. Dip them in the egg wash and remove, letting any excess drip off. Next toss them in the panko and coat well. Pour oil to a depth of 1 inch (2.5 cm) in a large sauté pan over high heat. When the oil is hot, fry the terrine slices on each side for about 2 minutes. Transfer to a plate lined with paper towels and add a squeeze of lemon juice and pinch of salt.

8. To make the sweetbreads, season the sweetbreads with salt and brush with a little oil. Preheat a gas grill or prepare a charcoal grill for cooking over high heat, or heat a grill pan on the stove top. Grill the sweetbreads for about 2 minutes on each side. Remove from the grill and season with lemon juice and salt.

{Continued}

9. To make the salad, combine the frisée, capers, cornichons, tomato, parsley, and tarragon. Add a tablespoon of gribiche and a squeeze of lemon and toss to combine.

10. Time for the bruléed eggs. Fill each cooked egg white with a raw egg yolk. This is slightly finicky, so you have to be patient. Torch the yolk with a kitchen torch, preferably on a baking dish outside so as not to ruin your countertops or burn the house down. If you haven't opened a nice bottle of wine yet, now is the time. You deserve it.

11. Put a slice of the terrine on each of four plates. Lean one sweetbread on a corner of each terrine slice. Arrange a large spoonful of salad on each plate and carefully place your bruléed egg next to the salad. Smear a swath of gribiche on each plate, dot with the pistou, and, finally, serve.

Real men hunt elk. Readers of Norman Maclean's *A River Runs Through It* may recall that "drinking beer is not considered drinking in Montana." Likewise, deer hunting is not necessarily taken seriously as "hunting" in Oregon. Those who do hunt elk (and this is not Gabriel) can bag a 500-pound animal that will produce 200 pounds of lean, boneless, totally organic meat.

We are most fortunate to work with Nicky USA (www.nickyusa.com), which supplies Roosevelt elk for the restaurant. The grandest of elk in America, usually weighing about 1,000 pounds, these animals make our hearts thump and our mouths water at the mere mention of their name. Raised on the free range in western Oregon, they are one of Nicky USA's most sought-after meats, and for good reason: the meat is leaner yet much richer than beef, with little gaminess. Unless hunting in the Alaskan wild is your beat, Nicky USA is the best alternative for us nonhunters.

We like to serve this atop Elk Tongue Stroganoff (page 35), but you can serve it with any warm vegetables or noodles. {SERVES 4}

ELK FILET

4 center-cut elk filets, cut from the tenderloin, each about 6 ounces (185 g)
Kosher salt
Neutral oil for searing
2 tablespoons unsalted butter

1. Preheat the oven to 400°F (200°C). Generously season the elk with salt.

2. In a large cast-iron pan over medium-high, heat the oil until it begins to smoke. Sear the elk on the first side until it turns a nice, rich brown on the bottom, about 3 minutes. Turn over and top each filet with ½ tablespoon of the butter. Place in the oven until a meat thermometer inserted into the center of the filet reads 135°F (57°C) for medium rare, 3 to 4 minutes. Remove the elk from the oven and place on a cutting board to rest for 5 minutes before serving.

As easy as it is to get your hands on beef heart, we Americans don't eat nearly enough of it. Like so many of the good things we love to serve at Le Pigeon, heart takes a good while to cook (unless you are dancing with the wolves and eating the still-beating heart from a buffalo). But, with a little TLC, the flavor gives back in a big way.

Because we slice the heart thinly in this recipe, we want to retain some texture rather than cooking it until it falls apart, as you may have seen in other recipes. Savory might be a little difficult to get your hands on, but fear not; you can substitute thyme if you must. The recipe calls for only half of a beef heart, so if you can't finagle just half from your butcher, you'll have enough heart leftover for tomorrow's scrambled eggs. {SERVES 4}

BEEF HEART, BROCCOLI, PARMESAN

Marinade

1 shallot
1 tablespoon savory leaves
1 teaspoon kosher salt
½ teaspoon freshly ground black
      pepper
3 teaspoons sherry vinegar

Dressing

¼ cup (12 g) savory leaves
1 teaspoon drained green peppercorns
1 tablespoon sherry vinegar
2 egg yolks
2 cloves garlic
A dash of Tabasco
¼ cup (60 ml) water
¼ cup (60 ml) neutral oil

Braised Heart

½ beef heart
4 cups (1 l) water
1 cup (250 ml) white wine
½ yellow onion, quartered
4 cloves
4 juniper berries, crushed
4 bay leaves
3 sprigs savory
2 tablespoons sugar
¼ teaspoon pink curing salt

Broccoli Salad

3 cups (180 g) broccoli florets
¼ cup (60 ml) Garlic Confit (page 323)
Kosher salt
1 red onion, thinly sliced
¼ cup (20 g) grated Parmesan
¼ cup (10 g) fresh flat-leaf parsley
A squeeze of fresh lemon juice

1. Preheat the oven to 400°F (200°C).

2. To make the marinade, combine the shallot, savory, salt, and pepper in a blender and blend until smooth. Add the vinegar and puree until all the ingredients are thoroughly mixed and you have a loose puree. Transfer to a small bowl and wash the blender.

3. To make the dressing, combine the savory, peppercorns, vinegar, egg yolks, garlic, Tabasco, and water in a blender. Set the blender to puree, and with the motor running, add the oil in a thin, steady stream to create an emulsion. When the dressing is smooth, turn off the machine and set the dressing aside.

4. To make the heart, in a large pot over medium heat, combine all of the ingredients for the braised heart. Bring to a boil, reduce the heat to a simmer, cover, and simmer until you can penetrate the heart with a fork but it's not tender, about 2 hours. Drain the heart, discarding the braising liquid, and set aside.

5. To make the broccoli, toss the florets with the oil from making the garlic confit and 1 teaspoon salt. Spread on a baking sheet and bake until tender with spots of golden brown, 10 to 12 minutes.

6. Slice the heart extremely thinly, like you would a roast beef, and do it with the panache of a banquet chef complete with toque. The consistency will be between that of roast beef and tongue. In a sauté pan over low heat, heat the heart slices and the marinade until just warmed through, about 5 minutes. Remove the heart from the pan with tongs and divide among four plates.

7. In a large bowl, toss together the broccoli, red onion rounds, garlic confit, Parmesan, and parsley with the dressing. Season with salt and lemon juice. Top the heart with the broccoli salad, drizzle a tablespoon or two of the dressing on top, and serve.

THE PIGEON POUR: This dish loves nebbiolo. If you want to spend the money, a Barbaresco would also be great, but it will probably be too young, unless you have a cellar full of it. Nearly all producers of Barbaresco and Barolo also produce nebbiolo, sometimes labeled "Nebbiolo d'Alba" or "Langhe Nebbiolo." The nebbiolos have the cherry fruit, earth, and herbs of Barbarescos and Barolos, but they are more approachable when young. If you see a Barolo or Barbaresco next to a nebbiolo from the same producer, buy it for this dish. Nebbiolos I love include those from Paitin, Vietti, De Forville, and Conterno (there are a few different Conternos, and any one of them will do).

Gabriel doesn't go bat-shit crazy for Buffalo wings, but he does for sweetbreads. And sitting at Claudia's Sports Pub in Portland eating wings, the idea for this recipe clicked—buffalo sweetbreads. If you're cooking these for dinner, you're going to want to start in the morning, as the sweetbreads need to be chilled for 6 hours. These are best enjoyed with Staropramen (a flavorful pilsner from the Czech Republic) or a Miller High Life. {SERVES 6}

BUFFALO SWEETBREADS, HOT SAUCE, CELERY, BLUE CHEESE

1½ pounds (680 g) veal sweetbreads
½ cup (70 g) kosher salt
Rice oil or other neutral oil
1 yellow onion, diced
2 carrots, peeled and diced
2 celery stalks, diced
1 head garlic, halved horizontally
1½ cups (375 ml) dry white wine
3 bay leaves
1 tablespoon black peppercorns
1 cup (125 g) all-purpose flour
1 cup (250 ml) Buffalo Bird Sauce
    (page 322)
Celery Salad (opposite)
1 cup (250 ml) Blue Cheese Dressing
    (page 321)

1. Rub the sweetbreads all over with the salt and set aside.

2. In a large sauté pan over medium heat, heat 1 tablespoon of oil. Add the onion, carrots, celery, and garlic and cook until softened, about 3 minutes. Add the wine, bay leaves, peppercorns, and finally the sweetbreads. Add just enough water to cover and bring to a boil. Reduce the heat to low and simmer until the sweetbreads are firm to touch, about 20 minutes. Remove with a slotted spoon. Place the sweetbreads in a colander and weigh them down with a heavy can. Removing the moisture like this will help you not get splattered when frying. Refrigerate for 6 hours with the can on top.

3. Now it's time to clean the sweetbreads, which can be slightly tricky and takes a little judgment. Using a paring knife, peel off as much of the outer membrane and connective tissue as possible. There is a happy medium here, as you also want to have nice-sized pieces to cook. So go for the big and ugly veins and membranes and try to keep the sweetbreads in pieces of about 1½ ounces (45 g). Remember that this is a take on wings.

4. In a large sauté pan over medium heat, add enough oil to come about halfway up the side of the pan. Heat until the oil reaches 350°F (180°C) on a thermometer, or it's hot enough so that a pinch of flour sizzles when dropped into the pan. Place the flour in a shallow bowl and toss the sweetbreads in the flour. Shake off any excess. Carefully fry the sweetbreads, turning occasionally, until brown on all sides, 2 to 3 minutes. Remove from the pan with a slotted spoon and drain on paper towels.

5. Toss the sweetbreads with the hot sauce and serve with celery salad and dressing alongside.

Celery Salad

¼ cup (35 g) thinly sliced red onion
4 celery stalks, peeled and thinly sliced on the diagonal
¼ cup (30 g) crumbled blue cheese
¼ cup (10 g) fresh flat-leaf parsley
3 tablespoons Blue Cheese Dressing (page 321)
½ cup (155 g) shredded roasted chicken meat (optional)
Kosher salt and freshly ground pepper

MAKES 1¼ CUPS (310 ML)

In a large bowl, toss all the ingredients together, seasoning with salt and a generous amount of pepper. Serve with the buffalo sweetbreads or, if you're including chicken, on its own.

If you or your kids are a little unsure about cooking with sweetbreads, this recipe—with noodles, Parmesan, meatballs, and crispy sweetbreads—is the perfect way to ease into it. Though we serve this dish as an appetizer at the restaurant, you can easily double the recipe to make enough for the main event. Add some nice roasted broccoli rabe and enjoy.

Note: The sweetbreads have to chill for 6 hours, so plan ahead.

{SERVES 4}

SWEETBREADS, SPAGHETTI, MEATBALLS

Sweetbreads

4 (3-ounce/90g) portions of
    sweetbreads
1 cup (125 g) all-purpose flour
1 teaspoon garlic powder
1 teaspoon onion powder
Neutral oil for frying
A squeeze of fresh lemon juice
Maldon flake salt

Meatballs

1 pound (450 g) ground veal or pork
2 tablespoons minced yellow onion
2 cloves garlic, minced
1 teaspoon chopped fresh oregano
2 tablespoons grated Parmesan
1 cup (60 g) fresh bread crumbs soaked
    in ½ cup (125 ml) whole milk
1 egg
1 teaspoon freshly ground black
    pepper
1 tablespoon kosher salt
Neutral oil for sautéing

Spaghetti and Sauce

Kosher salt
8 ounces (250 g) dry spaghetti
1 cup (250 ml) Parmesan Broth
    (page 325)
2 tablespoons Garlic Confit (page 323)
¾ cup (60 g) grated Parmesan, plus
    more for finishing
¼ cup (60 g) unsalted butter
Freshly ground black pepper

Chile Salsa Verde (optional)

¼ cup (60 ml) chile oil
2 tablespoons minced fresh flat-leaf
    parsley

1. To make the sweetbreads, combine the sweetbreads and just enough water to cover in a small saucepan over high heat. Bring to a boil and then reduce the heat to low and simmer until the sweetbreads are firm to the touch, about 20 minutes. Remove with a slotted spoon. Place the sweetbreads in a colander and weigh them down with a heavy can. Removing the moisture like this will help you not get splattered when frying. Refrigerate for 6 hours with the can on top.

2. Preheat the oven to 375°F (190°C).

3. To make the meatballs, in a large bowl, thoroughly mix the ground veal, onion, garlic, oregano, Parmesan, bread crumbs, egg, pepper, and salt. In a small sauté pan, heat a thin film of oil over medium-high heat. Cook a small portion of the mixture to taste for seasoning and adjust for salt as needed. Once it is seasoned to your liking, roll the mixture into twelve balls the size of a large gumball. Place on a baking sheet and bake until the meatballs are light gray and have released some of their fat, 10 to 12 minutes. Remove from the oven and set aside.

4. Time to cook the noodles. Bring a large pot of heavily salted water to a boil over high heat. Add the noodles and cook until soft but not mushy, about 8 minutes. Using a colander over the sink, drain the noodles and rinse with cold water to prevent sticking. Set aside.

5. To finish the sweetbreads, in a bowl, stir together the flour with the garlic powder and onion powder. In a sauté pan over high heat, heat ¼ inch (6 mm) of oil. Toss the sweetbreads in the seasoned flour and shake off any excess flour. Panfry until golden brown all over, about 2 minutes per side. Remove from the pan and drain on paper towels. Give a nice squeeze of lemon juice and sprinkle with a pinch of Maldon salt.

6. Now assemble the spaghetti and its sauce. In a sauté pan over medium-high heat, bring the broth to a boil and cook until reduced by half, about 3 minutes. Add the spaghetti, meatballs, and garlic confit. Cook until there are only about 2 tablespoons of liquid left in the pan, about 2 minutes. Remove from the heat and stir in the Parmesan and butter. Mix thoroughly to create a rich, creamy sauce.

7. Divide among four pasta bowls and top each bowl with one sweetbread. Grate more fresh Parmesan on top and give a few good grinds of pepper. If you want to get *titular* (see sidebar on page 14), make the salsa verde by stirring together the chile oil and parsley in a small bowl. Drizzle the chile verde on top and serve.

Every year Gabriel and Andy do a dinner at the Steamboat Inn on the Umpqua River in Southern Oregon. On the drive down, the two families always stop at Red Robin in Roseburg for a Banzai Burger. This steak fulfills that need for a Hawaiian-inspired burger without having to endure the boring scenery on Interstate 5.

This big ol' steak is meant to serve two, but if you eat it by yourself, you wouldn't be the first person to do so. {SERVES 2}

RIB EYE, PINEAPPLE, BLUE CHEESE

1 large boneless rib eye, about
    1½ pounds (680 g)
¼ cup (60 ml) soy sauce
Neutral oil for searing
1 tablespoon unsalted butter
Semolina Onion Rings (optional;
    page 327)

Pineapple Salad

¼ cup (10 g) fresh flat-leaf parsley
½ cup (60 g) crumbled blue cheese
½ cup (60 g) spring onions or sweet
    onions, thinly sliced
2 slices of pineapple, cored and cut
    into chunks ¼ inch (6 mm) thick
1 tablespoon good-quality balsamic
    vinegar
1 tablespoon good-quality olive oil
    (see sidebar on page 105)
A squeeze of fresh lemon juice
Maldon flake salt

1. In a baking dish, combine the rib eye and soy sauce and turn to coat. Marinate at room temperature for 2 hours.

2. About 20 minutes before you start to cook the steak, make the salad. In a large bowl, toss together the parsley, blue cheese, onions, pineapple, balsamic vinegar, olive oil, lemon juice, and Maldon salt to taste and set aside.

3. Preheat the oven to 400°F (200°C).

4. In a cast-iron pan over very high heat, heat a thin film of oil until smoking. Dry the steak with a paper towel and carefully transfer the steak to the pan (the soy sauce will make it spit). Cook for 4 minutes on the first side. Flip the steak and place the pat of butter on top. Cook for another minute, then transfer to the oven for 3 minutes. Remove from the oven, let rest for 8 minutes, and serve with the pineapple salad and semolina onion rings on top or on the side.

A note from Gabriel: The first time I saw carpaccio being prepared, the chef seasoned the beef heavily and then rolled it across a hot pan to sear the outer layer and provide a nice crust while keeping the beef raw on the inside. This is the way I have always done my carpaccio, as I love that heavily flavored crust yielding to raw pure beef flavor. For this preparation, I slice the beef by hand probably a little thicker than you are used to. Trust me, the beef will melt in your mouth. If you can't get your hands on the truffle caviar, your carpaccio won't be as visually stunning as it could be, but you can toss the trout roe with a couple drops of truffle oil for the same effect.

{SERVES 4}

BEEF CARPACCIO

Seared Beef
¼ cup (10 g) fresh flat-leaf parsley
¼ cup (60 ml) plus 2 tablespoons
    neutral oil
2 cloves garlic, peeled
½ teaspoon grated orange zest
1 tablespoon kosher salt
½ teaspoon pink peppercorns
½ teaspoon truffle oil
1 piece center-cut beef tenderloin,
    about 8 ounces (250 g)

Riesling Vinny
1 egg yolk
1 tablespoon riesling
1 tablespoon Katz honey-viognier
    vinegar (see sidebar on page 42)
    or Moscatel vinegar
¼ cup (60 ml) neutral oil
¼ teaspoon truffle oil
A pinch of kosher salt

A squeeze of fresh lemon juice
Maldon flake salt
Pickled Radish (page 326)
4 hard-cooked eggs, peeled
1 tablespoon trout roe
1 tablespoon cold truffle caviar
1 radish, thinly sliced
Radish leaves for garnish

1. To make the seared beef, using a mortar and pestle, combine the parsley, ¼ cup (60 ml) of the neutral oil, garlic, orange zest, salt, peppercorns, and truffle oil to make a paste. Rub the paste all over the beef and let marinate in the fridge for a minimum of 5 hours and up to 24 hours.

2. In a heavy sauté pan over hight heat, heat the remaining 2 tablespoons of oil until it begins to smoke. Add the beef and sear for 10 seconds on each side. You don't want to cook the meat, just make a delicious crust with the rub. Remove the beef from the pan and refrigerate until very cold, about an hour. (The beef can sit like this for up to 3 days as long as it is tightly wrapped.)

3. To make the riesling vinny, in a bowl, whisk together the egg yolk, riesling, and vinegar well. Whisk in the both the neutral oil and truffle oil in a thin, steady stream to create an emulsion. Season with salt. (At the restaurant, we whip it in a nitrous oxide charger to make it airy and foamy, but that's not necessary at home.)

4. Using a very sharp slicing knife, cut the beef across the grain into very thin slices, almost like beef sashimi. Divide among four chilled plates. Squeeze lemon juice and sprinkle Maldon salt on top to taste. Spoon some pickled radish next to the beef. Carefully cut the eggs in half and place two halves on top of the radishes. In a small bowl, gently stir together the trout roe and caviar. Top the eggs with the caviar mixture, spoon the vinny generously around the plate, top with radish slices and leaves, and serve.

This is pub fare, Le Pigeon style. We like to enjoy this venison with some simple roasted carrots, but you can add a veg of your choice.

These miniature Yorkshire puddings are one of Mr. Pickles's favorite things to make and he offers this note: "Yorkshire Pudding is one of those things you don't eat growing up in a kosher household. It is essentially flour, eggs, and milk cooked in beef drippings. I love fat, be it beef, lamb, or even that *other* animal. So one year I came back from visiting my wife's family over the holidays and we had cooked a rib roast and made Yorkshire pudding to go along with it. I think I talked Gabriel's ear off about it for a couple of weeks. So elementally delicious! And the fact that I couldn't shut up about it convinced him to play around with the Yorkshire pudding idea at Le Pigeon." You can just as well pair them with beef.

Note: You can buy black currant puree at many speciality food shops; our favorite brand is Boirin. {SERVES 4}

VENISON, CREAMED SPINACH, YORKSHIRE PUDDING

Venison
4 pieces venison loin, each about
    4 ounces (125 g) and 1 inch
    (2.5 cm) thick
Kosher salt
1 juniper berry, well ground
1 tablespoon extra-virgin olive oil
2 cloves garlic, crushed

Sauce
1 tablespoon unsalted butter
½ cup (70 g) thinly sliced red onion
2 cloves garlic, thinly sliced
1 teaspoon fresh thyme leaves
1 cup (250 ml) balsamic vinegar
1 cup (250 ml) red wine vinegar
6 black peppercorns
1 cup (250 ml) black currant puree,
    or 2 cups (280 g) pureed
    blackberries or black currants
6 cups (1.5 l) cheap red wine
2 quarts (2 l) Veal Stock (page 329)
1 tablespoon dried currants
2 tablespoons diced foie gras
    (see page 51)

4 slices Su Lien's Foie Gras Torchon
    (page 52)

1. Season the venison generously with salt and the ground juniper berry.

2. If you have the tools for sous-vide cooking, place the venison in a vacuum bag with the olive oil and garlic. Vacuum pack using the medium setting. Place the bag in a water bath at 130°F (55°C) for 15 minutes. Remove from the water and chill in an ice water bath. If you do not have the tools for sous-vide, preheat the oven to 300°F (150°C). Place the venison, olive oil, and garlic in a baking dish and cook until the meat is very rare, no more than 5 to 7 minutes. Remove from the oven and, using a spatula, transfer the venison to a plate. Refrigerate the venison until well chilled, about 45 minutes.

3. Now it's time to work on the sauce, which is basically a series of reductions. In a heavy saucepan over medium-high heat, melt the butter. Add the onion, garlic, and thyme and sauté until fragrant, 4 to 5 minutes. Add the vinegars, peppercorns, and currant puree and cook until reduced to a thin syrup, 12 to 15 minutes. Add the red wine and continue to cook until reduced to roughly ¾ cup (180 ml), about 30 minutes. Add the veal stock, reduce the heat to medium, and reduce further until you have about 1½ cups (375 ml) of sauce, about 40 minutes. Strain through a fine-mesh strainer and reserve.

4. Remove the venison from the refrigerator and top each piece with a slice of foie gras. Spread the top of the venison with a generous layer of creamed spinach, like you're making a deer layer cake. Finish with a sprinkle of bread crumbs.

1 cup Foie-Creamed Spinach
    (page 71)
2 tablespoons Seasoned Bread Crumbs
    (page 327)
Neutral oil for searing
1 tablespoon unsalted butter
4 individual Yorkshire Puddings (below)
Kosher salt

5. Preheat the oven to 400°F (200°C).

6. In a large cast-iron pan over high heat, heat a thin film of oil. Sear all four pieces of venison on the side without the spinach for 2 minutes. Add the pat of butter and baste well. Transfer to the oven and cook until the meat is heated through to about medium-rare and the foie is melted, about 5 minutes. Remember that the venison is already cooked.

7. While venison is in the oven, finish the sauce. Pour the sauce into a saucepan over medium heat and add the currants. Stir well. Now add the diced foie gras and cook until reduced by half, about 3 minutes.

8. Finally, time to plate: Very delicately remove the venison from the pan and place in a shallow bowl or on a large plate. Spoon some sauce next to the venison. Place 1 pudding next to the venison, sprinkle with salt, and serve.

Yorkshire Puddings

1 cup (125 g) all-purpose flour
½ teaspoon kosher salt
2 eggs
½ cup (125 ml) cup buttermilk
½ cup (125 ml) heavy cream
4 slices (2 ounces) white cheddar,
    crumbled
¼ cup (60 g) unsalted butter, melted

MAKES 4 TO 6 INDIVIDUAL PUDDINGS

Preheat the oven to 450°F (230°C) and place a muffin pan inside to heat; you want the muffin pan to be nice and hot. In a large bowl, sift together the flour and salt. In a separate bowl, whisk together the eggs, buttermilk, cream, and cheese. Whisk the dry ingredients into the egg mixture. Divide the melted butter between 4 large or 6 standard-sized muffin cups and ladle the batter into the cups. You want the mixture to fill about ¾ of each cup. Bake for 10 minutes, turn the heat down to 350°F (180°C), and continue to bake until the exterior is golden brown and puffy, about 10 minutes more. Serve immediately.

Roasted bone marrow has been the hot ticket ever since Fergus Henderson made it famous at his London restaurant, St. John, and Anthony Bourdain said it would be his death row meal. We agree wholeheartedly. That being said, big roasted bones full of marrow are served more often at Little Bird than at Le Pigeon. (Little Bird is more like a French bistro than its older and more deranged brother.)

These sandwiches make for great appetizers or a ludicrously rich lunch and eat like the most decadent grilled cheese sandwich ever. If you end up with more marrow than you know what to do with, it freezes very well. {MAKES 4 SANDWICHES}

BONE MARROW, CARAMELIZED ONION SANDWICH

4 ounces (125 g) bone marrow (from 6 to 8 bones)
¼ cup (60 g) unsalted butter, softened, plus 3 tablespoons cold unsalted butter
1 tablespoon olive oil
3 yellow onions, thinly sliced
½ teaspoon kosher salt
8 slices potato bread or other soft white bread
Maldon flake salt
4 sprigs fresh flat-leaf parsley
Aged balsamic vinegar for drizzling

1. Place the marrow and ¼ cup (60 g) of the butter in a food processor and puree until creamy. Set aside at room temperature while you caramelize the onions.

2. Heat the oil in a sauté pan over medium heat. Add the onions and salt and cook until translucent, about 5 minutes. Reduce the heat to low and continue to cook, stirring frequently with a wooden spoon, until well carmelized and sweet, about 20 minutes. Transfer the caramelized onions to a plate to cool to room temperature.

3. Divide the pureed marrow mixture among four slices of the bread, spreading it evenly. Divide the caramelized onions among the remaining four slices of bread, and sprinkle the onions with Maldon salt. Press together the slices of marrow-coated bread and onion-covered bread to form four sandwiches.

4. In a large sauté pan over medium heat, melt the remaining 3 tablespoons butter. Toast the sandwiches as if you were making grilled cheese, in batches as necessary, until lightly browned, 2 to 3 minutes per side. Cut each sandwich in half, arrange on a plate with a sprig of parsley and a healthy drizzle of balsamic vinegar, and serve.

When we first took over Le Pigeon—which was then "the restaurant we no longer mention"—we decided that we needed a burger to try to appeal to the clientele of East Burnside. It was Gabriel's first day in the kitchen and he was trying to sort out what exactly he had taken on. Ken's Artisan Bakery, our local bread supplier, makes a killer ciabatta, so we were covered for buns. Gabriel had discovered a square mold in the old restaurant, so that was pressed into service for shaping the patty. We love shredded lettuce, and, in our opinion, the best way to deliver said lettuce is to toss it with aioli or mayo for a creamy slaw. Adding a topping of Grilled Pickled Onions (page 323) was the obvious final flourish. We serve the LP Burger on a wooden board, knife-in, with butter lettuce dressed in Blue Cheese Dressing (page 321). East Burnside may have changed, but the burger has remained the same.

{MAKES 4 BURGERS}

THE LE PIGEON BURGER*

1¾ pounds (875 g) ground chuck
½ teaspoon kosher salt
4 slices cheddar cheese, preferably Tillamook
2 cups (90 g) shredded iceberg lettuce
¼ cup (60 ml) Aioli (page 321) or mayonnaise
1 tablespoon chopped fresh flat-leaf parsley
4 toasted ciabatta rolls
¼ cup (60 ml) Dijon mustard
½ cup (125 ml) LP Ketchup (page 324) or purchased ketchup
1 cup (160 g) Grilled Pickled Onions (page 323)

1.   Preheat a gas grill or prepare a charcoal grill for cooking over medium-high heat, or heat a grill pan on the stove top. Form the ground chuck into four 7-ounce (220g) square patties. Season the patties with the salt. Grill the patties until medium-rare, 3 to 4 minutes per side. Place 1 slice of cheese on each burger during the last 2 minutes of cooking to melt.

2.   In a bowl, toss together the lettuce, aioli, and parsley to make a slaw.

3.   On the bottom of each bun, spread an equal amount of the mustard, followed by the ketchup. Top generously with the pickled onions. Place the burger and the slaw on the bun and top with the second half before serving.

*A note from Gabriel: There are some who think putting a burger on the LP menu is a sacrilege of sorts, a sellout. I get that. However, as I've been known to board an airplane brown bagging twenty In-N-Out burgers, and I have a more than occasional yearning for a Slow Bar burger, it would be even more hypocritical *not* to serve a burger on my menu.

CHAPTER 10
LAMB

Green garlic is so abundant during the first few weeks of spring that it pretty much spills over every stall at the farmers' markets. At LP, we serve it with curry pickled fennel and *carnitas*-style lamb. If we had to reduce five years of Pigeon menu hits to an album of twelve dishes, this would surely be one of them. {SERVES 6}

LAMB, GREEN GARLIC RISOTTO

Lamb

½ teaspoon garlic powder
¼ teaspoon onion powder
½ teaspoon ground fennel seeds
2 tablespoons kosher salt
1 teaspoon freshly ground black pepper
1 boneless lamb shoulder, about 3 pounds (1.4 kg)
1 cup (250 ml) dry white wine
1 head green garlic, halved
Neutral oil for frying

Risotto

¼ cup (60 g) unsalted butter
½ yellow onion, diced
2 cloves garlic, thinly sliced
1½ cups (345 g) Arborio rice
Kosher salt
¾ cup (180 ml) dry white wine
4 cups (1 l) chicken stock, warmed
½ cup (40 g) grated pecorino
½ cup (100 g) thinly sliced radish

Salad

½ cup (20 g) fresh flat-leaf parsley
1 cup (160 g) halved cherry tomatoes
Pickled Fennel (page 325), strained and liquid discarded
2 tablespoons good-quality extra-virgin olive oil (see sidebar on page 105)
Kosher salt
A squeeze of fresh lemon juice

1. Preheat the oven to 300°F (150°C). To make the lamb, in a small bowl, stir together the garlic powder, onion powder, fennel seeds, salt, and pepper. Rub the lamb all over with the spice mixture. Place in a roasting pan with the wine and garlic. Cover with aluminum foil and roast for 5 hours. Remove the lamb from the oven and let cool. Refrigerate until cold. Cut into six equal portions.

2. To make the risotto, in a heavy pot over medium heat, melt 2 tablespoons of the butter. Add the onion and garlic and sauté until translucent, about 4 minutes. Add the rice and season with salt. Cook for 3 minutes, stirring frequently. Add the wine and cook, stirring, until the wine has evaporated, 7 to 8 minutes. Add half of the stock and cook, stirring continuously, until all of the stock has been absorbed, about 8 minutes. Add the remaining stock and cook until liquid is almost completely absorbed, about 8 minutes more. At this point the rice should be al dente. Stir in the remaining 2 tablespoons of butter and the pecorino. Stir in the radish and season with salt. Set aside and keep warm.

3. In a large sauté pan over high heat, heat ¼ inch (6 mm) of oil. Add the lamb and panfry until heated through and crispy, about 3 minutes on each side. Transfer to a plate lined with paper towels.

4. To make the salad, in a bowl, toss together the parsley, tomatoes, fennel, and olive oil to combine. Season with salt to taste.

5. Divide the risotto among six shallow bowls. Top each with a piece of lamb and an equal amount of the salad. Finish with lemon juice.

THE PIGEON POUR: This dish screams for something Italian. Great Italian wine speaks of the soil and exhibits dust and earthy notes; it can even be redolent of herbs and the veggies that come from the ground. Two Italian wines that we like to serve with this dish: Cabernet Franc from Girolamo Dorigo in Friuli, and Chianti from Colognole. The Dorigo Cab Franc is rich and has a ripe fruit flavor, but more importantly, it has an herbaceous hint of tomato stem, which is ideal here. The Colognole is a Chianti in the classic style, with notes of cherry, dusty roads, and tomato leaf.

The first time Gabriel made these lamb shanks it was a revelation. By first making a lamb confit and then frying it, we were able to create a great crust in seconds while still maintaining a moist, juicy interior. Since we don't have a purpose-built deep fryer at Le Pigeon, we fill two large pots with canola oil and heat them on the back of the stove. Considering the number of plates that we serve each night, it's a little crazy that we don't have a fryer, but our pots, which we call "the tub," work well enough, and we have come to love this technique. {SERVES 4}

LAMB SHANK, BBQ BEANS

Lamb Confit

2 tablespoons minced garlic

3 tablespoons chopped fresh rosemary

1 tablespoon freshly ground black pepper

2 tablespoons kosher salt

2 quarts (2 l) plus 3 tablespoons canola oil

4 lamb shanks, each about 14 ounces (400 g)

Beans

1 pound (450 g) dried pinto beans, soaked in water overnight

1 cup (250 ml) LP Ketchup (page 324) or purchased ketchup

1 (12-ounce/355 ml) can of Dr. Pepper

1 teaspoon Tabasco

1 teaspoon chili powder

1 teaspoon ground cumin

1 teaspoon mustard powder

1 teaspoon onion powder

1 teaspoon garlic powder

½ teaspoon red pepper flakes

1 yellow onion, thinly sliced

2 quarts (2 l) Veal Stock (page 329)

½ cup (100 g) firmly packed brown sugar

2 tablespoons molasses

1 tablespoon kosher salt

1. To make the confit, using a mortar and pestle or a very small food processor, grind the garlic, rosemary, pepper, salt, and 3 tablespoons of the oil to a paste. Rub the shanks all over with the paste; you want to really work it in there. At this point at the restaurant, we let them sit overnight to really get them seasoned up, but if you prefer you can go ahead and cook them right away.

2. To cook the shanks, we are going to confit them in oil. Preheat the oven to 300°F (150°C). Find a pot that will fit the lamb shanks snugly, add the shanks, and cover with the 2 quarts (2 l) of oil. Cover the pot and cook for about 5 hours. (At the restaurant, we cook them overnight at 200°F [95°C]; this is the method we prefer, but if you don't feel comfortable cooking overnight, the higher temperature for a shorter time will work just fine.) The shanks are done when the meat is soft and just starting to fall off the bone. Carefully remove the shanks from the oil using a slotted spoon or spatula and place on a cooling rack for 10 minutes. Transfer to a plate and cool in refrigerator for about 1 hour. Reserve the cooking oil for another use (see sidebar opposite).

3. Let's make some beans. Preheat the oven to 300°F (150°C) if it's not already on from the shanks. In a large roasting pan, combine the pinto beans, ketchup, Dr. Pepper, Tabasco, chili powder, cumin, mustard powder, onion powder, garlic powder, red pepper flakes, onion, veal stock, brown sugar, molasses, and salt. Bake, uncovered, stirring every 30 minutes, for about 2 hours. You will know the beans are done when they are soft and the liquid has reduced, thickened, and turned dark brown. Let's not beat around the bush folks; we want these to look like store-bought baked beans but to deliver a way tastier punch. Remove the beans from the oven and keep warm. Turn the oven up to 400°F (200°C).

4. To make the gremolata, in a small bowl stir together the parsley, garlic, lemon zest, and cumin. This is best served as fresh as possible. We make it every day right before service.

Cumin Gremolata

2 tablespoons minced fresh
   flat-leaf parsley
1 teaspoon minced garlic
½ teaspoon grated lemon zest
½ teaspoon ground cumin

4 cups (1 l) canola oil
A squeeze of fresh lemon juice

5. In a large, deep pot, heat the vegetable oil until it reaches 350°F (180°C) on a thermometer, or it's hot enough that it sizzles when you put a drop of water in it. Fry the shanks, two at a time, until they are beginning to crisp, 2 to 3 minutes. Transfer to the oven for another 5 minutes to ensure they are piping hot. Give the shanks a nice squeeze of lemon juice and serve with a healthy dose of gremolata on top and the baked beans alongside.

DON'T THROW AWAY YOUR COOKING OIL!

Not to sound like your Depression-era grandfather, but leftover oil is like gold. Strain the used frying oil through a coffee filter and let it come to room temperature. Cover and refrigerate for up to 2 weeks. You should be able to use it four or five times, and each time it will increase in flavor.

The oil will have a meaty flavor, so we wouldn't suggest using it to fry doughnuts or any dessert garnishes, but it would be great for preparing pork belly or any other savory dishes.

Ah, lamb neck, how we love you. An often underutilized part of the animal, lamb necks are long (from all of that grazing), fatty, and rich and are well suited to slow roasting. Sliced, they look almost like osso buco. Make sure to use domestic lamb for this dish, as they tend to be bigger and much meatier than their Australian counterparts. You can cook the lamb a day in advance to save yourself some time on the day you want to serve this. To reheat, simply heat in the oven for 20 minutes at 350°F (180°C). This dish hits the menu during the summer when corn (and mac 'n' cheese) is what we crave. {SERVES 4}

SLOW-ROASTED LAMB NECK, CORN, CHANTERELLE MAC 'N' CHEESE

4 slices lamb neck, sliced by the butcher between the vertebrae into slices 1½ inches (4 cm) thick

2 cloves garlic, minced, plus 4 cloves garlic, sliced

¾ teaspoon chopped fresh rosemary

½ teaspoon paprika

½ teaspoon onion powder

Kosher salt

¼ cup (60 ml) neutral oil

½ cup (125 ml) dry white wine

4 cups (600 g) corn kernels

3 tablespoons unsalted butter, melted, plus 2 tablespoons softened

1½ cups (175 g) dried elbow macaroni

8 ounces (250 g) chanterelle mushrooms

1 shallot, thinly sliced

1 teaspoon chopped fresh thyme

2 cups (500 ml) Corn Stock (page 322)

¾ cup (60 g) grated pecorino

1 tablespoon chopped fresh flat-leaf parsley

A squeeze of fresh lemon juice

1. Preheat the oven to 300°F (150°C).

2. Rub the lamb neck generously with the minced garlic, ½ teaspoon of the rosemary, the paprika, onion powder, and 1 tablespoon salt. You want to really work it in there. Place the neck in a single layer in a baking dish. Add the oil and the wine. Cover and bake about 2 hours. Check after the first hour: you'll know the neck is done when it is easily pierced with a fork. Uncover, turn the oven up to 375°F (190°C), and continue to cook until a nice crust has formed, about 20 minutes more.

3. Increase the oven temperature to 400°F (200°C). Toss the corn kernels with 2 cloves of the sliced garlic, 2 tablespoons of the melted butter, the remaining ¼ teaspoon rosemary, and ¼ teaspoon salt. Spread on a baking sheet and roast until nice and golden, but making sure not to burn the edges of the corn, 10 to 12 minutes. Remove from the oven and set aside.

4. Bring a large pot of heavily salted water to a boil over high heat. Add the macaroni and cook until al dente, about 5 minutes. Drain in a colander over the sink and rinse with cold water. Set aside.

5. In a bowl, toss the mushrooms with the shallot, the remaining 2 cloves of sliced garlic, the thyme, the remaining 1 tablespoon melted butter, and a pinch of salt. Spread on a baking sheet and roast until the edges are nice and browned and there is no liquid left on the baking sheet. This should take about 20 minutes, but the cooking time may vary depending on how wet the mushrooms are. Remove from the oven and set aside. Keep that oven on, and pop the lamb neck in to warm it up.

6. Now we're going to put it all together. In a sauté pan over medium heat, warm the corn kernels and corn stock. Add the chanterelles and cook until the liquid is reduced by half, about 8 minutes. Add the macaroni and toss well to combine. Continue cooking until you are left with ½ cup (125 ml) of liquid. Remove from the heat, stir in the 2 tablespoons of softened butter and the pecorino. Stir in the parsley. Place the mac and cheese in a serving dish. Give the piping-hot roasted lamb a squeeze of lemon juice and a pinch of salt and serve alongside.

Erik Van Kley, the sous-chef at Le Pigeon who is now at Little Bird, came up with this lamb belly BLT, a delicious combination of oozing lamb fat, fresh tomatoes, and a smoky bacon mayo. As you can guess, this is an intense BLT, so we only serve half a slice per person, as an appetizer. Warning: You have to cure the lamb belly for 3 days before making the dish. {SERVES 2}

LAMB BELLY BLT

Lamb Belly
¼ cup (35 g) kosher salt
½ teaspoon freshly ground black
  pepper
2 tablespoons brown sugar
⅛ teaspoon pink curing salt
1 teaspoon chopped fresh tarragon
1 lamb belly, about 1½ pounds (680 g)
Maldon flake salt

Bacon Mayo
½ cup (125 ml) neutral oil
4 ounces (125 g) bacon, coarsely
  chopped
2 egg yolks
½ teaspoon white vinegar
¼ teaspoon mustard powder
A pinch of onion powder

4 slices white bread, preferably Franz
  (see headnote on page 53), halved
4 leaves crisp baby romaine
4 slices of the most titular (see sidebar
  on page 14) heirloom tomatoes you
  can get your hands on

1. In a small bowl, stir together the kosher salt, pepper, sugar, curing salt, and tarragon to create the cure. Rub the belly all over with the cure; you want to really work it in there. Place the belly in a large resealable plastic bag and refrigerate for 3 days, turning it over every day to ensure it's evenly coated with the cure.

2. Preheat the oven to 300°F (150°C). Remove the belly from the fridge and rinse with cold water. Pat dry, place in a roasting pan, and cover with a lid or aluminum foil. Roast until the meat is easily penetrated with a fork, 2 to 2½ hours. Remove the belly from the pan and refrigerate while you prepare the bacon mayo.

3. To make the bacon mayo, in a small, heavy saucepan over low heat, heat the oil. Add the bacon and cook until the bacon has rendered all of its fat, about 12 minutes. It's ready when the bacon looks like, well, cooked bacon. Strain, reserving the rendered bacon fat for the mayo. Nibble on the cooked bacon as you work.

4. Let the rendered bacon fat cool to room temperature (the mayo emulsion will break if it's too warm). In a bowl, combine the egg yolks, vinegar, mustard powder, and onion powder. Using a whisk and whisking constantly, slowly drizzle the bacon fat into the bowl in a thin, steady stream to create an emulsion. Stop and add a few drops of water when when it starts to look like a thick paste rather than mayo. Refrigerate until ready to use.

5. Remove the belly from the refrigerator and cut into four equal portions. Preheat a gas grill or prepare a charcoal grill for cooking over medium-high heat, or heat a grill pan on the stove top. Grill the belly pieces, being careful to not let them scorch (if the dripping fat is causing the fire to flare up, move the belly to the cooler side of the grill and cook an extra minute or so on each side). Grill until you have light char marks and the fat is bubbling and hissing, 2 to 4 minutes per side. Remove from the grill and season with Maldon salt.

6. Toast the bread. Spread bacon mayo on one side of each piece of toast. Add the romaine and tomatoes and top with lamb belly. Add another slice of mayo-slathered bread and serve.

This is a simple, pared-down recipe rather than the gussied-up version of this dish (which is usually composed with micro-this and micro-that) that might be served in a bad Italian restaurant. This is a one-stop-shop, knock-it-out-of-the-park dinner. (See photo on pages 236–7.)

There are some really great lamb producers here in Oregon that breed beautifully flavorful animals—I'm talking about Cattail Creek and Anderson Ranch—with just the right amount of fat-to-meat ratio. They are a magical thing to eat. {SERVES 4}

LAMB T-BONE, CAPRESE

4 lamb T-bone steaks, each about
    8 ounces (250 g)
Kosher salt
1 cup (30 g) basil leaves
1 tablespoon grated Parmesan
2 cloves garlic
1 tablespoon toasted pine nuts
¼ cup (60 ml) extra-virgin olive oil, plus
    more for drizzling
Neutral oil for searing
1 large ball fresh mozzarella, at room
    temperature
1 large heirloom tomato
Maldon flake salt
A squeeze of fresh lemon juice

1. Preheat the broiler and season the lamb with salt.

2. In a food processor, combine the basil, Parmesan, garlic, pine nuts, olive oil, and kosher salt to taste. Pulse to create a thick pesto.

3. Get a large cast-iron pan ripping hot and add a film of oil. Sear the lamb hard (it will generate lots of smoke) to create a nice brown crust on each side. It should take no more than a minute on each side. Remove from the pan and place on a baking sheet. Spread a layer of the pesto on the top of each lamb T-bone, like you would cream cheese on a bagel. Slice the mozzarella thickly, about the thickness of a slice of bread, and place a piece on each T-bone. Broil the lamb until the cheese is bubbling and crispy brown, about 4 minutes. Remove from oven and let rest for 4 to 5 minutes.

4. While the T-bones are resting, slice the tomato and sprinkle with Maldon salt. Drizzle with olive oil and give a squeeze of lemon juice. Serve the tomatoes alongside the broiled T-bones.

Spring is a great time to eat carbonara because lamb and peas are in season at that time. One day we had lamb belly trimmings around the restaurant, so we fried them for this dish and decided they worked well as an alternative to lardons. Mr. Pickles will shovel this carbonara down by the quart. When we tested the recipe for this book, he did just that. And it's likely that you will too.

Note: The belly has to cure for 5 days before you make this dish. If you don't have that much time, cut the rub recipe in half and cook the belly immediately after coating it with the rub. It won't have the same cured flavor, but it still does the trick. {SERVES 4}

SPAGHETTINI, LAMB BELLY, PEAS, PARMESAN (YES, CARBONARA)

¼ cup (35 g) kosher salt, plus more for blanching
¼ teaspoon pink curing salt
¼ cup (60 g) sugar
1 teaspoon freshly ground black pepper
1 teaspoon chopped fresh thyme
1 teaspoon chopped garlic
1 boneless lamb belly, about 1½ pounds (680 g)
1 cup (250 ml) dry white wine
2 yellow onions, thinly sliced
1 cup (155 g) fresh green peas
8 ounces (250 g) dried spaghettini
1 cup (80 g) grated Parmesan
3 egg yolks
Freshly ground black pepper

1. In a small bowl stir together the kosher and curing salts, sugar, pepper, thyme, and garlic. Rub the belly all over with the cure and transfer to a resealable plastic bag, pressing as much air out of the bag as possible. Store the belly in the refrigerator for 5 days, turning it every other day to ensure it's evenly coated with the cure.

2. Preheat the oven to 350°F (180°C).

3. Remove the belly from the refrigerator and give it a quick rinse. Place it in a Dutch oven with the wine and one of the onions and cook until a fork can be inserted into the belly with very little resistance, 2 to 3 hours. Remove from the oven and let cool completely in the liquid; it's fine to pop it in the fridge for a few minutes to speed things along. Reserve the braising liquid. Once cooled, dice the belly into batons about ¼ inch (6 mm) thick and long (the size of pencil erasers).

4. Prepare an ice water bath. Bring a large pot of heavily salted water to a boil over high heat. Add the peas and blanch for 1 minute. Using a spider or large slotted spoon, transfer the peas to the ice water bath and cool for 5 minutes. Remove the peas and pat dry; set aside. Toss the spaghettini in the same boiling water and cook until al dente, about 7 minutes. Drain in a colander over the sink and rinse with cold water.

5. In a large pot over medium-high heat, crisp up the lamb belly, stirring with a wooden spoon and letting the fat render, 4 to 5 minutes. Remove the lamb from the pot, but leave the fat. Add the remaining onion to the pot with the fat and cook until the onion just starts to break down but still retains some of its texture, 2 to 3 minutes. Add 1½ cups (375 ml) of the braising liquid and the pasta to the pot. Cook until the liquid is reduced to about ½ cup (125 ml). Remove the pan from the heat.

6.   Add the crispy belly back to the pot, half of the Parmesan, and the peas. Turn the heat down to low, stir in the egg yolks, and return the pot to the heat. Stir, stir, stir. Keep stirring constantly for about a minute, minding that you're making a carbonara here, not scrambled eggs.

7.   Stir in the rest of the Parmesan and pepper to taste. Divide among four bowls and serve.

We included this recipe in the book because brains, which were once popular, are disappearing from American menus. When lamb brains are poached, chilled, and fried, the experience of eating them is like biting into a beautiful cloud.

Brains do take some detective work to procure because some farmers are a little squeamish about selling them. The best way to get your hands on some lamb's brains is to cut out the middle-man and go straight to the source. Find a farm that produces lamb, call them up, and then beg, plead, and grovel to get the brains. If you ask your butcher to get them for you, give him or her at least a week's notice. {SERVES 4}

LAMB BRAINS, LAMB'S LETTUCE

Brains
4 lamb brains (yes, 1 brain per person)
2 cups (250 g) all-purpose flour
Kosher salt
Neutral oil for sautéing
2 tablespoons unsalted butter
A squeeze of fresh lemon juice
Maldon flake salt

Poaching Broth
1 tablespoon neutral oil
½ yellow onion, diced
2 celery stalks, diced
1 carrot, peeled and diced
3 bay leaves
4 sprigs thyme
1 tablespoon black peppercorns
1 cup (250 ml) dry white wine
3 cups (750 ml) water
1 tablespoon kosher salt

Mustard Crème Fraîche
¼ cup (60 ml) crème fraîche
2 tablespoons whole-grain mustard
A dash of Tabasco
1 tablespoon chopped fresh flat-leaf
    parsley
Juice of 1 lemon
Kosher salt

2 cups (185 g) mâche (lamb's lettuce)

1.   Soak the brains in ice water to cover for 1 to 2 hours to firm them and allow them to release some of their remaining blood.

2.   While the brains are soaking, let's make a flavorful broth to poach them in: warm the oil in a saucepan over medium heat. Add the onion, celery, and carrot and sauté for 4 minutes. Add the bay leaves, thyme, peppercorns, wine, and water. Season with the salt and bring to a simmer. Once the liquid comes to a simmer, turn off the heat and let it cool to room temperature.

3.   After the brains have soaked, add them to the poaching liquid and return to medium heat, slowly bringing them up to a simmer. Using a slotted spoon, transfer the brains to a plate lined with paper towels. Let the brains chill out a little bit while we make our mustard crème fraîche.

4.   To make the mustard crème fraîche, in a small bowl stir together the crème fraîche, mustard, Tabasco, parsley, and lemon juice. Season with salt to taste and set aside.

5.   Time to cook the brains! In a shallow dish, season the flour generously with kosher salt and mix well. Roll the brains in the seasoned flour and shake off any excess. In a sauté pan over medium-high heat, heat ¼ inch (6 mm) of oil. When the oil is hot, add the brains. Cook for 2 minutes, then turn the brains over. Add the butter to the pan and baste the brains until golden brown and crisp all over, 1 to 2 minutes. Using a slotted spoon, transfer the brains from the oil to a plate lined with paper towels. Give a squeeze of lemon juice and a sprinkle of Maldon salt.

6.   Arrange the brains on a platter alongside the mâche. Spoon the mustard crème fraîche over each brain and serve.

A note from Gabriel: After my son, Gus, was born, a good friend and colleague, Naomi Pomeroy—wild woman/chef/owner of Beast restaurant here in Portland—brought us a shepherd's pie (the only energy I had for cooking had to be reserved for Le Pigeon). That pie was so good that I started thinking about how to tweak it for the Le Pigeon menu. The curried mashed potatoes are the showstopper; applause may ensue. {SERVES 4 TO 6}

LAMB SHEPHERD'S PIE, CURRY MASH

Kosher salt
1 cup (155 g) fresh or frozen green peas
1 tablespoon extra-virgin olive oil
1 pound (450 g) ground lamb
1 cup diced (140 g) yellow onion
1 cup (155 g) finely diced carrots
1 tablespoon tomato paste
2 teaspoons chopped fresh oregano
3 cloves garlic, minced
1 tablespoon curry powder
¼ cup (60 ml) dry white wine
1 cup (250 ml) chicken stock
1 tablespoon cornstarch
1 teaspoon white wine vinegar
1½ pounds (675 g) Yukon gold potatoes, peeled and quartered
⅓ cup (80 ml) heavy cream
2 tablespoon unsalted butter, softened
2 eggs, lightly beaten

1. Prepare an ice water bath. Bring a large pot of heavily salted water to a boil over high heat. Add the peas and blanch for 1 minute. Using a spider or large slotted spoon, transfer the peas to the ice water bath and cool for 5 minutes. Remove the peas and pat dry; set aside.

2. In a sauté pan over medium-high heat, heat the olive oil. Add the lamb and sauté, stirring occasionally, until browned, about 10 minutes. Season with a pinch of salt. Using a slotted spoon, remove the lamb from the pan, leaving the fat in the pan. Add the onion, carrots, tomato paste, oregano, and garlic. Add 1½ teaspoons of the curry powder and season with a pinch of salt. Sauté for 3 minutes. Add the white wine and continue to cook until the liquid has reduced to about 1 tablespoon, 2 to 3 minutes more. Add the stock and bring to a boil.

3. Meanwhile, in a small bowl stir together the cornstarch, vinegar, and 2 teaspoons of water. We're forming a thick paste here, called a slurry. Add the slurry to the vegetable mixture along with the browned lamb and the peas. Cook for 4 minutes longer; it should thicken quite a bit. This is our first layer for the pie. Spread this mixture in the bottom of a 9-inch-square (22.5cm) baking dish, smoothing it out with a spatula.

4. Onto the potatoes: In large pot of heavily salted water, add the potatoes and bring to a boil. Once at a boil, reduce the heat to a simmer and cook until the potatoes give no resistance when pierced with a knife, 10 to 12 minutes.

5. While potatoes are cooking, in a small saucepan over low heat, warm the cream and the remaining 1½ teaspoons curry powder. We're just trying to let the flavor of the curry bloom here, about 6 minutes.

21 Frozen Peas
A wise old chef
once told me: Wait till
peas are in season,
then use frozen.
—Fergus Henderson, St. JOHN, London

6. Using a colander, drain the potatoes. If you have a ricer, push the potatoes through the ricer back into the pot. If not, return the potatoes to the pot and mash them using a potato masher. Add the cream, butter, and eggs. Stir with a wooden spoon to combine and season to taste with salt.

7. Preheat the oven to 400°F (200°C). Using a spatula, evenly spread the potatoes over the lamb layer. Bake for 20 minutes, turning the heat up to broil for the last 5 minutes, to get nice and brown potatoes. Remove from the oven and let cool for 10 minutes before serving family-style.

ENTER THE CHEESE BAR: STEVE JONES'S KILLER CASE

In Portland, we're lucky to have one of America's best cheesemongers,[1] Steve Jones, who runs the Cheese Bar in the Mount Tabor neighborhood. It's the best place in Portland to kill an afternoon. Ideally, go with a group of four or more so you can order a few big chunks of cheese—no little slices, please—and some big bottles of beer from Steve's carefully selected list. It's easy to let a couple of hours slip by. We asked Steve to compile a list of his go-tos—the cheeses that he always wants in his case—and to pontificate on the reasoning behind his choices. He kindly sent us the following.

---

1. When we say "the best," we mean it. Steve's accolades include winning the international Cheesemonger Invitational and routinely popping up on all the best monger lists.

My dad was a herdsman for the Iowa-based Maytag Dairy Farm in the 1940s. So you might say that I was genetically predisposed to work with cheese.

After graduating with an art degree in Missouri, I took up cooking to pay the bills. I hated the hours. It was in 1996 when I guess you could say I went from noncheese to cheese, making my way from cooking to working in a deli to focusing on American artisanal cheeses at the Wine Merchant in St. Louis. Before long, I was the cheesemonger at all three of the Wine Merchant stores. I loved it, but having spent time in the greater Pacific Northwest, I couldn't wait to get back.

In 2000, I began working for a large distributor in Portland. It was a formative experience, but I was responsible for $2 million worth of cheese, and the job included endless spreadsheets and keeping track of cheese traveling on ships across the Atlantic. Although I was thankful for the opportunity, such a large-scale operation just wasn't my passion. Then I rented space in a corner of a large wine shop where I had two cheese cases: this was the beginning of Steve's Cheese. Finally, around 2007, I started to save

for my own place. In addition to cheese, I wanted to carry Olympic Provisions meats such as loukaniko and mortadella; local beverages, such as beers from Upright Brewing, The Commons Brewing, and Logsdon Organic Farmhouse Ales; and wines and ciders from small regional producers.

The cheese bar I designed in my mind is exactly the Cheese Bar I now have. It's simple, it's located in a cool neighborhood, I have drawings by Evan Harris on the walls, and my kids feel comfortable parading around the shop in their pajamas demanding stinky cheese.

I have around 200 cheeses in the case and the case turns over about every ten days. Of those 200 cheeses, only about a quarter of them are static. I am constantly changing the cast of characters. Some cheeses are seasonally significant; others are in the case because I was given a perfect opportunity to snatch something and I did. Still others came to me from cheese mules, travelers who bring back cheeses from where the getting is good. In the course of a couple of years, I probably offer more than a thousand cheeses.

There are usually three stages that happen between the time we receive a cheese and it goes out

the door: the cheese arrives, we unpack it and check its state of health (determining what we need to do to make it better and how quickly it needs to be sold), and then we start making calls. There are forty to fifty cheeses that people have signed up to receive as soon as the cheese arrives. So quite often a cheese will land here and be gone within an hour.

We have a good number of wholesale customers and a lot of restaurants, like Le Pigeon, that have been with us from the beginning. The wholesale business is the wheel that keeps the Cheese Bar turning. I have to move everything I get within ten days. And I do. So I'm happy.

Gabriel and the LP staff are some of my favorite people to work with. When he wanted to take his own cheese menu to the next dorky level, being the king of cheese dorks myself, I was like "woo hoo!"

When reading this list, keep in mind that I'm a bit of a whore when it comes to cheese. My favorites change with the rotation of our case and whatever is new that day. However, if I could create a killer case for all time, it would look like this:

CATO CORNERS "HOOLIGAN"

Colchester, Connecticut
Cow's Milk Cheese

I love this cheese because I cannot get it. I admit that.

Mark Gillman at Cato Corners only sells cheese within 100 miles of his farm. I thought to myself, *If I go there, he will sell me his cheese.* So I went. His response? "No way. I sell my cheese only within 100 miles. Why would I put it in a box for you to sell in Portland?" You can't argue with that. But it just makes me want it more.

If you live in New York, you can get Hooligan at the Union Street market, where there's always a long, completely justified line. This cheese is aptly named, as it's big, wild, and manly. A washed-rind cheese,[2] with a strong fragrance of stinky feet, it's pugnacious, smoky, and peaty, redolent of bacon fat.

RODOLPHE LE MEUNIER "PUITS D'ASTIER"

Auvergne, France
Sheep's Milk Cheese

I described this big, funky doughnut-shaped cheese to Gabriel as having the flavors of "root vegetables and roasted peanut shells." Gabriel then took it and designed a dish around it; it's a cheese collaboration. He made a turnip peanut butter with it that completely blew my mind. He's an alchemist! This is a cheese dork's cheese, as it has truly insane depth and looks like a wheel from a medieval cart.

"A REALLY KICK-ASS CAMEMBERT"

Normandy, France
Cow's Milk Cheese

Occasionally, raw milk Camembert makes its way into the United States, but more often than not it has arrived here illegally. Why is it illegal? Because the laws in the United States require cheese to age for at least sixty days, and the peak for Camembert is usually forty-five days. So I can't sell illegal Camembert, but my killer cheese case list doesn't have rules, so I'm including it here.

When I travel to France, the first thing I buy is Camembert or Brie. Nothing compares to it. *When you're in France, buy young cheese.*

At Cheese Bar, I can give you cheese as fresh as you could get in the Jura, but with Camembert, no way. Eating fresh cheese can be like chasing the dragon, you're always looking for the taste of that first hit.

NEAL'S YARD DAIRY "BEENLEIGH BLUE"

Devon, United Kingdom
Sheep's Milk Cheese

In pulling together this list, it would have been easy for me to make each and every cheese a Neal's Yard Dairy cheese. But then I would have sounded like a company man. But straight up, if I had to pick one cheese selector/ager to deal with for the rest of my life, it would be Neal's Yard Dairy. When I did my internship there, I was in the cellar flipping these pink little piggies of cheeses, and they were so delicious that every day I went upstairs and ate them for lunch. By now, I've been buying from Neal's Yard Dairy for fifteen years. During that time, there were *maybe* two or three cheeses that I didn't like. That record is unbeatable. And not only do their cheeses ship well, but owner Randolph Hodgson's palate is unmatchable. One day we tasted seventeen Stiltons, and I was lost at number four.[3]

What I love most about this cheese is its ice-creamy sweetness. More accurately, it's the edge-of-the-bowl part of the ice cream, where it's melting and dripping. Lauren Fortgang agreed, and she took it one step further and, indeed, made Beenleigh Blue Ice Cream (page 310).

---

2. When you wash the rind, you're encouraging a bacteria strain called *B. linens* to grow on the outside, and that's what gives cheese that stinky-foot aroma.

3. If you think seventeen Stiltons sounds intense, Steve judges for the American Cheese Society, where 1,500 cheeses are judged in two days and they have huge KFC-style paper buckets for spitting. Steve doesn't use the buckets.

PURE LUCK DAIRY "HOPELESSLY BLEU"

Dripping Springs, Texas
Goat's Milk Cheese

American cheese names—like Australian wine names—are brutal. For every "Little Penguin" or "Yellow Fish," you have "Little Boy Blue," "Bad Axe," "Holy Cow," or "Off Kilter." (I love most of these cheeses; I just hate the silly names.)

Goat's milk blues always have an egg yolky taste to me. I fell in love with this cheese in Austin, but unfortunately, like the Hooligan, the producer is only willing to sell it within 100 miles of the shop. Déjà vu.

Regardless, this means Pure Luck Dairy is doing its job well. So, for now, I'll be making special trips to Texas.

CAPRIOLE "WABASH CANNONBALL"

Greenville, Indiana
Goat's Milk Cheese

Judy Schad, a Southern gentlewoman, brings this cheese to us. You can find her at almost any cheese conference; she's the one at the bar drinking bourbon. One of the grand dames of American cheeses (the list also includes Mary Keehn, Paula Lambert, and Debra Dickerson), Judy has never stopped producing perfect cheese.

This is a little 3-ounce (90g) ball of ash-encrusted goat cheese with a bloomy rind on top. Amazingly well made, it is slightly cost-prohibitive, seeing as you can eat the whole thing in a couple of bites, but it's always worth the price.

PHOLIA FARM "ELK MOUNTAIN"

Rogue River, Oregon
Goat's Milk Cheese

This is a regional pick. A grand dame in the making, Gianaclis Caldwell is one of the best cheese makers in America. She is a retired artist and her husband is a former Marine. They live off the grid and their farm relies totally on solar energy. Gianaclis only makes five or six cheeses throughout the year, only striking when the humidity is right. This is the alchemy of a great cheese maker: she doesn't make cheeses during seasonal dips.

This cheese is made from Nigerian Dwarf goats. How great is that? Nigerian Dwarf goats were originally brought to the United States to

{Continued on page 260}

Beenleigh Blue   Puits d'Astier   Lou Bergier Pichin

feed animals in zoos and circuses, but then someone had the wise idea to use their milk to make cheese. The cheese is more similar to a sheep's milk cheese than a goat cheese; it has the richness of sheep's milk but with goat's milk's sweetness. A lot of goat cheeses don't have depth, but this one has it in spades.

You take a talented cheese maker and an unusual animal that gives milk with this amount of depth and the result is a cheesemonger's dream.

"BEAUFORT D'ÉTÉ" (THE KING OF COMTÉ)

Savoie, France
Cow's Milk Cheese

Usually the size of a tractor tire or a small human, the typical Beaufort weighs more than 100 pounds. This is a big cheese with big problems: because of its size, producers can only make a few wheels in a week. And because of the limited number, it's expensive, like my entire budget for a week. Also, it fills half of my two-door cooler, which is all of my stock space. And finally, it fissures, meaning it's so big the cheese can't even handle its own weight.

Some of you are probably wondering, "Why can't you cut it?" Well, because cutting cheese brings about its eventual death. A wheel in its full form is the best it will ever be, like a wine uncorked. Once it's cut, the quality drops off quickly. When we cut a big cheese like that—the moment you cut it—that moment is magic.

A good Comté should be on everyone's list. Comté should be in your fridge like Cheddar. You should have a chunk of Cheddar, a chunk of Parmesan, and a chunk of Comté. You have Cheddar because you have kids or you're just American. You have Parmesan because you like to cook. And you have Comté because you like to cook and it's kick-ass with every wine. Like Camembert, Comté is an origin-controlled cheese, which means that it's made in a certain region with a particular cow's milk. All Comté is made by cooperatives, which belong to a bigger consortium. It's very difficult to go back to the actual producer of this cheese because it's all pooled milk. So whether you're the milker, the fruitiére, or the affineur, you're all part of the bigger production.

You might say that stocking this cheese is illogical due to its expense, volatility, and size. So why is Beaufort on every monger's list? Because it's that good.

"FARMHOUSE OSSAU-IRATY"

Pyrénées, France
Sheep's Milk Cheese

Farmhouse Ossau-Iraty is made by shepherds on high pasture in the French Pyrénées. The act of *transhumance* (taking the animals to high alpine pastures) is where the magic comes from in this cheese; it has big, grassy, nutty, buttery, and creamy notes and is infinitely satisfying.

It's also a perfect cheater cheese: when you don't know what to bring to a party, this is your ace in the hole because it pairs well with almost all beverages and is loved by all.

When people step up to the counter with that deer-in-the-headlights look, I hand them this cheese so they're not scared, they're just happy. It's a great baseline from which to gauge a customer's tastes (whether a cheese is too mild, too sharp, too grassy, too sheepy, or just right). The main point of handing them the cheese, though, is to break the ice, take away any overwhelming aspects of the transaction, and make people feel comfortable and welcome.

If you're having a dinner party, don't get five different cheeses, please. Get a 5-pound wheel of one and just chip away at it and then send the leftovers home with your guests. Setting out 10 pounds of Iraty is like throwing down a magnum, or maybe a jeroboam. Cut into it and hand it around.

TILLAMOOK "CHEDDAR"

Tillamook, Oregon
Cow's Milk Cheese

Okay, so this isn't technically on my top-ten list as a cheesemonger, but it's worth mentioning because it's a great local cheese. Most people have a cheddar like this in the fridge. Tillamook started their cooperative in 1909. It was, and still is, a Pacific Northwest institution. Kids—mine, and most of them in general—eat a ton of cheese, like ¼ pound a day. So I would rather have them eat this than cheese from a multinational corporation. The cheese is hormone free, and the animals eat actual grass. I don't sell it at the shop, but it is a point of Oregon pride. And it's also good to note that Gabriel serves it on The Le Pigeon Burger (page 234).

"LOU BERGIER PICHIN"

Piedmont, Italy
Cow's Milk Cheese

This cheese uses thistle flower as the coagulant rather than calf's rennet, which is used in most cheeses. Thistle rennet is used almost exclusively in Spain and Portugal, not Italy, so this is an unusual cheese indeed. It has bright, creamy wild strawberry notes, with the emphasis on the wild, like a weasel on a leash. I get this only once a month or so because it's rare and difficult to procure.

"REBLOCHON"

Savoie, France
Cow's Milk Cheese

Reblochon is a washed-rind cheese that people usually cook with, but it should really be eaten from a cheese board. It's like pizza in that when it's really good it's amazing, and when it's not that great . . . it's still good! This is a cheese lover's cheese, and, like Camembert (see page 256), it's kind of in an illegal zone now due to the aging requirements. But really creative importers keep renaming it and bringing it into the United States. When we do have it, we show it to our best customers.

One of my favorite memories of all time is when I came across a hut on a hike in the French Alps and was served a reblochon omelet and a delicious regional beer—the perfect cheese moment!

long bea
$ 3.95

Green
Cabbage
$1.2 /lb

Nicola
Potatoes
$2.5 /lb

Carrots
$3.00/bunch

$3.95/lb.

Romano
Beans
$3.95/lb.

CHAPTER 11
VEG

Colorado
Rose Potatoes
$2.50/lb.

Vitaly Paley is the godfather of Portland's food scene. If you look at any top kitchen in Portland, you will probably see a Paley alum, as almost every chef has at one time passed through Paley's Place.

Gabriel had never had his ass kicked in a kitchen before working for Vitaly. And there were many ass kickings. In fact, the two years he worked at Paley's Place were the most formative of his career. Vitaly Paley is a skilled teacher of French cooking technique, and he gave Gabriel the freedom to try out many new ideas. Simply put, it's because of Paley that Le Pigeon's cuisine is what it is today. We mention him here because both toasting the bread in an herb-flavored butter and including vinegar in the custard are both nods to the master.

You can make the fennel puree up to 4 days in advance, as it will keep in the fridge. {SERVES 6}

BREAD PUDDING, LEEK, FENNEL

Bread Pudding
¼ cup (60 g) unsalted butter
1 tablespoon chopped fresh sage
½ teaspoon Tabasco
1 baguette, sliced into ½-inch
　(12mm) pieces
Kosher salt
1½ sweet onions, sliced
2 leeks, white and light green parts
　only, cut into half-moons
6 cloves garlic, thinly sliced
4 eggs
1½ cups (375 ml) heavy cream
¼ cup (20 g) grated San Andreas or
　other aged sheep's milk cheese
¼ cup (60 ml) sherry vinegar

1.　Preheat the oven to 350°F (180°C). Butter a 9-inch (23cm) square baking dish and set aside.

2.　To make the bread pudding, in a small sauté pan over medium heat, melt 3 tablespoons of the butter with the sage and Tabasco. In a bowl, toss the melted butter with the baguette slices, season with salt, and toast in the oven until golden brown on the outside and slightly soft on the inside, about 10 minutes.

3.　While bread is toasting, in a sauté pan over medium heat, melt the remaining 1 tablespoon butter. Add the onions, leeks, and garlic and sauté until soft and slightly translucent, about 6 minutes. Season with salt, remove from the heat, and set aside.

4.　In a bowl combine the toasted bread with the sautéed onion mixture. In a separate bowl, whisk together the eggs, cream, cheese, and vinegar and season with salt. (We are seasoning all the components separately to build depth of flavor.) Pour the egg mixture over the bread and vegetable mixture. Work it together well with your hands, but don't turn it to mush.

5.　Pour the mixture into the prepared baking dish and bake until it is set and the top is golden brown, 30 to 35 minutes. Remove from the oven and allow the bread pudding to cool for 30 to 40 minutes in the pan.

Fennel Puree

1 tablespoon unsalted butter
1 fennel bulb, cored and thinly sliced
½ sweet onion, sliced
¼ teaspoon fennel pollen
¼ teaspoon ground fennel seeds
Kosher salt
½ cup (125 ml) dry white wine

Cauliflower

2 tablespoons unsalted butter
Kosher salt
A squeeze of fresh lemon juice
2 cups (185 g) cauliflower florets
1 teaspoon minced garlic
½ teaspoon paprika
A pinch of red pepper flakes

6.   To make the fennel puree, in a small saucepan over medium heat, melt the butter. Add the fennel and onion and sauté until fragrant, about 3 minutes. Add the fennel pollen and fennel seeds and season with salt. Add the white wine and reduce the heat to low. Cook until the fennel is soft and falling apart, about 20 minutes. Transfer to a blender and puree. If you find the puree is slightly too thick, loosen with 2 to 3 teaspoons of water.

7.   To make the cauliflower, preheat the oven again to 350°F (180°C). In an ovenproof sauté pan over medium heat, melt the butter and cook, stirring constantly, until light brown. Season with salt and lemon juice. Add the cauliflower and garlic. Stir in the paprika and red pepper flakes and roast in the oven until just tender, about 10 minutes. At this point, if need be, you can easily rewarm the bread pudding in the oven for a couple of minutes. Slice the pudding into six equal pieces and serve with warm fennel puree and cauliflower alongside.

 THE PIGEON POUR: We always have one vegetarian entrée on the menu, and when we are looking for a pairing for it, we often end up with a local pinot. This is usually because the dish is flavorful and complex but doesn't have the meaty protein component, so a wine that has complexity and bright fruit but softer tannins is ideal. A big, chewy tannic wine needs some protein and fat to cut through it; it will shred more delicate foods. At its best, Oregon pinot has lively fruit and good acid and exhibits great layers of complexity. I hesitate to mention my favorites in this book because I don't want to leave anyone out. When pressed, however, I would say that Belle Pente, Soter, J. Christopher, St. Innocent, Cameron, and Bethel Heights are often on the Pigeon wine list.

We are often asked why we don't have more local wines on our list and are accused of not being behind the home team. To clear the air, we love the local juice. At any given time, we have ten to twelve wines from the Willamette Valley on the list, and we try to rotate through different wines so we can feature as many of our favorites as we can. No area of the world is better represented on our wine list than Oregon. Okay, Burgundy is, but they've had 900 years to make their wines so good. Oregon is doing pretty damn well in a fraction of the time.

We love radishes, cooked or raw. They are emblematic of Le Pigeon: colorful, spirited, and zesty. When cooked, they mellow a little but still have some zip. We use them here to make a vichyssoise that's a little brighter than the classic version. The large, sweet mussels we get from Totten Inlet in Washington are a great contrast for the soup. Mussels don't make it on the menu that often, but we love them for this dish. {SERVES 4}

RADISH VICHYSSOISE, MUSSELS, PESTO

1 tablespoon unsalted butter
1 large white onion, diced
3 cloves garlic, minced, plus 4 cloves garlic, chopped
4 bunches red radishes, leaves reserved for the pesto and radishes coarsely chopped
3 cups (750 ml) of water
2½ cups (625 ml) dry white wine
3 tablespoons Moscatel vinegar
Kosher salt
Neutral oil for sautéing
3 shallots, minced
1 teaspoon red pepper flakes
1 tablespoon chopped fresh tarragon
2 pounds (900 g) mussels
⅓ cup (80 ml) heavy cream
8 Grilled Pickled Onions (page 323)
½ cup Radish Pesto (see recipe below)

1. In a stockpot over medium heat, melt the butter. Add the onion and the 3 cloves minced garlic and sauté until translucent, about 5 minutes. Add the radishes and cook for 5 minutes more. Add the water, 1½ cups (375 ml) of the white wine, the vinegar, and salt to taste and bring to a simmer.

2. While that's simmering, heat a thin film of oil in a large sauté pan over medium heat. When the oil is hot, add the shallots, the 4 cloves chopped garlic, and the red pepper flakes. Sauté until aromatic, 1 to 2 minutes. Add the remaining 1 cup (250 ml) wine, the tarragon, 1 teaspoon salt, and the mussels. Cover and cook until the mussels have opened, about 4 minutes. Discard any mussels that don't open and then remove the pan from the heat and strain, reserving the solids and liquid separately. Add the liquid to the stockpot and continue to simmer for another 20 minutes. Meanwhile, let the mussels cool.

3. Remove the soup from the heat and let it cool to room temperature. Transfer to a blender and puree, slowing adding the cream while the blender is running. Salt to taste.

4. Ladle the soup into four large shallow bowls and, with your hands, gently place the mussels in the center of each bowl. Top the mussels with two pickled onions per bowl. Divide the pesto equally among the bowls, drizzling it lightly around the mussels, and serve.

Radish Pesto

½ cup (15 g) chopped radish leaves (reserved from making the vichyssoise)
1 clove garlic
¼ cup (60 ml) extra-virgin olive oil
Zest of ½ lemon
A dash of kosher salt

MAKES ½ CUP (125 ML)

In a blender, puree the radish leaves, garlic, olive oil, and lemon zest until you have a rich and oily pesto texture. Season to taste with salt and serve.

A few days per week Gabriel gets up at the crack of dawn to do lunch service at Little Bird. His saving grace is the quiche he grabs at Lauretta Jean's, an espresso shack turned baked goods shop two doors down from Little Bird. It specializes in pies, both savory and sweet, and their goat cheese and bacon quiche is absolutely killer.

Lauretta Jean's quiche inspired Gabriel to come up with this recipe. On its own, this quiche makes a great lunch. But for dinner, paired with Rabbit in a Pig Blanket (page 107), it sings.

The quiche dough is extremely versatile. Take the cheese out and you can use it for just about any type of tart you want to make. It is very forgiving, and you can easily double or triple a batch without any issues. The addition of cream cheese adds to the flakiness. Whether it holds a juicy filling or something dense and rich, this dough will hold up. You may not want to have a love affair with it, but this crust will definitely be your best friend through thick and thin.

{SERVES 4}

MUSTARD GREENS QUICHE

Crust

½ cup (60 g) plus 2 tablespoons all-purpose flour
¼ teaspoon kosher salt
¼ cup (60 g) cold unsalted butter, cubed
2 tablespoons (35 g) cream cheese
1½ tablespoons ice water
2 tablespoons grated Gruyère cheese

1. Preheat the oven to 350°F (180°C).

2. To make the crust, in a food processor combine the flour, salt, butter, and cream cheese. Pulse until the mixture starts to resemble coarse pebbles. Add the ice water and pulse until the dough just begins to come together. Turn the dough out onto your work surface and knead the grated cheese into it. Divide the dough into four equal pieces. Roll each portion of dough into a ball. Place each ball between two pieces of waxed paper or parchment paper and, using a rolling pin, roll each into a 4-inch (10cm) diameter circle. (Wrap the dough rounds tightly in plastic wrap and place them in the refrigerator to rest if you aren't going to make the tart shells immediately.)

3. On a baking sheet lined with parchment paper, place four tart rings, each 3¼ inches (8 cm) across by 1 inch (2.5 cm) high. Peel the parchment paper away from the dough and lightly flour both sides of each dough round. Use your fingers to push the dough into the bottom of the rings and also against the sides. Smooth out any creases. There will be excess dough at the top of the ring. That's okay. Once all the rings have tart dough in them, place them in the freezer for 5 minutes. Pull them out and trim the excess dough with a paring knife until the dough is flush with the top of the rings. Prick the bottom of each tart shell several times with the tip of a paring knife. Place the dough back in the freezer for a minimum of 10 minutes.

Filling

1 tablespoon unsalted butter
½ cup (70 g) diced yellow onion
2 cloves garlic, thinly sliced
1 teaspoon chopped fresh thyme
1 cup (30 g) mustard greens
1 teaspoon freshly ground black
    pepper
A pinch of freshly grated nutmeg
4 eggs
¼ cup (60 ml) heavy cream
1 tablespoon Dijon mustard
A dash of Tabasco
1 cup (125 g) grated Gruyère cheese
Kosher salt

Mizuna Salad

1 cup (15 g) mizuna or arugula leaves
¼ cup (28 g) very thinly sliced radishes
A squeeze of fresh lemon juice
Radish Vinny (page 327)
Kosher salt

4.   Remove the dough from the freezer and bake in the oven for 10 minutes. Rotate the baking sheet and bake until the crust is golden brown, another 10 to 15 minutes. Let the tart shells cool to room temperature and remove the rings before adding the filling.

5.   To make the filling, reduce the oven temperature to 325°F (165°C). In a sauté pan over medium heat, melt the butter. Add the onion, garlic, and thyme and sauté until aromatic, about 5 minutes. Add the mustard greens, pepper, and nutmeg and cook, stirring occasionally, 10 minutes. Remove from the heat and transfer the contents of the pan to a food processor. Pulse until the mixture is pureed, about 3 minutes. Add the eggs, cream, Dijon, Tabasco, and Gruyère and pulse to combine well. Season to taste with salt.

6.   Use a spatula to fill each tart shell about three-quarters of the way to the rim. Transfer to a baking sheet and bake until the egg mixture has set and does not wiggle in the middle when gently shaken, about 17 minutes.

7.   To make the salad, in a large bowl toss together the mizuna and radishes. Add a squeeze of lemon juice and dress with the radish vinny, tossing to coat. Season to taste with salt.

8.   Top each quiche with an equal amount of the salad and serve.

What would this book be without some local nettles? These grow like wildfire in Oregon. This recipe is a relatively tame LP creation and a good example of how to add a little tang to simple crepes.

We buy nettles from our urban wizard Lars (see page 198), who buys them from the magical foraging enthusiasts. These forest dwellers love tea, nettles, mushrooms, and watercolor portraits of mushrooms. There are as many mushrooms growing in their beards as there are thriving on the forest floor. Also, they're not scared of the dark. {SERVES 4 TO 6}

NETTLE CREPES, RADISH, RICOTTA

Radishes

¼ cup (60 g) unsalted butter
1 bunch radishes, cut into slices the size of a quarter
⅛ teaspoon ground coriander
½ teaspoon chestnut honey (see Note on page 165)
1 cup water (250 ml)
1 tablespoon sugar

Mushrooms

1 tablespoon unsalted butter
8 ounces (250 g) oyster mushrooms
Pinch of kosher salt

Filling

8 ounces (250 g) ricotta cheese
Zest and juice of 1 lemon
1 bunch of chives, chopped
2 tablespoons grated Parmesan
2 egg yolks
1 teaspoon chopped fresh oregano

Nettle Crepes (opposite)
2 ounces sheep's milk cheese, thinly sliced
½ cup (20 g) frisée

1. First we're going to reduce the radishes. In a sauté pan over medium-high heat, melt the butter. Add the radishes, coriander, chestnut honey, water, and sugar and cook until there is ¼ cup (60 ml) of liquid along with the radishes. Remove from the heat and set aside.

2. To make the mushrooms, in a small sauté pan over high heat, melt the pat of butter. Add the mushrooms and salt and sauté until cooked through and the edges are just starting to crisp, 4 to 5 minutes. Remove from the heat and keep warm.

3. To make the filling, in a large bowl, combine the ricotta, lemon zest and juice, chives, Parmesan, egg yolks, and oregano. Mix well.

4. Preheat the oven to 400°F (200°C).

5. Spoon about 2 tablespoons of the filling onto each crepe and fold the crepe in half, and then in half again to form a triangle. Arrange the crepes on a baking sheet and top each crepe with an equal amount of the sheep's milk cheese. Bake just until the cheese is melted, 4 to 6 minutes. Remove from the oven and top each crepe with a few mushrooms.

6. In a bowl, toss together the radish mixture with the frisée. Serve two or three crepes per plate with the radish salad alongside.

Nettle Crepes

Kosher salt
2 cups (70 g) packed nettles, cleaned
1 cup (125 g) all-purpose flour
4 eggs
1 cup (250 ml) whole milk
½ cup (125 ml) water
¼ cup (60 g) unsalted butter, melted, plus 2 tablespoons softened
1 teaspoon kosher salt
1 teaspoon truffle butter
1 teaspoon freshly grated nutmeg

MAKES 12 CREPES

Prepare an ice water bath. Bring a large pot of heavily salted water to boil over high heat. Wearing rubber gloves, add the nettles to the pot and blanch for 30 seconds. Using a spider or large slotted spoon, transfer the nettles to the ice water bath and cool for 2 minutes. Remove the nettles from the ice water, wrap them tightly in a kitchen towel, and wring out any excess water. In a blender, combine the flour, eggs, nettles, milk, water, ¼ cup (70 g) of melted butter, the salt, truffle butter, and nutmeg. Blend until smooth. Refrigerate for 30 minutes to let the batter rest. Lightly grease an 8-inch (20cm) nonstick pan over medium-high heat with the 2 tablespoons of softened butter. Add 2 tablespoons of the crepe batter to the pan (you can use a 1-ounce/30g ladle, if you have one). Swirl the pan in a circular motion to evenly coat the pan with a thin layer of batter. Cook until brown and pliable, about 1 minute. Using a rubber spatula, gently flip the crepe over and cook for 30 seconds longer. Remove from the pan and repeat with the remaining batter, adding more butter to the pan if necessary.

This is a nice simple tart to serve in the summer. Alternatively, you can make the tomato filling in the summer, freeze it, and then revisit this recipe during the dark depths of winter, when you're jonesing for good tomatoes. This tart is also great to serve as a side dish with a salad or a steak, or even for breakfast. {SERVES 4}

TOMATO TART, EGG SALAD

Tomato Jam
2 tablespoons olive oil
1 large shallot, minced
2 cloves garlic, minced
¼ teaspoon red pepper flakes
6 large red tomatoes, peeled and
    seeded
2 tablespoons extra-virgin olive oil
1 tablespoon balsamic vinegar
1 teaspoon chopped tarragon
1 teaspoon kosher salt

4 pieces of puff pastry, each about
    3 inches (7.5 cm) square
4 hard-boiled eggs
½ cup (60 ml) Gribiche (page 215)
Fresh tarragon leaves as garnish
Maldon flake salt
Good-quality olive oil (see sidebar on
    page 105), for drizzling

1.   To make the tomato jam, warm the olive oil in a sauté pan over medium heat. Add the shallot, garlic and red pepper flakes and sauté until aromatic, about 1 minute. Add the tomatoes, extra-virgin olive oil, balsamic vinegar, tarragon, and salt. Continue to cook, stirring occasionally, until the mixture is the consistency of tomato paste, about 45 minutes. Remove from the heat and let cool.

2.   Preheat the oven to 425°F (220°C).

3.   Arrange each square of puff pastry on a baking sheet and poke the middle of each with a fork. Place 2 tablespoons of the tomato filling in the center of each square. Bake until puffy and golden brown, 10 to 12 minutes.

4.   Place a warm tomato tart on the center of each plate. Slice each egg lengthwise into four or five slices. Place one egg on each plate, fanning the slices out next to the tart. You want to get a bit of tart and egg in each bite. Top with the gribiche. Garnish with the tarragon leaves, sprinkle with Maldon salt, drizzle with olive oil, and serve.

BAKED CARROTS, ALMOND CREAM

½ cup (125 ml) crème fraîche
¼ cup (40 g) toasted almonds
2 tablespoons Moscatel vinegar
1 pound (450 g) carrots, peeled and cut
    into ½-inch (12mm) rounds
2 tablespoons unsalted butter, melted
Kosher salt
1 tablespoon chopped fresh flat-leaf
    parsley

1. Preheat the oven to 400°F (200°C).

2. In a food processor or blender, combine the crème fraîche, almonds, and vinegar and pulse until the mixture is coarsely pureed but still slightly chunky, about 1 minute.

3. In a bowl, toss together the carrots and the melted butter. Season with salt. Spread the carrots evenly on a baking sheet and roast until fork-tender, about 10 minutes. Remove from the oven.

4. Place the carrots in a shallow baking dish. Spread the crème fraîche mixture over the carrots and bake for 5 minutes more. Remove from the oven and sprinkle with parsley. Serve family style from the baking dish.

We asked our favorite cheesemonger, Steve Jones, owner of Portland's Cheese Bar (see page 254), to tell us which Gouda he would use with cauliflower, a cheese so good that it would trick his son, Oscar, into eating vegetables. This was his response:

"In America, Gouda has a bad reputation as being plasticky, flavorless, and boring. When people come into my shop, they eye the Gouda, but I can tell that they feel too embarrassed to ask for some. Wilde Weide Gouda changes the game. This cheese is made on an island in southern Holland that is only accessible by boat. How crazy is that? I always say, 'This is what Gouda wants to be when it grows up.' Wilde Weide is aged 15 months, so it stays on the savory side of the spectrum, with the big caramel and toffee notes that you get with longer-aged Goudas."

These potatoes are perfect with Pork Shoulder Confit (page 186) or Lamb Shank (page 240). {SERVES 6}

CAULIFLOWER, AGED GOUDA, MASHED POTATOES

Kosher salt
3 pounds (1.4 kg) russet potatoes, peeled and quartered
1 head cauliflower, cut into florets
½ cup (125 g) unsalted butter
½ cup (125 ml) heavy cream
4 ounces (125 g) aged Gouda, grated

1. In a large pot of salted water, combine the potatoes and cauliflower and bring to a boil. Turn down to a simmer so the potatoes don't explode. Cook until the potatoes are fork-tender, about 15 minutes, and drain in a colander.

2. In the same pot and off the heat, combine the butter, cream, and cheese. If you have a ricer, push the potatoes and cauliflower through the ricer into the pot. If not, return the potatoes and cauliflower to the pot and mash them with the butter, cream, and cheese using a potato masher. Stir to combine. Season with salt and serve.

We invited Lars (see page 198) to briefly wax poetic on the art of finding morels to inspire you to make this recipe: "Morels! They grow everywhere in the northern two-thirds of the United States and everywhere in Canada south of the tundra. In most places they are rare, not a commercial commodity. They are also famous in the Midwest, where people pick them in hardwood forests along river bottoms. The entire midwestern harvest between February and June—from Missouri and Kansas north to Canada—probably does not come close to equaling a single day's harvest at the peak of the season in Oregon. Look for morels in the high mountains of eastern Oregon where coniferous forest is dead or dying, whether from insect infestations, recent logging activity, or forest fires. When wild strawberries are blooming and bracken fern is a few inches tall, the ground will be warm enough for morels to fruit." {SERVES 4}

MOREL TEMPURA, GOAT CHEESE, MÂCHE

Morel Tempura

1 cup (125 g) all-purpose flour
1 teaspoon baking powder
1 egg
⅔ cup (160 ml) very cold club soda
Kosher salt
½ cup (120 g) goat cheese, softened
1 small shallot, minced
1 tablespoon minced chives
1 teaspoon minced Preserved Lemons (page 326)
2 tablespoons crème fraîche
16 large fresh morel mushrooms
Rice oil for frying

Salad

2 cups mâche
A handful of radishes, thinly sliced
A squeeze of fresh lemon juice
Extra-virgin olive oil
Kosher salt

1. To make the tempura, in a blender, combine the flour, baking powder, egg, club soda, and a pinch of salt and blend until smooth. Refrigerate the batter until you're ready to use it, though it's best if used within 1 hour.

2. In a bowl, whisk together the goat cheese, shallot, chives, preserved lemon, crème fraîche, and a pinch of salt. Place in a pastry bag fitted with a small tip. Carefully fill the morels with the goat cheese mixture all the way to the top. You may have to snip the tops of those morels that are closed and much smaller than the rest.

3. In a large, heavy pot over high heat, pour rice oil to a depth of 4 inches (10 cm) and heat to 375°F (190°C). Very carefully drop the filled morels into the batter and, in batches, fry until golden brown and crispy, 3 to 4 minutes each. With a slotted spoon, remove the mushrooms from the oil and transfer to a plate lined with paper towels. Sprinkle with salt.

4. To make the salad, in a large bowl, toss together the mâche and radishes. Add the lemon juice and a drizzle of olive oil and toss to combine. Season with salt. Serve the salad alongside the hot tempura morels.

Gabriel's first real cookbook obsession—and probably yours, too—was *The French Laundry Cookbook* by Thomas Keller. One dish that always stood out to him was the angolotti. After a little research, he realized that, as far as stuffed pasta goes, agnolotti are much easier to make than ravioli. In this recipe, we pair agnolotti with a variety of parsley preparations, but feel free to have fun with different fillings and sauces of your choosing. The first time we put this on the LP menu, the impact in the dining room was huge. {SERVES 4}

Dough

1¾ cups (225 g) all-purpose flour, plus more for kneading and rolling
1½ tablespoons olive oil
9 egg yolks
1 egg
1 tablespoon whole milk
Semolina flour for dusting

Filling

1 yellow onion, thinly sliced
6 cloves black garlic, peeled (see sidebar on page 81)
2 cloves garlic
¼ cup (60 g) unsalted butter
½ cup (125 ml) water
1 pound (450 g) parsley root or celery root, peeled and thinly sliced
½ cup (125 ml) dry white wine
1 cup (250 ml) heavy cream
½ cup (40 g) grated Parmesan

Parsley Butter

1 cup (250 g) unsalted butter
6 cloves garlic, minced
¼ cup (60 ml) parsley juice

Mushrooms

2 ounces (60 g) maitake mushrooms
Neutral oil for frying
Maldon flake salt

Kosher salt
1½ cups (375 ml) Parmesan Broth (page 325)
1 clove garlic minced
1 tablespoon olive oil
2 tablespoons chopped fresh flat-leaf parsley
½ cup (60 g) Seasoned Bread Crumbs (page 327)
¼ cup (20 g) grated Parmesan

AGNOLOTTI, PARMESAN BROTH

1. To make the dough, in a food processor combine the all-purpose flour and olive oil and pulse to combine. Add the egg yolks and whole egg and pulse until well incorporated. With the motor running, sprinkle in the milk a little at a time. The dough should start coming together but not be wet. Remove the dough from the processor and knead briefly on a work surface lightly dusted with flour to combine. Wrap in plastic wrap, let rest for 30 minutes at room temperature, and knead again for 5 minutes. Rewrap the dough, let rest for another 30 minutes, and then knead again for 5 minutes; set aside.

2. To make the filling, in a small saucepan over low heat, combine the onion, black garlic, regular garlic, butter, and water and bring to a simmer. Cover and simmer for 45 minutes. Add the parsley root and continue cooking, stirring occasionally, for 10 minutes. Add the wine and reduce until the pan is almost dry and there's only about 1 tablespoon of liquid left. Add the cream and cook, with the pan covered and still on low heat, until the root parsley is tender. It should take about 20 minutes, but check every 5 minutes to check on its doneness. If it's getting close to the end and the parsley root isn't tender, add a touch of water and continue cooking until it's done. Remove from the heat and transfer the mixture to a food processor. Add the Parmesan and process for 2 minutes. Set aside.

3. To make the agnolotti, place the filling in a pastry bag fitted with a ½-inch (12mm) tip. Divide the dough into 2 pieces. You will be working with one at a time, so cover the remaining piece with plastic wrap to keep it from drying out. Dust your work surface with a light coating of all-purpose flour and flatten your piece of dough as much as possible with the palm of your hand. Set a pasta machine to the number one setting. Roll the dough through your pasta machine, fold it over on itself, dust it with a little flour, and roll it through the machine again. Repeat, rolling the dough through

{Continued}

the machine four or five times, until it has an elastic, rubbery texture. This is building the gluten in the flour and giving the pasta the correct texture. Set the machine to the number two setting and roll the dough through the machine again, going slowly and keeping the dough from folding over on itself. (If you make a mistake and let the dough fold on itself, you can always go back to number one setting and start the process over.) Continue the process, increasing the machine to the number three and then the number four setting. Now you should have a nice long sheet of pasta. Repeat with the remaining piece of dough. Dust your work surface with all-purpose flour and prepare to fill these little guys.

4.   Trim the edges of your pasta to make nice squared corners, discarding the scraps. Cut each sheet of pasta lengthwise to create two long sheets, with the long sides facing you. Brush the middle of each sheet lightly with water (using too much water will cause the pasta to stick to the table). Pipe a steady tube of filling along each sheet from left to right, leaving ½ inch (12 mm) of exposed dough at the bottom (the side closest to you). Now you are going to gently roll the ½ inch (12 mm) of exposed dough over the filling. Using your thumb, press it down to make a long cylinder; the water will help the pasta seal. Once you have completed this, trim the top of each sheet with a cutter, to give a nice rippled appearance. Using your thumb and forefinger, pinch the cylinder at 1-inch (2.5cm) intervals to create a long line of little pouches that are soon to become separate agnolotti. You want ½ inch (12 mm) between each pouch so you have ample space to cut them. Roll a pastry cutter through the middle of each ½-inch (12mm) space and the pasta will roll up on itself to form little agnolotti; you might need to give a little pinch to ensure they are stuck together. Transfer them to a baking sheet, dusting them with semolina flour so they don't stick together. If you're not serving immediately, freeze until you're ready to use.

5.   To make the parsley butter, in a food processor combine the butter, garlic, and parsley juice and process until smooth. Set aside. (You won't use all of the parsley butter. The leftovers can be stored in an airtight container in the freezer for up to 2 months.)

6.   To make the mushrooms, cut the root off the maitake mushrooms and separate them. In a medium sauté pan over high heat, heat ¼ inch (6 mm) of oil until it begins to smoke. Add the mushrooms and sauté for 1 minute. Remove from the oil with a slotted spoon to a plate lined with paper towels. Sprinkle with Maldon salt to taste. Keep warm until ready to serve.

7.   To cook the pasta, heat a large pot of water and add enough salt to taste like seawater. Add the agnolotti and cook until tender, about 4 minutes. You don't want this pasta to be al dente. Meanwhile, in a sauté pan over medium heat, combine the Parmesan broth, garlic, and olive oil. Cook until reduced to about ½ cup (125 ml), 5 or 6 minutes. With a slotted spoon, transfer the pasta from the water to the sauté pan. Stir in ¼ cup (60 g) of the parsley butter and the chopped parsley. Season with salt to taste.

8.   To serve, divide among four bowls. Top with the bread crumbs, Parmesan, and fried mushrooms and serve.

Though we usually serve this as a side dish with rabbit at Le Pigeon, it doubles as a satisfying vegetarian main. The twist here is that we use crepes rather than pasta sheets to give this veggie lasagna an extra-buttery richness. If you're new to making crepes, be warned that some may not come together the first time around. That's pretty standard, and there's enough batter in this recipe to allow a few mistakes. Feel free to make this one day ahead of time, as it helps to have everything set in the refrigerator overnight. {SERVES 8}

CREPE LASAGNA, CHARD, SWEET ONION

Crepes

2 cups (250 g) all-purpose flour
8 eggs
2 cups (500 ml) whole milk
1 cup (250 ml) water
½ cup (125 g) unsalted butter, melted, plus 2 tablespoons softened
1 teaspoon kosher salt
1 teaspoon truffle butter
1 teaspoon freshly grated nutmeg

Béchamel Sauce

¼ cup (60 g) unsalted butter
¼ cup (30 g) all-purpose flour
2 cups (500 ml) whole milk, warmed
1 teaspoon kosher salt
1 teaspoon freshly grated nutmeg

Filling

2 tablespoons unsalted butter, plus more for greasing
2 sweet onions, thinly sliced
4 cloves garlic, thinly sliced
¼ cup (60 ml) white balsamic vinegar
½ teaspoon kosher salt
3 bunches white Swiss chard, stems removed
¾ cup (60 g) grated Parmesan
¾ cup (60 g) grated pecorino
2 cups (500 g) fresh ricotta

1.   To make the crepes, in a blender combine the flour, eggs, milk, water, ½ cup (125 g) of melted butter, salt, truffle butter, and nutmeg. Blend until smooth. Refrigerate for 30 minutes to let the batter rest.

2.   Lightly grease an 8-inch (20cm) nonstick pan over medium-high heat with the 2 tablespoons of softened butter. Add 2 tablespoons of the crepe batter to the pan (you can use a 1-ounce/30g ladle, if you have one). Swirl the pan in a circular motion to evenly coat the pan with a thin layer of batter. Cook until brown and pliable, about 1 minute. Using a rubber spatula, gently flip the crepe over and cook for 30 seconds longer. Remove from the pan and repeat with the remaining batter, adding more butter to the pan if necessary. Lay a piece of parchment paper on top of each crepe before you stack the next one on top. (This process can be done a day ahead of time and the stacked crepes covered and stored in the refrigerator. You will need 24 crepes for this recipe.)

{Continued}

3.   To make the béchamel sauce, in a heavy saucepan over medium heat, melt the butter. Add the flour and stir using a wooden spoon. (We are making a roux, a mixture of flour and butter that will thicken the sauce.) Cook the roux, stirring constantly, until it starts to smell nutty, about 2 minutes. You don't want it to color much. Once the roux is cooked, use a whisk to mix in the warm milk; season with the salt and nutmeg. Cook gently until it comes up to a simmer and thickens, about 10 minutes. Remove from the heat and let cool to room temperature.

4.   To make the filling, in a large, heavy pot over medium heat, melt the butter. Add the onions, garlic, balsamic vinegar, and salt. Cook, stirring occasionally, until the onions are soft, about 5 minutes. Add the chard and cook until wilted and softened, about 5 minutes. Remove from the heat, transfer the contents of the pan to a colander, and let drain for 10 minutes. Chop coarsely and set aside.

5.   Preheat the oven to 350°F (180°C) and grease a 9 by 13-inch (23 by 33cm) baking dish with butter. In a bowl, stir together the Parmesan and pecorino.

6.   To assemble the lasagna, layer six crepes in the bottom of the prepared dish. Next, spread a quarter of the béchamel over the crepes. Sprinkle a quarter of the ricotta and a quarter of the chard mixture on top. Layer six more crepes on top of the chard and sprinkle with a quarter of the Parmesan mixture. Spread a quarter each of the béchamel, ricotta, and chard mixture on top. Repeat two more times with the crepes, Parmesan mixture, béchamel, ricotta, and chard mixture. Sprinkle the remaining Parmesan mixture on top to create a nice brown crust.

7.   Cover the baking dish with aluminum foil and bake for 45 minutes. Remove the foil and continue to bake until golden brown, about 10 minutes more. Remove from the oven and let cool slightly. You can eat it right away, but it will be slightly messy. If you want to cut nice squares, simply refrigerate overnight. Remove the next day, cut portions, and reheat for about 10 minutes at 350°F (180°C) before serving.

Due to the richness of this dish, we like to serve these leeks with a lean piece of pork or a nice Lamb T-Bone (page 246). It is also a great pasta substitute for that gluten-free friend you have. The idea of using leeks cut in the shape of pasta has made its way onto the LP menu quite a few times, including in leek pesto and leeks with Parmesan and butter. However, this carbonara version was the first, and it's still Gabriel's favorite. {SERVES 4}

LEEK CARBONARA

4 large leeks, white and light green parts only
Kosher salt
7 ½ ounces (210 g) pancetta, thinly sliced into batons
1 yellow onion, thinly sliced
A small pinch of red pepper flakes
½ cup (125 ml) water
2 egg yolks
½ cup (40 g) grated Parmesan, plus more for serving
Freshly ground black pepper
A squeeze of fresh lemon juice

1. Cut the leeks into a thick julienne, so that the pieces are roughly the same size and shape as fettucine. Prepare an ice water bath.

2. Bring a large pot of salted water to a rolling boil over high heat. Add the leeks and blanch for 30 seconds. Using a spider or large slotted spoon transfer the leeks to the ice water bath to cool for 5 minutes. Remove the leeks from the ice water bath, wrap them in a cloth towel, and wring out any excess water.

3. In a heavy sauté pan over medium heat, sauté the pancetta until the fat is rendered, about 5 minutes. Drain off half of the fat and return the pan to the heat. Add the onion and red pepper flakes and continue to cook until the onion is translucent, about 2 minutes. Add the leeks to the pan and, using tongs, toss to combine. Add the water and cook for 1 minute longer. Remove from the heat and, stirring rapidly, add the egg yolks and Parmesan. Season with salt, pepper, and the lemon juice.

4. Divide the leeks among four bowls and sprinkle each bowl with Parmesan to serve.

CHAPTER 12

CHOCO, TART, PROFIT

This chapter is a collaboration between Gabriel and Lauren Fortgang, LP's excellent pastry chef and Andy's wife: a look back at five years of desserts, as told by Lauren.

According to dessert expert and Portland bon vivant Paul "Big Paulie" Rosenfeld, "Lauren can make all the classical desserts from anywhere in the world, but in Portland she is the classic." And Paul is right.

This was the first dish I put on the dessert menu at Le Pigeon. It was actually 2 years before I started working there. Nate Flansburgh, the pastry chef at the time, was out of town, and I had volunteered to help out in his absence. I didn't realize until the week before that I would be working a crazy amount of overtime at Paley's Place because it was Thanksgiving week, so I had to come up with a dessert that would please the people and not kill me.

And so I give to you that dish. We sold out of it halfway through the first night and I had to come back to the restaurant to make more. Did anyone ask for a description before they ordered? No. If they had, they would have been reassured that the cake is a simple flourless one, there are no pickles, and "jazz" is just a Le Pigeon term for sauce. {SERVES 8 TO 10}

MRS. PICKLES'S CHOCOLATE CAKE, CARAMEL CORN, MILK JAZZ

Milk Jazz

¾ cup (185 g) sugar
¼ cup (60 ml) heavy cream
1 tablespoon unsalted butter
1 (14-ounce/400g) can sweetened condensed milk
½ teaspoon kosher salt

Caramel Popcorn

2 tablespoons vegetable oil
¼ cup (50 g) popcorn kernels
1½ cups (375 g) sugar
1½ tablespoons unsalted butter
¼ cup (60 ml) water
1 tablespoon kosher salt
¼ teaspoon baking soda

Chocolate Cake

¼ cup (30 g) all-purpose flour
¼ cup (20 g) unsweetened cocoa powder
½ teaspoon kosher salt
4 ounces (115 g) dark chocolate (we use Theo 70% Dark Chocolate), roughly chopped
6 tablespoons butter
3 eggs
1 cup (250 g) sugar
1 teaspoon coffee extract or vanilla extract
¼ cup (60 ml) sour cream

1. The first thing to do is make the milk jazz (for a shortcut, see the variation on page 288). In a small saucepan over high heat, combine the sugar with about 2 tablespoons of water—just enough so the sugar resembles wet sand. Cook until the sugar turns an amber color and begins to caramelize, 5 or 6 minutes. Using a whisk, whisk in the cream and butter. Be careful: the mixture will release a lot of steam and the sugar will seize up. Reduce the heat to medium and continue cooking until the sugar is dissolved again, 2 or 3 minutes. Whisk in the sweetened condensed milk and salt, transfer to a bowl, and let cool.

2. Next, make the caramel popcorn. Grease a large bowl and set it aside. To pop the corn on the stove top, use a pot with a lid that will hold at least 4 quarts (4 l). Heat the vegetable oil over high heat. When the oil is very hot, add the popcorn and cover the pot with the lid. Using oven mitts or a thick towel, shake the pot from time to time, like you did with Jiffy Pop during sleepovers. Continue to shake every few seconds even when the kernels start popping. Keep shaking the pot until the popping slows down and almost stops. Remove the pot from the heat and pour the popcorn into the greased bowl.

3. Place a silicone baking mat on a baking sheet. Have a whisk and a heat-proof spatula set aside and ready to use. In a medium pot over high heat, combine the sugar, butter, and the water. Meanwhile, measure out the salt and the baking soda separately and set them next to the stove. As the sugar

{Continued}

and butter cook, swirl the pan (do not stir) until the sugar is just beginning to turn a light caramel color, 5 to 7 minutes. When the sugar is light caramel, whisk in the salt and then the baking soda. (Keep an eye on the sugar while it is cooking because the caramelization happens very fast and it can go from light caramel to blackened sugar in a matter of seconds.) Quickly remove the caramel from the heat and pour it over the popcorn in the bowl. Using the spatula, stir the caramel into the popcorn. Try to get it all coated. Pour the caramel popcorn out onto the silicone baking mat and press it out with the spatula into a thin layer. When the popcorn is cool, break it up and store it in an airtight container until you are ready to use it.

4. To make the chocolate cake, grease an 8-inch (20cm) round cake pan and line the bottom with a parchment paper circle. Preheat the oven to 350°F (180°C). In a bowl, sift together the flour, cocoa powder, and salt and set aside. Heat a pan of water over medium heat on the stove top. Set a metal bowl on top of the pan and add the chocolate and butter. Stir frequently until the chocolate is melted and thoroughly combined with the butter. Remove from the stove top and set aside. In a medium bowl, whisk together the eggs and sugar until smooth. Whisk in the coffee extract followed by the sour cream. Add the chocolate mixture and whisk just until everything is incorporated. Whisk in the dry ingredients until just blended. Pour the batter into the prepared cake pan and bake until the center looks set when you jiggle the pan slightly, 25 to 30 minutes. Remove the cake from the oven and let cool. Run a knife around the sides of the pan before inverting the cake onto a plate.

5. To serve, place the cake on a large plate or (preferably) on a well-deserved cake stand. Drizzle the milk jazz over the top. You will have more than you need, so you can save the rest for a delicious treat another time. Pile the caramel popcorn in the center of the cake and enjoy.

VARIATION: If you have a pressure cooker, you can use this shortcut to make the milk jazz. Peel the label off a 14-ounce (400g) can of sweetened condensed milk, place the unopened can in a pressure cooker, and add enough water to submerge the can by at least ½ inch (12 mm). Seal the pressure cooker and bring it up to high pressure over high heat. Once you reach that, reduce the heat to the lowest possible setting. Cook for 40 minutes. Remove the lid of the pressure cooker and allow the can to cool before opening. This is very important! If you try to open the can while it is too hot, the hot dulce de leche could explode and burn you.

Portland is a coffee and doughnuts town. Actually, no, let us rephrase: Portland is *the* coffee and doughnuts town.

Why? I can only guess. Maybe it's the city's history of logging camps and shipyards. Or maybe it's the endless months of drizzle and *Twin Peaks* chill (if the show had been filmed in Oregon, Agent Cooper would have surely swapped his cherry pie for a maple bar).

Yes, it seems there has always been a coffee and doughnut vibe here. The only difference now is that there are *more* coffee and *more* doughnut shops. And, of course, there's the inflation. What was once black coffee in a thermos and an old-fashioned glazed is now a $4 single-origin Peruvian with a "VooDoo Doll" doughnut.

These somewhat healthier doughnuts are not fried but instead baked in doughnut pans that you can find at any specialty kitchen-ware store. {SERVES 8 TO 12}

ZUCCHINI DOUGHNUTS

2 tablespoons freshly squeezed lemon juice
1¼ cups (160 g) powdered sugar
2 eggs
½ cup (125 ml) vegetable oil
1 cup (250 g) sugar
½ teaspoon vanilla extract
1¾ cup (220 g) all-purpose flour
1 teaspoon baking soda
½ teaspoon baking powder
½ teaspoon kosher salt
⅛ teaspoon ground cinnamon
2 cups (300 g) finely grated zucchini

1. Preheat the oven to 325°F (165°C) and grease two doughnuts pans. (If you only have one, you can cook the doughnuts in batches.)

2. In a small bowl, whisk together the lemon juice and powdered sugar until smooth. It should look like a relatively thick paste. Set this aside for dipping the doughnuts when they come out of the oven.

3. In a large bowl, combine the eggs, vegetable oil, sugar, and vanilla extract and whisk to combine; it should look thick and creamy. In a separate bowl, sift together the flour, baking soda, baking powder, salt, and cinnamon. Add the dry ingredients to the large bowl and whisk until fully incorporated. Fold in the zucchini.

4. Pour the batter into the greased pans, filling each well about halfway. Bake the doughnuts until they are golden brown around the sides and spring back when the tops are lightly pressed, 15 to 20 minutes.

5. Flip the doughnuts out onto a cooling rack. While the doughnuts are still warm, dip them into the glaze on the rounded side of each doughnut. Place the doughnuts back on the cooling rack so that any excess glaze can fall off. Serve warm or at room temperature.

Although it's one of my favorite traditional desserts, I have a beef with many a restaurant's carrot cake: too often it arrives with an unwanted parade of chunky nuts, raisins, and pineapple; the frosting is either a cream cheese bomb or completely flavorless; and, contrary to its name, it's often difficult to find even a trace of carrots. So here is my solution: this cake has two different forms of carrots in the cake itself, both a cooked puree of carrots and freshly grated carrots. Then, because I couldn't help myself, I've added a carrot tuile (a thin cookie that comes from the French word for *roof tile*, which it resembles) and a carrot gelée. Yes, it's a bit precious, and there are a lot of steps to work through, but I promise, it's worth it.

Carrot cake is synonymous with spring. The bunnies are out, the carrots are growing, and flowers are blooming. Chamomile is one of those early spring flowers, so it seemed fitting to pair this cake with a delicate chamomile ice cream. {SERVES 12}

CARROT CAKE, RAISINS, PECANS, CHAMOMILE ICE CREAM

Cooked Carrots

12 ounces (340 g) carrots, peeled and
    sliced ½ inch (12 mm) thick

Tuiles

¼ cup plus 2 tablespoons (90 g)
    Cooked Carrots (see above)
1 egg white
1 tablespoon sugar
⅛ teaspoon kosher salt

Cake

1½ cups (190 g) all-purpose flour
1½ teaspoons baking soda
½ teaspoon ground cinnamon
½ teaspoon kosher salt
2 eggs
¾ cup (180 ml) vegetable oil
1¼ cups (315 g) sugar
1½ teaspoons vanilla extract
⅔ cup (170 g) Cooked Carrots
    (see above)
¾ cup (120 g) finely grated carrot

1. The cooked carrots are used in both the tuiles and the cake, so you'll make enough for both. Place the sliced carrots in a small pot over medium-high heat with enough water to cover. Bring to a boil and cook until soft, 15 to 20 minutes. Remove from the heat, drain the water, and transfer the carrots to a food processor. Pulse, scraping down the sides as necessary, until the carrots are smooth. (If you're feeling fanciful and would like to make the tuiles with different colored carrots—purple or yellow, for instance—cook those 4 ounces/115 g of carrots separately.)

2. Next, make the tuiles. Preheat the oven to 225°F (105°C). Place the ¼ cup plus 2 tablespoons (90 g) cooked carrots in the blender with the egg white, sugar, and salt. Blend them on low until the ingredients are combined. Slowly turn the blender speed up until the mixture looks smooth. Pour the puree through a fine-mesh strainer to make sure there are no carrot chunks remaining.

3. Using an offset spatula, spread the tuile batter on a silicone baking mat placed on a baking sheet. Spread it as evenly as you possibly can. The slightest difference can be a matter of one part of the tuile being sticky while the other part is crisp. Bake until you can touch the top of the batter without it sticking to your finger, 25 to 30 minutes. Using a pizza cutter, cut ½- to ¾-inch (1 to 2cm) strips. Continue cooking until the tuiles feel totally dry, about 10 minutes more. Carefully pull each strip off of the baking mat and twist to shape. (See illustrations on page 292.) Transfer them to a cooling

Cream Cheese Frosting

1 pound (450 g) cream cheese
1 cup (125 g) powdered sugar

Riesling Raisins

½ cup (125 ml) riesling
2 tablespoons sugar
½ cup (90 g) golden raisins

Candied Pecans

½ cup (60 g) pecans
2 teaspoons maple syrup

Carrot Gelée (page 293)
Chamomile Ice Cream (page 311),
    made at least 6 hours ahead

rack and let cool completely before storing. These will keep for 2 or 3 days in an airtight container.

4.   Now onto the main event, the actual cake. Preheat the oven to 325°F (165°C). Grease an 18 by 26-inch (45 by 66 cm) sheet pan and line with parchment paper. In a bowl, sift together the flour, baking soda, cinnamon, and salt. Set aside. In a separate large bowl, whisk together the eggs, vegetable oil, and sugar until smooth and creamy. Whisk in the vanilla extract, then the sifted dry ingredients. The batter will seem really stiff at first, but it will get easier to whisk as the ingredients become combined. Whisk in the remaining ⅔ cup (170 g) cooked carrots and then fold in the grated carrots. Spread the batter evenly onto the baking sheet. Bake until a toothpick inserted comes out clean and the cake bounces back when lightly pressed, 20 to 25 minutes. Set aside to cool.

5.   To make the frosting, cut the cream cheese into cubes and place in a food processor with the powdered sugar. Pulse until the cream cheese is smooth. You will likely need to scrape down the sides from time to time to make sure that there are no lumps.

6.   To make the riesling raisins, in a small saucepan over medium-high heat, combine the riesling and sugar. Bring to a boil, add the raisins, and reduce the heat to a simmer. Simmer until the raisins are plump, about 5 minutes. Remove from the heat and set aside to cool.

{Continued}

CARROT TUILE

Peel, slice, and cook carrots until they are soft.

Fill blender with cooked carrots, egg whites, sugar, and salt. Blend on low until it comes together, then turn speed up until mixture is smooth.

Strain mixture to filter out carrot chunks.

Spread mixture out on a baking mat using an offset spatula. Make it as even as possible!

Bake for 25–30 minutes.

Take out of oven and cut vertical strips with a pizza cutter.

Place back in oven for 10 or so minutes.

Carefully pull each strip and twist to shape.

Let cool, place on top of cake, and serve!

7.   To make the candied pecans, preheat the oven to 275°F (135°C). Grind the pecans in a food processor until they are very fine. Place them in a small bowl and stir in the maple syrup until the pecans are thoroughly coated in the syrup. Spread them out on a baking sheet and bake, stirring every 10 minutes or so, until they no longer feel wet or sticky, 20 to 25 minutes. Set aside to cool until you are ready to serve the dessert. These can be made ahead and stored in an airtight container for up to a week.

8.   To assemble the cake, trim off the edges of the cake. Cut the cake in thirds lengthwise. Cover a cutting board, an upturned rectangular pan, or other sturdy surface with parchment paper and place one of the cake thirds on top. Spread a thin layer of the frosting on top of the cake. It helps to use an offset spatula to make the frosting even. Place another piece of cake on top. Repeat with more frosting and the third piece of cake. Finish by frosting the top of the cake. Place the cake in the refrigerator for an hour; this will make it easier to cut into pieces.

9.   Remove the cake from the fridge and, using a warm knife, cut the cake into rectangles, with two rows on the short end and six on the long side. The cake can be stored in the refrigerator, cut, until you are ready to serve it.

10. To serve the cake, begin by cutting small cubes of the carrot gelée. Place each piece of carrot cake on the side of a plate. Sprinkle the top of each piece of cake with the candied pecans. Place five or six cubes of the gelée on the plate. Add some raisins next to the gelée and drizzle a little bit of the raisin syrup around the plate. Arrange a carrot tuile on top of each piece of cake. Finally, place a scoop of chamomile ice cream in the middle of the gelée cubes and raisins and serve.

Carrot Gelée

¾ cup (180 ml) plus 1 tablespoon
   carrot juice
1½ teaspoons (½ package) gelatin
   powder
3 tablespoons sugar
¼ vanilla bean
⅛ teaspoon kosher salt

MAKES 1 CUP

Grease a 4-inch (10cm) square bowl (a storage container works well here). Put ½ cup (125 ml) of the carrot juice in a small bowl. Sprinkle the gelatin over it and whisk them together. Meanwhile, place the sugar in another small bowl. Scrape the seeds out of the vanilla bean into the sugar and stir them in. Discard the pod. In a small saucepan over medium heat, warm the remaining ¼ cup plus 1 tablespoon carrot juice and add the vanilla sugar and salt. As soon as the sugar is dissolved, pull the saucepan off the heat. Add the carrot juice and gelatin mixture to the saucepan and whisk until smooth. Pour into the prepared bowl and place in the refrigerator for at least 2 hours. Once the gelée is set, the dish should be covered. The gelée will keep in the refrigerator for up to 1 week.

A note from Gabriel: People always ask me how much pot I was smoking when I came up with the idea for this dessert, and I can honestly respond, "I don't remember." I *do* know that when I was a kid and came home from school with my parents still at work, an Eggo waffle with ice cream and maple syrup was my favorite forbidden snack. I'm shocked that people are so surprised that we added bacon to the mix. What else do you want to eat with maple syrup? It seems so logical to me, and I would like to think that we were at the forefront of the bacon and dessert revolution, a combo that is pretty played out by now. Still, this one isn't going anywhere. When Lauren started as pastry chef, she took the maple ice cream to a completely new (and creamier) level by changing the maple syrup to maple sugar.

If you would like to serve this like we do at the restaurant, double the amount of bacon that you cook so you can sprinkle some on top when you serve it. {SERVES 12}

HONEY BACON APRICOT CORNBREAD, MAPLE ICE CREAM

3 slices bacon, finely diced
¾ cup (90 g) all-purpose flour
¼ cup (60 g) sugar
2 teaspoons baking powder
½ teaspoon baking soda
½ teaspoon kosher salt
1¼ cups (190 g) cornmeal
2 eggs
¾ cup (180 ml) buttermilk
½ cup (125 ml) milk
3 tablespoons honey
1 tablespoon molasses
½ cup (60 g) thinly sliced dried apricots
Maple Ice Cream (page 311)

1. Preheat the oven to 325°F (165°C). Butter and flour an 8-inch (20cm) square baking pan and set aside.

2. In a large sauté pan over medium-high heat, cook the bacon, stirring occasionally, until crisp. Transfer to a plate lined with paper towels to drain. Set aside.

3. In a large bowl, sift together the flour, sugar, baking powder, baking soda, and salt, then stir in the cornmeal. In a medium bowl, whisk the eggs until well combined. Stir in the buttermilk and milk, then whisk in the honey and molasses. Even though these are thick ingredients, try to get them as thoroughly mixed in as possible. Pour half of the wet mixture into the large bowl with the dry ingredients. Whisk by hand until smooth. Add the rest of the wet ingredients to the dry and continue to whisk until the mixture is smooth again. Fold in the apricots and most of the bacon; reserve a little bacon for topping at the end.

4. Pour the batter into the prepared pan and bake for 25 minutes. Rotate the pan in the oven and continue to cook until the cornbread has risen and the center is firm and dry when a toothpick is inserted, about 25 minutes more. Remove from the oven and let cool on a cooling rack. Once cool, run a knife around the edges of the pan to release the cornbread and flip it onto a cutting board. Cut the cornbread into twelve squares.

5. To serve, return the cornbread squares to the oven for 5 minutes to warm up. Place each square on a plate, top with a large scoop of maple ice cream and a few sprinkles of bacon.

My grandmother made the best piecrust in the world, and the pie she was best known for was her apple pie. She worked magic with anything she made with apples. My grandfather was so enamored with her applesauce that he insisted on putting it on ice cream. This dessert is inspired by them.

Crostada is another word for a free-form tart, also called a *galette*. I've included four different accompaniments for the crostada; they are all delicious, so just choose the one that sounds best (or make them all and let your guests choose). The brown butter ice cream adds a nutty quality, and the cider caramel brings out the juiciness in the apples and softens the tart apple flavor with buttery goodness. The vanilla crème fraîche is so supple and creamy that it's like a pillow for your taste buds. And the cheddar, well, if it's good cheddar, it's just damn good. {SERVES 8}

APPLE CHEDDAR CROSTADA, CHOOSE-YOUR-OWN CONDIMENT

1¼ cups (155 g) all-purpose flour, plus more for kneading and rolling

½ teaspoon kosher salt

½ cup (125 g) cold unsalted butter, cubed

2 tablespoons crème fraîche

3 tablespoons cold water

½ cup (60 g) grated aged cheddar

4 apples, preferably tart

¼ cup (60 g) granulated sugar

¼ cup (50 g) turbinado sugar

Brown Butter Ice Cream (optional; page 311)

Cider Caramel Sauce (optional; page 298)

Vanilla Crème Fraîche (optional; page 298)

Slices of cheddar cheese (optional)

1. In a food processor, combine the flour, salt, and butter. Pulse until the mixture starts to resemble coarse pebbles. Add the crème fraîche and water and pulse until the dough just begins to come together. Turn the dough out onto a floured work surface and knead the grated cheese into it. Divide the dough into eight equal pieces. Roll each portion of dough into a ball, wrap in plastic wrap, and refrigerate for 15 minutes.

2. Preheat the oven to 350°F (180°C).

3. Peel the apples and slice them ¼ inch (6 mm) thick. Place them in a medium bowl and toss them with the granulated sugar. Set aside.

4. Line two baking sheets with parchment paper. Pull the dough out of the refrigerator and, on a floured work surface, roll each ball into a disk about ⅛ inch (3 mm) thick. Place the circles of dough onto the prepared baking sheets. Arrange the apple slices to your liking on each circle of dough, leaving a 1-inch (2.5cm) border uncovered. Fold the edges of the dough over the edges of the apple slices. Pinch the sides together where there are cracks. Brush the tops of the crostadas with the remaining liquid from the sliced apples. Sprinkle the turbinado sugar over each crostada. Bake until the crust is golden brown, 30 to 35 minutes. Let cool and then serve with any or all of the suggested accompaniments.

VARIATION: To make one large crostada, roll out all of the dough into a single circle 12 inches (30 cm) in diameter. Follow the steps for assembling the individual crostadas. Bake at 350°F (180°C) until the crust is golden brown, 35 to 45 minutes.

Cider Caramel Sauce

1 cup (250 g) sugar
¼ cup (60 ml) heavy cream
¼ cup (60 ml) apple cider
2 tablespoons unsalted butter
¼ teaspoon kosher salt

MAKES 1 CUP

In a small saucepan over high heat, combine the sugar with just enough water so that it resembles wet sand, about ¼ cup (60 ml). Cook until the sugar begins to caramelize and turns an amber color, 5 or 6 minutes. Whisk in the cream. The mixture will send up a lot of steam, so be careful not to get burned. The sugar will also seize up. Reduce the heat to medium and continue cooking until the sugar is dissolved again, 2 or 3 minutes. Whisk in the cider, butter, and salt. Transfer to a bowl and let cool.

Note: This sauce is delicious as is, but if you want to give it even more flavor, cook down 2 cups (500 ml) of cider to ¼ cup (60 ml). This will intensify the flavor of the cider in the sauce.

Vanilla Crème Fraîche

1 vanilla bean
1 cup (250 ml) crème fraîche

MAKES 1 CUP (250 ML)

Cut the vanilla bean in half lengthwise and scrape out the seeds using the tip of a paring knife. Discard the pod. In a medium bowl, combine the crème fraîche and vanilla seeds and whisk until the mixture forms medium-stiff peaks (this happens more quickly than with heavy cream, so be careful not to overwhip).

If Hawaii had a flavor, it would taste like this. Every February, Andy and I go to Oahu for our wedding anniversary. It's smack in the middle of the winter, and I come back wanting even more sun and tropical fruit. February is also a few months into the season when you can get apples and pears but hardly anything else, which is the perfect time for a dessert that is bright and bursting with flavor. The pie is tasty on its own, but it's even more delectable with the macadamia topping, milk foam, rum-soaked pineapple, and pineapple sorbet. I've included these recipes but kept them separate so that you can choose how adventurous you'd like to be with your accompaniments.

{MAKES 8 INDIVIDUAL PIES}

BANANA CREAM PIE, PINEAPPLE, MACADAMIA NUTS

Piecrust

7 tablespoons (110 g) unsalted butter, softened
¼ cup (60 g) sugar
1 egg yolk
½ teaspoon vanilla extract
¼ teaspoon kosher salt
1¼ cups (155 g) all-purpose flour

Banana Filling

1 tablespoon unsalted butter
3 tablespoons sugar
½ teaspoon kosher salt
2 ripe bananas
1 cup (250 ml) heavy cream
½ cup (125 ml) whole milk

Banana Cream Topping

¼ cup Banana Filling (see above)
1 cup (250 ml) heavy cream
1 tablespoon sugar

Optional Accompaniments

Macadamia Praline (page 302)
Macadamia Milk Foam (page 302)
Rum Pineapple (page 303)
Pineapple Sorbet (page 315)

1. To make the piecrust, in a stand mixer fitted with the paddle attachment, combine the butter and sugar. Begin mixing on low speed. Once the mixture is smooth, add the egg yolk, vanilla extract, and salt and continue to mix on low speed. Once the ingredients are incorporated and the mixture looks smooth again, add the flour all at once. Continue to mix until the dough comes together.

2. Divide the dough into eight equal pieces. Roll each portion of dough into a ball. Place a ball between pieces of wax or parchment paper and then roll it out to a circle 4 inches (10 cm) across. Repeat with the remaining pieces of dough.

3. Preheat the oven to 350°F (180°C).

4. Place eight tart rings, each 3¼ inches (8 cm) across by 1 inch (2.5 cm) high, onto a baking sheet lined with parchment paper. Peel the parchment paper away from the dough rounds and lightly flour both sides. Use your fingers to push the dough into the bottom of the ring and also against the sides. Smooth out any creases. There will be excess dough at the top of the ring. That's okay. Once all the rings have dough in them, place them in the freezer, still on the baking sheet, for 5 minutes.

5. Remove the piecrusts from the freezer and trim the excess dough with a paring knife until the dough is flush with the top of the rings. Prick the bottom of each piecrust several times with the tip of a paring knife. Place the dough back in the freezer for a minimum of 10 minutes.

{Continued}

6. Bake the piecrusts on the baking sheet in the oven for 10 minutes. Rotate the baking sheet and bake until golden brown, 5 minutes more. Allow the piecrusts to cool and remove the rings. If they stick to the rings at all, put them back in the oven for a couple minutes. The heat should help the piecrusts release from the rings. Place the piecrusts back on the baking sheet.

7. To make the banana filling, in a medium saucepan over medium heat, melt the butter. Sprinkle the sugar and the salt around the surface of the butter. Peel the bananas and slice them lengthwise. When the sugar has started to melt, add the bananas to the pan, cut side down. Continue to cook until the bananas start to brown on the cut side, 2 to 3 minutes. Flip each banana half over and cook until the other side has browned, 2 to 3 minutes more. Pour ½ cup (125 ml) of the cream into the pan. Remove the pan from the heat and set aside to cool.

8. Once the bananas have cooled, transfer the contents of the pan to a food processor. Add the remaining ½ cup (125 ml) heavy cream and the milk. Pulse the mixture until it is smooth. (You can make the filling ahead of time and refrigerate it for up to 1 day. When you are ready to fill the piecrusts, remove the filling from the fridge at least 1 hour in advance so it can soften up.)

9. To make the topping, measure out ¼ cup (50 g) of the banana filling. In a stand mixer fitted with the whisk attachment, combine it with the cream and sugar. Whip on medium speed until the mixture has become light and fluffy.

10. To serve, spoon the banana filling into the piecrusts, filling them three-quarters of the way. There may be a little filling leftover depending on the size of the bananas you used. Top the banana filling with the banana cream topping. Sprinkle with the praline. Spoon some milk foam onto the plate and serve with a spoonful of the rum pineapple and a scoop of pineapple sorbet.

 THE PIGEON POUR: This dessert sounds very rich, but it's actually quite light. A dessert wine that is similarly light on its feet is an ideal match. My absolute favorite riesling producer is Dönnhoff, and serving a bottle of their Auslese with this dish will blow your mind. If you are shopping for German wine, ask the salesperson to help you find an Auslese, a late-harvest wine that is sweet but still packs a lot of acidity. It won't be cheap, but it will be cheaper than Sauternes!

{Continued}

Macadamia Praline

½ cup (75 g) unsalted macadamia nuts
¼ teaspoon baking soda
½ teaspoon kosher salt
½ cup (125 g) sugar
2 tablespoons unsalted butter
2 tablespoons water

MAKES ABOUT 1 CUP (225 G)

1.   Preheat the oven to 325°F (165°C). Spread the macadamia nuts on a baking sheet and toast in the oven until just golden brown, 10 to 15 minutes. Remove from the oven and let cool.

2.   Measure out the baking soda, salt, and macadamia nuts separately and set them aside near the stove. Lay a piece of buttered parchment paper on a baking sheet and have a heatproof spatula ready to use.

3.   In a small saucepan over medium-high heat, stir together the sugar, butter, and water. Cook, without stirring, until the sugar begins to cara-melize and turns a light amber color. (Stirring might cause the mixture to crystallize.) Once the sugar has reached the right color, whisk in the baking soda followed by the salt. Take the mixture off the heat and fold in the macadamia nuts with the spatula. Pour the praline onto the prepared bak-ing sheet and, using the spatula, spread it in a thin layer. Let cool for about 20 minutes.

4.   Once it is cool, break it up into large pieces and place the pieces in a food processor. Pulse until the praline is broken up into tiny pieces. Store in an airtight container until ready to use. It will keep for up to 2 weeks at room temperature.

Note: While this praline puts the crowning touch on the banana cream pie, it is also delicious on its own. Instead of grinding it up in the food proces-sor, you can just break it into small pieces for a tasty snack. The recipe can also easily be doubled or tripled.

Macadamia Milk Foam

2 cups (300 g) unsalted macadamia
    nuts
1 cup (250 ml) soy milk
2 tablespoons sugar
½ teaspoon kosher salt
1 teaspoon soy lecithin

MAKES ABOUT ¾ CUP (180 ML)

Preheat the oven to 325°F (165°C). Spread the macadamia nuts on a bak-ing sheet and toast in the oven until just golden brown, 10 to 15 minutes. Transfer the hot macadamia nuts to a blender and add the soy milk, sugar, salt, and soy lecithin. Begin blending on low speed and slowly turn up the speed to high. Blend until smooth, 1 to 2 minutes. Strain the macadamia milk into a sealable container and discard the ground macadamia nuts. The foam can be refrigerated for up to 3 days.

Note: This foam really adds macadamia nut flavor to the banana cream pie, and its frothiness enhances the many textures on the plate. If you make it ahead of time, just blend it for a few seconds before serving to make it frothy again.

Rum Pineapple

2 cups (500 ml) water
¼ cup (60 ml) dark rum
¼ cup (50 g) firmly packed brown sugar
2 cinnamon sticks
10 whole cloves
2 whole star anise
½ of a pineapple

MAKES 1 PINT (500 ML)

1.　In a medium saucepan over medium-high heat, combine the water, rum, and brown sugar. Bring the liquid to a boil and then reduce the heat to a simmer. Add the cinnamon sticks, cloves, and star anise and continue to cook on very low heat for 15 minutes.

2.　Meanwhile, cut the pineapple. Take the pineapple half and cut it in half again lengthwise. Cut the core out. Cut each piece into four slices lengthwise. Cut these into pieces ¼ inch (6 mm) thick. Set aside.

3.　Back to the pot: Strain the spices out, reserving the liquid. Put the liquid back in the saucepan and add the pineapple. Bring the mixture back up to a boil and then reduce the heat to medium-low. Cook the pineapple for 10 minutes, or until it becomes translucent. Remove the saucepan from the heat. Keep the pineapple in the liquid until you are ready to serve it. The longer it sits, the stronger the flavor will become. The pineapple will keep in the refrigerator for up to 1 week.

Note: In addition to being very complementary to the banana cream pie, the pineapple is also great served with a scoop of ice cream for a quick dessert.

This dessert, which we make with Valrhona Jivara Lactee chocolate, was a big summer hit when we first served it, and now it returns to the menu annually. It's also great in the fall, served with roasted pears. The pepper in the ice cream really sets off the fruit and mellows the richness of the tart. It would be hard to find a dessert that's easier to make and will have as big an impact on your guests.

{SERVE 8 TO 10}

DOUBLE CHOCOLATE TART, STRAWBERRIES, BLACK PEPPER ICE CREAM

1½ cups (130 g) finely ground Oreos or other chocolate cookie crumbs
2½ tablespoons unsalted butter, melted
18 ounces (560 g) milk chocolate
1½ cups (375 ml) heavy cream
1 pint strawberries
2 tablespoons sugar
Candied Hazelnuts (page 306) for garnish
Black Pepper Ice Cream (page 310), made at least 6 hours ahead

1. Preheat the oven to 325°F (165°C) and place ten tart rings, each 3¼ inches (8 cm) across by 1 inch (2.5 cm) high, on a baking sheet lined with parchment paper. To help you unmold the tarts, the tart rings must be lined with parchment paper. Cut 10 strips of parchment paper, each 1¼ inches (3 cm) wide by 10½ inches (26.5 cm) long. Make a loop with the strip and place it inside the tart ring as a liner. Put a piece of tape between the parchment paper and the ring to keep it in place.

2. In a medium bowl, stir together the cookie crumbs and butter. Press the mixture into the bottom of each tart ring. Bake for 12 minutes. Set aside and let cool while you make the filling.

3. Place the chocolate in a medium heatproof bowl. In a small saucepan over medium heat, bring the cream to a boil. Remove from the heat and pour over the chocolate. Stir until the chocolate is melted and the mixture is smooth. Divide the mixture evenly among the cooled crusts. Place the tarts in the freezer for at least 2 hours and up to overnight. (This is to make removing the parchment paper easier.)

4. Slice the strawberries. In a medium bowl, toss the strawberries with the sugar and set aside. To serve, pop the tarts out of the rings and remove the parchment paper strips. Sprinkle the hazelnuts on top of the tarts and serve the strawberries and ice cream on the side.

VARIATION: Alternately, you can make one large tart by using a 9-inch (23cm) springform pan, following the instructions above, and using the same oven temperature and baking and freezing times. Cut into slices while still chilled.

{Continued}

Double Chocolate Tart, Strawberries, Black Pepper Ice Cream, *continued*

Candied Hazelnuts

¼ cup (60 g) sugar
2 tablespoons egg white
¼ teaspoon kosher salt
¾ cup (110 g) hazelnuts

MAKES 1 CUP

Preheat the oven to 250° F (120°C) and line a baking sheet with a silicone baking mat or parchment paper. In a medium bowl, whisk together the sugar, egg white, and salt until frothy. Stir in the hazelnuts until coated. Spread the hazelnuts on the prepared baking sheet and bake, stirring every 10 minutes, until the hazelnuts feel dry, about 50 minutes. Store in an airtight container until ready to use. They will keep for up to 2 weeks at room temperature.

This dish oozes summer to me. When it's hot outside and you can't even imagine eating anything rich, let alone sweet, you will want this. Blackberries and peaches are one of my favorite fruit combinations, so it's good that they happen to be at their peak of ripeness at the same time. I wanted to make a napoleon-type dish with them, but instead of using a flaky pastry like puff pastry, I wanted something with a crunch. Hence the cornmeal cookies that you see here. The honey cream serves as a delicate barrier between the layers and really pulls everything together. {SERVES 8}

PEACH NAPOLEON

Cornmeal Cookies
½ teaspoon baking powder
¾ teaspoon kosher salt
2 cups (250 g) all-purpose flour
1 cup (250 g) plus 2 tablespoons unsalted butter, softened
¾ cup (95 g) powdered sugar
2 teaspoons vanilla extract
¼ cup (40 g) plus 2 tablespoons finely ground cornmeal

Blackberry Sauce
2 pints (600 g) blackberries
½ cup (125 g) sugar

Honey Cream
2 cups (500 ml) heavy cream
¼ cup (60 ml) honey

4 peaches
Peach Caramel Sauce for garnish (optional; page 308)

1. To make the cornmeal cookies, in a bowl, sift together the baking powder, salt, and flour and set aside. In the bowl of a stand mixer fitted with the paddle attachment, combine the butter and powdered sugar and mix on low speed. When the mixture is smooth, add the vanilla extract and mix for a few more seconds. Add the sifted ingredients to the mixer and continue to blend until the ingredients are combined. Add the cornmeal and mix until the dough is smooth.

2. Divide the dough into four equal parts. Roll each portion of dough into a ball. Place a ball between pieces of wax or parchment paper and then roll it out to a rectangle ⅛ inch (3 mm) thick. Repeat with the remaining pieces of dough. Place the sheets of dough on a baking sheet and place them in the refrigerator until they are firm to the touch, about 20 minutes.

3. Preheat the oven to 350°F (180°C).

4. Remove the parchment paper from one side of each sheet of dough and, using a 3-inch (7.5cm) round cutter, cut circles out of the dough. You will need 24 circles. The dough can be rolled out a second time if necessary to get enough circles. Place them on baking sheets and bake in the oven until golden brown, 10 to 15 minutes. Set aside to cool.

5. To make the blackberry sauce, in a small saucepan over medium-low heat, combine half of the blackberries with the sugar. Cook until the blackberries begin to break down and get mushy, about 10 minutes. Reduce the heat to low and cook for another 5 minutes, stirring from time to time so that the sauce doesn't scorch on the bottom. Remove the sauce from the heat and transfer to a food processor. Pulse a few times (too much and it will break up the seeds and make the sauce bitter). Strain the sauce through a fine-mesh sieve and set aside.

{Continued}

6. Next, make the honey cream. In a stand mixer fitted with the whisk attachment, combine the cream and honey. Whip on medium-high speed until it's the consistency of shaving cream. Refrigerate until ready to serve.

7. Just before serving, in a small bowl, mix the remaining half of the blackberries with the blackberry sauce. Cut the peaches into thin slices. To serve, place a cornmeal cookie onto each plate. Arrange the peach slices on top of the cookie to cover it. Place a generous spoonful of honey cream on top of the peaches. Repeat this process and then top with one more cookie. Place a spoonful of blackberries and their sauce on top of the napoleon. Drizzle the caramel sauce around the plate. Repeat this process to make eight napoleons and serve.

Peach Caramel Sauce

½ cup (125 g) granulated sugar
2 tablespoons water
½ peach, peeled and chopped
1 tablespoon unsalted butter
½ cup (125 ml) heavy cream
¼ teaspoon kosher salt

MAKES ABOUT 1 CUP (250 ML)

In a small saucepan over high heat, combine the sugar and water. Bring to a boil and continue to cook until the sugar turns golden brown, about 4 minutes. Stir in the peach and cook until glazed, 2 to 3 minutes. Stir in the butter, followed by the cream and salt. The sugar will seize up and become brittle. Cook until the sugar has melted again and the peaches are soft, about 4 minutes. Pour into a blender and blend on high speed until the sauce is smooth. The sauce can be stored in the refrigerator for up to 4 days.

A dessert's success or failure may be determined by the ice cream it is served with. Making homemade ice cream is not difficult—especially if you keep things simple and forget the xantham gum and glucose—as long as you have a decent ice cream machine.

I have tested and adjusted my basic ice cream recipe over the years, working to create the creamiest and most lush ice cream possible. This base recipe can be adapted to create any of the flavors listed here. {MAKES 1½ QUARTS (1.5 L)}

ICE CREAMS

2 cups (500 ml) heavy cream
2 cups (500 ml) whole milk
1 cup (250 g) sugar
1 teaspoon kosher salt
9 egg yolks

1. In a medium saucepan over medium-high heat, combine the cream, milk, and ½ cup (125 g) of the sugar. Stir in the salt. Cook, whisking from time to time, until the mixture just comes to a boil.

2. While the cream mixture is heating, in a medium bowl whisk together the egg yolks and the remaining ½ cup (125 g) sugar. When the cream mixture comes to a boil, whisk about 1 cup (250 ml) of it into the yolk mixture. Whisking constantly, pour the yolk and cream mixture into the saucepan. Reduce the heat to low and cook, whisking, until the custard coats the back of a wooden spoon, about 1 minute. Using a fine-mesh sieve, strain the custard into a bowl and place over an ice water bath to chill.

3. Once chilled, pour the custard into an ice cream machine and freeze according to the manufacturer's instructions. Store in a sealable container in the freezer for at least 6 hours before serving.

Beenleigh Blue

Crumble 2 ounces (60 g) of Beenleigh Blue (see page 256) or any rich and creamy blue cheese and add it to the ice cream machine just as the ice cream is beginning to thicken. Continue to freeze until it reaches the desired thickness.

Black Pepper

Add 4 teaspoons of freshly ground black pepper to the milk and cream as it comes to a boil. Continue the recipe as directed, straining out the pepper when you strain the custard after tempering the egg yolks.

Brown Butter

In a small saucepan over medium heat, melt ¼ cup (60 g) unsalted butter. Stir in ¼ cup (35 g) milk powder and cook until the butter is browned. (This happens really fast, so be sure to keep your eye on it.) Transfer to a bowl and set aside to cool slightly. When it is still warm but not hot, whisk it into the egg yolk mixture and continue with the recipe as directed.

Chamomile

Add ¼ cup plus 2 tablespoons (5 g) of chamomile tea or whole dried chamomile flowers to the milk and cream as it comes to a boil. Remove the pan from the heat and let the chamomile steep in the liquid for 20 minutes, then continue with the recipe as directed. Strain out the chamomile when you strain the custard after tempering the egg yolks.

Maple

Replace the sugar with 1⅓ cups (225 g) maple sugar. (If you can't find maple sugar at your local grocery store, you can purchase it from www.vermont puremaple.com or a number of other websites.)

Noyaux

You will need 20 apricots pits. (You can save them over time and keep them in the freezer until you are ready to make the ice cream.) Break open the apricot pits with a hammer to remove the kernels inside. Discard the pits and crush the kernels with a mortar and pestle or chop them into small pieces. Add the kernels to the cream and milk. Bring to a simmer, remove from the heat, and steep for 45 minutes. Continue with the recipe as directed, straining out the pits when you strain the custard after tempering the yolks.

Clockwise from top: maple, brown butter, noyaux, black pepper, chamomile

Clockwise from top: pineapple, elderflower, gooseberry, raspberry-honey, rhubarb-vanilla

Who knew that something made from rhubarb could be as dreamy as a Creamsicle? In the springtime, when you can't come up with anything else to do with all that damn rhubarb that's growing like a weed in your garden, give this recipe a try. The addition of vanilla bean gives it an incredibly creamy flavor and a great texture from those tiny little seeds, like you'll find in any high-end vanilla bean ice cream. {MAKES 1½ QUARTS (1.5 L)}

RHUBARB-VANILLA SORBET

1½ pounds (680 g) rhubarb
3 cups (750 ml) water
3 cups (750 g) sugar
1 vanilla bean

1. Cut the rhubarb into pieces 1 inch (2.5 cm) long and put them in a pot with the water and sugar. Cut the vanilla bean in half lengthwise, scrape out the seeds, and add them to the pot along with the pod. Cook over medium heat, stirring from time to time, until the rhubarb breaks down and turns completely mushy, 15 to 20 minutes. Remove from the heat and remove the vanilla bean pod and discard.

2. In batches as necessary (it will probably require two or three batches), transfer the mixture to a blender. Begin blending on the lowest speed and gradually increase the speed to high. When the mixture is completely smooth, transfer it to a bowl and let cool over an ice water bath. Once cool, freeze in an ice cream machine according to the manufacturer's instructions. Store in the freezer for up to 2 weeks.

SORBET

Most pastry chefs probably don't sweat over the quality of their sorbets quite the way I do. My dad has always said that you can judge how good a restaurant is based on how good its sorbet is. Every time we put a new sorbet on the menu, I always have to ask myself, what would Dad say about this?

There is an art to making sorbets. With ice cream, with a few exceptions, the recipe is pretty straightforward. With sorbets, however, the amount of sugar you need to add varies greatly depending on what type of fruit is being used. A surefire way to know if a sorbet base has the right amount of sugar, which in turn will make it freeze properly, is to place a whole egg (in the shell) in the base and see if it floats. If the egg is floating and a patch the size of a quarter is above the surface of the liquid, you've got it in the bag. If more of the egg is above the surface, then there is too much sugar. If the egg isn't floating at all, then it doesn't have enough sugar.

The flavor of elderflower is most commonly associated with St. Germain liqueur. For the liqueur, fresh elderflowers are used. However, there is a very short season for elderflowers, and it's difficult to find them even when they are in bloom. For this reason, I use dried elderflowers for the sorbet. Even with the dried flowers, this sorbet maintains the delicate flavor that is part tropical fruit with just a hint of exotic French perfume. This is the perfect complement to fresh summer fruit and cake. {MAKES 1½ QUARTS (1.5 L)}

ELDERFLOWER SORBET

¾ cup (30 g) dried elderflowers
5½ cups (1.3 l) water
2 cups (500 g) sugar
½ teaspoon kosher salt
¼ cup (60 ml) freshly squeezed
  lemon juice

1.   In a saucepan over medium-high heat, combine the elderflowers, water, sugar, and salt. Stir well and bring to a boil. Remove from the heat and let steep for 10 minutes. The elderflowers will absorb a lot of the liquid and form a sort of cap on top of the liquid.

2.   Strain the liquid into a bowl and stir in the lemon juice. Place over an ice water bath to cool. Freeze in an ice cream machine according to the manufacturer's instructions. Store in the freezer for up to 1 week.

We get our gooseberries from a lovely lady, Tommie van de Kamp, and her husband, Peter. She mostly grows heirloom apples at her farm, Queener Fruit Farm, but she also grows small amounts of red and black currants, marionberries, and gooseberries. I look forward to their short season every year and the chance to make this sorbet, which comes out very creamy and bright from the tartness of the fruit. {MAKES 1½ QUARTS (1.5 L)}

GOOSEBERRY SORBET

2 pounds (900 g) gooseberries
2 cups (500 g) sugar
2 cups (500 ml) water

1.   Start by rinsing the gooseberries. In a saucepan over medium-low heat, combine the gooseberries, sugar, and water. Cook, stirring from time to time, until the gooseberries are completely mushy, about 30 minutes.

2.   Place the warm gooseberries in a blender and blend on medium speed until smooth. Strain with a fine-mesh sieve and place the sorbet base over an ice water bath to cool. Freeze in an ice cream machine according to the manufacturer's instructions. Store in the freezer for up to 2 weeks.

Raspberries are tart, and the addition of honey helps to mellow the fruit just perfectly. It also helps add some richness, resulting in a truly vibrant sorbet. {MAKES 1¼ QUARTS (1.25 L)}

RASPBERRY-HONEY SORBET

2 pints raspberries
1 cup (250 g) sugar
¾ cup (180 ml) honey
1¾ cups (415 ml) water

1. In a saucepan over medium heat, combine the raspberries, sugar, honey, and water. Cook, stirring from time to time to make sure that the sugar doesn't burn on the bottom, just until all of the raspberries are mushy and the sugar is dissolved, 10 to 15 minutes.

2. In two batches (if you put too much liquid in at once, you will have red juice splattered all over the place), transfer to a food processor and pulse until smooth, about 1 minute. Be careful not to pulse too long or the seeds will break and cause the sorbet to become bitter. Strain with a fine-mesh sieve and discard the seeds.

3. Place the sorbet base over an ice water bath to cool. Freeze in an ice cream machine according to the manufacturer's instructions. Store in the freezer for up to 2 weeks.

We serve this with our Banana Cream Pie (page 299), but it is also fantastic on its own. My personal favorite way to eat it is with a shot of rum poured over the top. Consider it a staycation in a glass! {MAKES 1¼ QUARTS (1.25 L)}

PINEAPPLE SORBET

1⅓ cups (330 g) sugar
1⅓ cups (315 ml) water
1 pineapple

1. In a medium saucepan over medium-high heat, combine the sugar and water and bring to a boil. Remove from the heat and let cool to room temperature.

2. Peel and core the pineapple and cut it into 1-inch (2.5cm) pieces. Place the pineapple chunks in a blender with the sugar syrup. Begin blending on the lowest speed and gradually increase the speed to high. When the mixture is completely smooth, strain into a bowl.

3. Freeze in an ice cream machine according to the manufacturer's instructions. Store in the freezer for up to 2 weeks.

A note from Gabriel: It was fall 2007 and we were having huge success with our Honey Bacon Apricot Corn Bread (page 294). Naturally, being the young Turk that I was, I wanted to push the meat-for-dessert concept further, and using foie gras was a natural choice since it pairs well with sweet components.

FOIE GRAS PROFITEROLES

I started out by stuffing foie gras ice cream inside a profiterole with a Cognac crème anglaise and shaving some chocolate on top. It was good, but it needed something more. Erik, my partner in crime, suggested caramel sauce and Maldon flake salt as a better fit. Good man.

The profiteroles started attracting attention, and that's when we knew we had something good. But like all things on our menu, they evolve. One day I thought, "Why aren't we putting foie gras in the caramel?" As it turns out, the rich, livery taste of foie takes caramel sauce to another level. Then I thought, "If it works for caramel, why not for pastry?" One part butter and one part pure foie gras gave the profiteroles an extra kick as well. Now we had traction.

Another year passed and these profiteroles had become an LP fixture. We couldn't have stopped selling them even if we wanted to. But we didn't want to. We wanted to add another layer. So Erik and I started messing around with tapioca maltodextrin (don't judge us; it was 2008), a starch that will turn fat into powder. Since foie gras is pretty much pure fat, when you blend it with tapioca maltodextrin and fold it into powdered sugar, it becomes foie gras powdered sugar—the final piece of the puzzle. Having said all that, this is a complicated recipe. If there is one thing that could be left off, it would be the powdered sugar. We've put that part of the recipe at the end so you can decide for yourself just how ambitious you want to be. {MAKES 18 PROFITEROLES, SERVES 6}

Foie Gras Base

¼ cup (60 g) unsalted butter, cut into 1-inch (2.5cm) cubes and softened

2 ounces (60 g) foie gras, cut into 1-inch (2.5cm) cubes (see page 51)

Foie Gras Caramel Sauce

½ cup (125 g) plus 2 tablespoons sugar

¼ cup (60 ml) water

½ cup (125 ml) heavy cream

2 ounces (60 g) Foie Gras Base (see above)

Profiteroles

¼ cup (60 g) unsalted butter, cubed

1 ounce (30 g) Foie Gras Base (see above)

1 cup (250 ml) water

1 teaspoon sugar

1 teaspoon kosher salt

1 cup (125 g) all-purpose flour

2 to 3 eggs

Foie Gras Ice Cream (page 319)

Foie Gras Powdered Sugar for garnish (optional; page 319)

1. Preheat the oven to 300°F (150°C).

2. To make the foie gras base, place the butter and foie gras in a small baking dish and cover with foil. Warm in the oven until both the butter and foie gras are just slightly softened, about 5 minutes. Transfer to a food processor and blend until smooth. Store in an airtight container in the refrigerator until ready to use, up to 5 days. Leftovers can be stored in the freezer for up to 6 months.

3. To make the caramel sauce, in a medium saucepan over medium-high heat, combine the sugar and water. Swirl the pan (do not stir) until the sauce is just beginning to turn amber. Whisk in the cream. The sauce will bubble up a lot, so be careful. Quickly remove from the heat and whisk in 2 ounces (60 g) of the foie gras base. The sauce can get dark very fast, so have a bowl ready to pour the sauce into. Set aside and let cool at room temperature. If the sauce separates at all, simply whisk it some more and it will come back together. The caramel sauce may be stored in the refrigerator for up to 1 week; let it come to room temperature before using.

4. Preheat the oven to 400°F (200°C).

5. To make the profiteroles, in a medium saucepan over medium heat, combine the butter, 1 ounce (30 g) of the foie gras base, the water, sugar, and

{Continued}

salt. When it comes to a rolling boil, add the flour all at once and stir with a wooden spoon. Reduce the heat to medium-low and cook, stirring vigorously, until a film begins to form on the bottom of the pan, 4 to 5 minutes. Transfer the dough to a stand mixer fitted with the paddle attachment and mix on medium speed until the outside of the bowl is lukewarm and no steam can be seen rising, 5 to 6 minutes. Reduce the speed of the mixer to low and add the eggs one at a time, thoroughly incorporating each egg before adding the next. (You may not need the third egg. Test the dough by putting a small amount between your forefinger and thumb and pulling apart to make a thread. If it doesn't break, the dough has enough eggs and is ready.)

6. Transfer the batter to a pastry bag; the dough will be very sticky. On a parchment-lined baking sheet, pipe 18 (1-inch/2.5cm) mounds (about the diameter of a quarter) about 1 inch (2.5 cm) apart. (If you're not using the profiteroles right away, cover and freeze the raw, piped mounds for up to 1 week. Let them thaw to room temperature before baking.) Bake for 15 minutes, reduce the oven to 350°F (180°C), and bake until the profiteroles are golden brown and sound hollow when tapped, 10 to 15 minutes more. Let the profiteroles cool before assembling.

7. To assemble the profiteroles, warm the caramel sauce over low heat. For each serving, cut three of the profiteroles in half horizontally. Place a small scoop of ice cream inside. Place the top half of each profiterole on top of the ice cream. Garnish with a small amount of caramel sauce. Sprinkle the foie powdered sugar over the top of each and serve.

THE PIGEON POUR: Sometimes when pairing wine with a rich dish, you want a contrast, something to cut the richness. But in this case, screw that! You need to wallow in the richness, swim in it, make it even richer. There is an expression in Yiddish that translates to "When you eat pig, it should drip from your beard." For these profiteroles, Sauternes is the only way to go. We often pair this with a glass of Castelnau de Suduiraut, the second wine of Château Suduiraut. It is a tremendous value for its quality. Really, any Sauternes would work with this dish, but I would recommend splurging here.

Foie Gras Ice Cream

8 ounces (240 g) foie gras, diced
  (see page 51)
½ cup (125 g) sugar
2 egg yolks
¼ cup (60 ml) dry white port
½ cup (125 g) unsalted butter, cut into
  small pieces
½ cup (125 ml) heavy cream

MAKES 2 CUPS (425 G)

1.   Preheat the oven to 250°F (120°C).

2.   Place foie gras in a small baking dish, cover with foil, and render in the oven for 10 minutes (some of the fat will have melted out so it resembles softened butter).

3.   Meanwhile, bring water to a simmer in the bottom half of a double-boiler. In the top bowl of the double-boiler, whisk together the sugar and egg yolks off the heat. Whisk in the port and place the bowl on top of the simmering water. Whisk continually until the mixture thickens and forms a long, thick stream, like a ribbon, when you lift the whisk, 5 to 6 minutes. Transfer to a food processor.

4.   With the food processor running, slowly add the foie gras (both the solids and rendered fat). Add the butter one piece at a time. Continue to run the food processor until all the butter is incorporated before slowly pouring in the cream. Watch very carefully and as soon as it begins to look thick, stop the machine. (Due to the high fat content, it can turn to butter if it is churned too much.) Pour the mixture through a fine-mesh strainer into a bowl. Immediately pour the mixture into an ice cream machine and freeze according to the manufacturer's instructions. Store in an airtight container in the freezer for up to 2 weeks until ready to use.

Foie Gras Powdered Sugar

3 ounces (90 g) foie gras (see page 51)
1¼ cups (25 g) lightly packed tapioca
  maltodextrin
¼ cup (30 g) powdered sugar
Kosher salt

MAKES 2 CUPS (120 G)

1.   Before you start making the foie gras powdered sugar, I have to emphasize one word: *dry*. It is very important that everything you use to make this is as dry as humanly possible. The slightest bit of liquid can ruin it.

2.   Preheat the oven to 250°F (120°C).

3.   The first thing you must do is render the fat out of the foie gras. Yes, there are a few solids besides fat in a lobe of foie gras. Place the foie gras in a shallow baking dish and cover it with foil. Bake until the foie has melted, 10 to 15 minutes. Skim off any solids and discard. This should leave you with approximately 2 tablespoons of rendered foie fat. Refrigerate the fat for at least 20 minutes before proceeding.

4.   Place the tapioca maltodextrin and the rendered fat in a dry food processor. Pulse until they combine into a powder. Place in a dry bowl and fold in the powdered sugar. Add a little salt to taste. Store in a dry container at room temperature for up to 1 week until ready to use.

LE PIGEON PANTRY

By now you've gotten the gist that at Le Pigeon there are a few codes by which we live and breathe. One is that salt, fat, and acid are the holy trinity. Salt is used in multiple layers in many dishes, and a big squeeze of lemon is ever-present.

We use unique vinaigrettes, marinades, and braises throughout our recipes, many of which include weirdo elements like vermouth vinegar, white balsamic vinegar, anchovy extract, chestnut honey, and yuzu juice. We understand that collecting many different vinegars is a hassle both in terms of time and your wallet, but after experimenting, you'll see how much they add to your cooking arsenal.

In the depths of the LP basement, we have a prep kitchen where the team spends the first half of the day. This is where the pantry is, and where we concoct the basics that go into many of our dishes.

AIOLI

Makes 1 cup (250 ml)

2 egg yolks
Juice of 1 lemon
2 large cloves garlic, minced
½ teaspoon kosher salt
¾ cup (180 ml) neutral oil

In a large bowl, whisk together the egg yolks, lemon juce, garlic, and salt. Using a whisk, whisk in the oil in a thin, steady stream to create an emulsion. Refrigerate in an airtight container for up to 2 days.

DEVILED AIOLI

Makes 1 cup (250 ml)

We like to serve this with crab or other seafood that needs a little kick.

2 egg yolks
2 anchovy fillets
1 teaspoon chopped garlic
1 teaspoon espelette pepper
1 teaspoon paprika
1½ tablespoons sherry vinegar
1 tablespoon Dijon mustard
1 cup (250 ml) neutral oil
Kosher salt

In the bowl of a food processor, combine the egg yolks, anchovies, garlic, pepper, paprika, vinegar, and mustard. Puree until smooth, then, with the motor running, add the oil in a thin, steady stream to create an emulsion. Season to taste with salt. Refrigerate in an airtight container for up to 4 days.

HERB AIOLI

Makes 1¼ cups (310 ml)

1 cup (250 ml) Aioli (above)
1 tablespoon minced fresh flat-leaf
    parsley
1 teaspoon minced fresh tarragon
1 teaspoon minced fresh chervil
1 teaspoon minced chives

1 tablespoon Katz sauvignon blanc
    vinegar or other white wine vinegar
    (see sidebar on page 42)
Kosher salt

In a small bowl, stir together the aioli, parsley, tarragon, chervil, chives, and vinegar. Mix well and season with salt to taste. Let sit for about 30 minutes prior to serving to let the flavors marry. Refrigerate in an airtight container for up to 2 days.

BLACK GARLIC VINNY

Makes 1 cup (250 ml)

1 head black garlic, peeled (see sidebar
    on page 81)
¼ cup (60 ml) balsamic vinegar
1 shallot, minced
1 teaspoon kosher salt
⅔ cup extra-virgin olive oil

In a blender, combine the black garlic, vinegar, shallot, and salt. Puree until smooth, then, with the motor running, add the oil in a thin, steady stream to create an emulsion. Refrigerate in an airtight container for up to 2 weeks. Like women, this gets better with age.

BLOOD ORANGE MARMALADE

Makes about 2 cups (500 ml)

5 pounds (2.25 kg) blood oranges
1 teaspoon Chinese five-spice powder
1 pound (450 g) sliced shallots
6 cloves garlic, thinly sliced
¼ cup (60 ml) soy sauce
1 tablespoon sugar
1 tablespoon kosher salt
1 cup (250 ml) mirin
Juice of 2 lemons

Cut each orange in half, juice both halves, and reserve the peels and juice. Cut the peels in half again,

leaving you with thick strips with pulp attached. Using a sharp knife, cut away and discard the pith. Cut the peels in very thin strips. In a large saucepan over medium heat, combine the reserved juice and peels, five-spice powder, shallots, garlic, soy sauce, sugar, salt, and mirin and cook until syrupy and jammy, 30 to 40 minutes. Stir in the lemon juice. Transfer to a jar and refrigerate overnight before using. This will keep up to 1 month in the refrigerator.

BLUE CHEESE DRESSING

Makes 2 cups (500 ml)

⅓ cup (80 ml) apple cider vinegar
2 shallots, minced
1 cup (120 g) crumbled Oregon or
    other good-quality blue cheese
¾ cup (180 ml) sour cream
½ cup (125 ml) buttermilk
1 tablespoon finely chopped fresh
    tarragon
Kosher salt and freshly ground black
    pepper

In a medium bowl, combine the vinegar and shallots and let stand for 20 minutes. Stir in the blue cheese and sour cream until combined but still slightly lumpy. Stir in the buttermilk and tarragon. Season with salt and pepper to taste, stir well, and cover with plastic wrap. Chill for at least 1 hour before using. Refrigerate in an airtight container for up to 4 days. (It's actually best on the second day, when all of the flavors have had a chance to meld.)

BUFFALO BIRD SAUCE

Makes about 2¼ cups (560 ml)

½ cup (125 g) unsalted butter
¼ cup (60 ml) hot pepper sauce, such as Frank's RedHot sauce
¼ cup (60 ml) Moscatel vinegar
¼ cup (60 ml) white wine vinegar
¼ cup (60 ml) good-quality balsamic vinegar
¼ cup (25 g) minced shallots
¼ cup (35 g) pureed sun-dried tomatoes in oil
2 tablespoons garlic, minced
1 teaspoon kosher salt

In a heavy saucepan over medium heat, combine the butter, hot pepper sauce, the vinegars, shallots, sun-dried tomatoes, and garlic and bring to a boil. Reduce the heat to medium and simmer gently for 30 minutes. Season with salt and remove from the heat. Refrigerate in an airtight container for up to 2 weeks.

CORN STOCK

Makes 2 cups (500 ml)

4 ears of corn
½ yellow onion, sliced
1 celery stalk, coarsely chopped
1 teaspoon black peppercorns
2 bay leaves
1 cup (250 ml) dry white wine
4 cups (1 l) water

Remove the kernels from the cobs and reserve them for another use. Cut the corncobs into 2-inch (5cm) pieces. In a large stockpot combine the cobs, onion, celery, peppercorns, bay leaves, white wine, and water. Bring to a boil and then immediately reduce to a simmer. Simmer for 20 to 25 minutes, with the goal of reducing it by half. Strain and reserve. Yes, it should look like Depression-era corn water.

DUCK CONFIT

Makes 6 legs or 1 pound (450 g) of shredded duck

Leaves from 1 bunch fresh thyme
Leaves from ½ bunch rosemary
8 cloves garlic
6 Muscovy duck legs (or 8 legs if they're smaller), each about ¾ pound (375g)

In a food processor, combine the thyme, rosemary, and garlic and puree until it forms a thick paste. Rub the duck legs with the herb mixture and then refrigerate for a minimum of 4 hours, and preferably overnight.

Preheat the oven to 300°F (150°C). Remove the duck legs from the fridge and transfer to a Dutch oven. Cover and cook until the meat is easily penetrated when poked with a fork. It will probably take 4 to 5 hours, but start checking for doneness around the 3-hour mark. If you want to shred the meat right away (it's easier to do this when it's warm), as soon as the legs are cool enough to handle, pick them apart with your fingers, discarding the bones and skin. If you're not using the confit right away, let it cool to room temperature and refrigerate in an airtight container for up to 1 week or store in the freezer for up to 2 months.

FOIE GRAS MOUSSE

Makes 8 ounces (250 g)

8 ounces (240 g) foie gras (see page 51)
1 teaspoon kosher salt
1 tablespoon Sauternes or other sweet white wine

Preheat the oven to 300°F (150°C). Place the foie gras in a Dutch oven and put it in the oven; you're not trying to cook it (or render too much fat) but just to soften it, about 10 minutes max. Transfer the foie gras to a food processor and puree for about 10 seconds, adding the salt and wine while the motor is running. If the foie gras mixture separates, add a couple of ice cubes and continue to process. Transfer to the fridge and store in an airtight container until about 10 minutes before use. Refrigerate in an airtight container for up to 3 days.

GARLIC CHIPS

Makes ¼ cup (30 g)

2 cloves elephant garlic
Neutral oil for frying
Maldon flake salt

Using a mandoline, thinly slice the garlic. In a bowl, soak the garlic slices in hot water to cover for 10 minutes. Drain and pat dry. Add the garlic slices to a saucepan filled with 2 inches (5 cm) of cold oil. Over medium-high heat, and stirring frequently so the garlic doesn't stick, slowly bring the oil up to a very hot frying temperature, about 300°F (150°C). Once the chips are a light brown (be careful not to let them get too brown or they will turn bitter), transfer them to a plate lined with paper towels and sprinkle with Maldon salt. These are best eaten the day they are made.

GARLIC CONFIT

Makes ¼ cup (75 g)

2 heads garlic, cloves separated and sliced about ⅛ inch (3 mm) thick
½ cup (60 ml) extra-virgin olive oil

In a small saucepot over low heat, combine the garlic and olive oil. Simmer until the garlic is translucent, about 7 minutes. Strain and reserve the garlic; save the oil to use in salad dressings or as a simple dip for bread. Refrigerate the confit in an airtight container for up to 2 weeks.

GOAT CHEESE VINNY

Makes 1 cup (250 ml)

1 tablespoon minced shallots
2 tablespoon Katz sauvignon blanc vinegar or other white wine vinegar (see sidebar on page 42)
½ cup (180 g) soft goat's milk cheese
¼ cup (60 ml) buttermilk
1 teaspoon freshly ground black pepper
A pinch of kosher salt

In a small bowl, combine the shallots and vinegar and let stand for about 5 minutes. Add the cheese, buttermilk, pepper, and salt and mix until smooth. Refrigerate in an airtight container for up to 1 week.

GRILLED PICKLED ONIONS (GPOs)

Makes 2 cups (500 g)

½ cup (125 ml) red wine vinegar
¼ cup (60 ml) water
2 tablespoons sugar
1 tablespoon kosher salt
2 sprigs thyme
3 bay leaves
1 teaspoon black peppercorns
1 clove garlic, crushed
¼ teaspoon red pepper flakes
1 large red onion, cut into ½-inch (12mm) rings
Neutral oil for drizzling

Preheat a gas grill or prepare a charcoal grill for cooking over high heat. In a large saucepan over high heat, combine the vinegar, water, sugar, and salt. Wrap the thyme, bay leaves, peppercorns, garlic, and red pepper flakes in cheesecloth and secure with a piece of string. Add to the saucepan and bring to a boil. Remove from the heat and set aside to cool.

Put the onions in a bowl, drizzle a little oil on top, and toss to coat. Grill the onions until you have grill marks on each side and the onion still has some of its texture, 3 to 4 minutes per side. Add the onions to the pickling liquid in the saucepan. Transfer the onions and their pickling liquid to an airtight container and refrigerate. Dig in as early as the next day. The onions will keep indefinitely in the refrigerator.

HERB PISTOU

Makes 1 cup (250 ml)

This is great with fish, poached eggs, or langoustines from the Scottish sea.

Leaves from 1 bunch tarragon
15 chives, coarsely chopped
1 cup (40 g) loosely packed flat-leaf parsley
¾ cup (180 ml) neutral oil
¼ teaspoon kosher salt

Combine all the ingredients in a blender and blend until smooth. Refrigerate in an airtight container for up to 3 days.

LP KETCHUP

Makes 2 cups (500 ml)

¼ cup (60 ml) apple cider vinegar
½ cup (70 g) diced yellow onion
⅛ teaspoon ground cloves
⅛ teaspoon ground allspice berries
6 black peppercorns, ground
⅛ teaspoon mustard powder
¼ cup (50 g) firmly packed brown sugar
1 (14-ounce/440g) can crushed tomatoes
1 clove garlic, minced
1 teaspoon kosher salt

In a heavy saucepan over medium heat, combine the vinegar and onion. Bring to a simmer and simmer for 5 minutes. Add the clove, allspice, peppercorns, and mustard powder and simmer for a minute longer. Add the brown sugar, tomatoes, garlic, and salt. Reduce the heat to medium-low and cook until the ketchup is thick and aromatic—and you're craving French fries—about 45 minutes. Remove from heat and puree in a blender. Refrigerate in an airtight container for up to 10 days.

SPANISH KETCHUP

Makes 2 cups (500 ml)

2 cups (500 ml) LP Ketchup (left) or purchased ketchup
⅛ teaspoon ground cloves
1 teaspoon pimento smoked paprika
½ teaspoon paprika
½ teaspoon ground Chimayo chile or cayenne pepper
1 tablespoon sherry vinegar

In a saucepan over medium heat, combine all of the ingredients. Cook, stirring frequently, for 45 minutes. Remove from the heat and let cool to room temperature. Refrigerate in an airtight container for up to 10 days

SPICY ROSEMARY KETCHUP

Makes 2 cups (500 ml)

1 tablespoon minced fresh rosemary
1 tablespoon olive oil
2 cups (500 ml) LP Ketchup (left) or purchased ketchup
1 teaspoon Tabasco

In a small sauté pan over medium-low heat, warm the rosemary in the olive oil for 2 minutes. In a bowl, fold the rosemary and oil into the ketchup and add the Tasbasco. Refrigerate in an airtight container for up to 10 days.

MUSTARD VINAIGRETTE

Makes ¾ cup (180 ml)

2 tablespoons white balsamic vinegar
2 teaspoons whole-grain mustard
2 tablespoon Dijon mustard
1 small shallot, minced
1 tablespoon chopped fresh flat-leaf parsley
1 teaspoon freshly squeezed lemon juice
½ cup (125 ml) neutral oil
Kosher salt

In a bowl, whisk together all of the ingredients until smooth. Refrigerate in an airtight container for up to 3 days.

ORANGE RELISH

Makes ¼ cup (60 ml)

1 orange
2 tablespoons minced Preserved Lemons (page 326)
1 tablespoon minced red onion
A dash of espelette pepper, or more to taste
½ cup (125 ml) olive oil
Kosher salt

Supreme the orange (remove the peel and cut into segments) and then cut the segments to the size of a pencil eraser; you should have about ¼ cup (20 g). In a bowl, stir together all of the ingredients, adding more espelette pepper if you prefer a spicier relish. Cover and refrigerate. The relish is best if used within 2 days.

OYSTER MAYONNAISE

Makes about 2 cups (500 ml)

6 medium oysters, shucked and drained, with liquid reserved
Juice of ½ lemon
A pinch of kosher salt
½ teaspoon fish sauce
2 dashes of Tabasco
1 large clove garlic
1¼ cups (310 ml) neutral oil

In a blender, combine the oysters and their liquid, the lemon juice, salt, fish sauce, Tabasco, and garlic. Puree until smooth. With the motor running, add the oil in a thin, steady stream to create an emulsion. Refrigerate in an airtight container for up to 2 days.

PARMESAN BROTH

Makes 2 1/2 quarts (2.5 L)

Like shellfish shells, Parmesan rinds are gems that most people throw in the garbage. I wish I could buy just the rinds so I could make this all the time and not just when I've saved up enough to make a batch.

1 pound (450 g) Parmesan rinds
1½ cups (40 g) parsley stems
1 onion, peeled and quartered
1 head garlic, halved
3 quarts (3 l) water

In a 12-inch (30cm) square of cheesecloth, wrap up the Parmesan rinds, parsley stems, onion, and garlic and tie it closed with a piece of butcher's twine. In a large pot over medium heat, bring the water to a simmer. Add the cheesecloth to the pot and simmer for 1½ hours. Remove the cheesecloth and discard. Refrigerate the broth in an airtight container for 1 week or store in the freezer for up to 1 year.

PARSNIP PEAR BUTTER

Makes 1/2 cup (100 g)

¾ cup (140 g) peeled and chopped Bosc pear
¾ cup (120 g) peeled and chopped parsnips
1 cup (250 g) unsalted butter
A pinch of freshly grated nutmeg

Preheat the oven to 300°F (150°C). Place the pears and parsnips in a small baking dish with half of the butter and bake until tender, about 25 minutes. Remove from the oven and pour the contents of the dish into a food processor. Add the remaining butter and process until emulsified. Refrigerate in an airtight container for up to 3 days.

PEPPER JAM

Makes 1 1/2 cups (430 g)

Neutral oil for sautéing
3 orange bell peppers, seeded and diced
1 yellow onion, diced
3 cloves garlic, sliced
1½ teaspoons pimentón paprika
¼ cup (60 ml) balsamic vinegar
¼ cup (60 ml) honey
2 tablespoon chopped chives
½ teaspoon Tabasco
1 tablespoon kosher salt

In a heavy sauté pan over medium heat, heat a thin film of oil. Add the bell peppers, onion, and garlic. Cook until the vegetables have become soft and translucent, about 5 minutes. Add the pimentón paprika, balsamic vinegar, honey, chives, Tabasco, and salt. Reduce the heat to low and cook for 30 minutes more. Remove from the heat, transfer to a food processor, and pulse 4 or 5 times, until it is the texture of a slightly chunky jam. Refrigerate in an airtight container for up to 1 week.

PICKLED FENNEL

Makes 1 1/2 cups (375 ml)

1 cup (250 ml) champagne vinegar
1 tablespoon curry powder
½ cup (125 ml) water
2 tablespoons sugar
2 tablespoons kosher salt
1 tablespoon ground fennel seeds
1 small fennel, bulb, cored and thinly sliced
½ small yellow onion, thinly sliced

In a saucepan over medium heat, combine the vinegar, curry powder, water, sugar, salt, and fennel seeds. Bring to a boil and remove from the heat. In a heatproof bowl, pour the pickling liquid over the fennel and onion. Let the mixture cool to room temperature and serve. Refrigerate in an airtight container for up to 1 week.

PICKLED GARLIC

Makes 1 cup (250 ml)

1¼ cups (310 ml) water
½ cup (125 ml) white wine vinegar
2 tablespoons sugar
1 tablespoon kosher salt
4 heads garlic, cloves separated, peeled, and sliced about ¼ inch (6 mm) thick

In a small saucepan over high heat, combine the water, vinegar, sugar, and salt. Bring to a boil and remove from the heat. In a heatproof bowl, pour the pickling liquid over the garlic. Let cool to room temperature and serve. Refrigerate in an airtight container for up to 1 month.

PICKLED MUSTARD SEEDS

Makes 1/4 cup (60 ml)

¼ cup (35 g) yellow mustard seeds
⅓ cup (80 ml) Moscatel vinegar
1 cup (250 ml) water
3 tablespoons sugar
½ teaspoon kosher salt

In a small saucepan over medium-low heat, combine all the ingredients. Bring to a simmer and simmer until the seeds turn plump and soften, about 45 minutes. Transfer to an airtight container and refrigerate. Will last until infinity and beyond covered in the refrigerator.

PICKLED RADISH

Makes 1 ½ cups (375 ml)

¾ cup (180 ml) cider vinegar
¼ cup (60 ml) water
1 tablespoon sugar
1 tablespoon honey
1 teaspoon dried oregano
2 teaspoons kosher salt
2 cloves garlic, crushed
1 bunch radishes, cut into quarter-sized
    disks

In a small saucepan over high heat, combine the vinegar, water, sugar, honey, oregano, salt, and garlic to a boil, stirring occasionally to dissolve the sugar and salt. In a heatproof bowl, pour the pickling liquid over the radish slices. Let cool to room temperature and serve. Will keep indefinitely in an airtight container in the refrigerator.

POBLANO CREMA

Makes 1 cup (250 ml)

Use this to mellow out any spicy dish. A nice dollop in a hot Mexican soup, for example, can do wonders.

2 poblano peppers (80 g)
1 teaspoon neutral oil
½ cup (125 ml) sour cream
1 tablespoon fresh lime juice
1 tablespoon chopped cilantro
½ teaspoon ground cumin

Preheat a gas grill or prepare a charcoal grill for cooking over high heat, or heat a grill pan on the stove top. Rub the peppers with the oil and grill until the skin is blackened and blistered on all sides, 5 to 6 minutes. Transfer the peppers to a bowl, cover with plastic wrap, and let sit for 20 minutes. Remove the peppers from the bowl and, under cool running water, gently scrape off the blistered skin. Slice the peppers in half, wash away the seeds, and discard the stems.

In a blender, puree the poblanos until smooth. Add the sour cream, lime juice, cilantro, and cumin and pulse until smooth. Refrigerate in an airtight container for up to 3 days.

PRESERVED LEMONS

Makes 2 ½ cups (200 g)

When you preserve citrus in salt and sugar it brings out a whole new aromatic side to the fruit, diminishing the bitterness from the peel and thus letting you use the entire thing. Most people simply cut lemons in half, pack them in a salt-and-sugar mixture in a jar, and leave them to cure. However, we thinly slice the lemons and incorporate other savory ingredients, giving the lemons a whole new depth of flavor. Plus they don't take weeks to cure! These are great in dressings (like the Preserved Lemon Dressing, page 23) or just tossed with some salad greens. They also make a great addition to olive tapenade. Like curing, preserving demands attention to ratios, so be sure to measure the salt and sugar precisely.

5 lemons
¼ cup (60 g) sugar
½ cup plus 1 tablespoon (90 g)
    kosher salt
1 shallot, minced
1 clove garlic, minced
1 teaspoon minced fresh thyme
¼ teaspoon red pepper flake
1 tablespoon good-quality olive oil
    (see sidebar on page 105)

Slice the lemons as thinly as possible, removing the seeds as you go. We use an electric slicer, but a mandoline or even a sharp serrated knife and steady hand should do the trick. In a small bowl, stir together the sugar and salt.

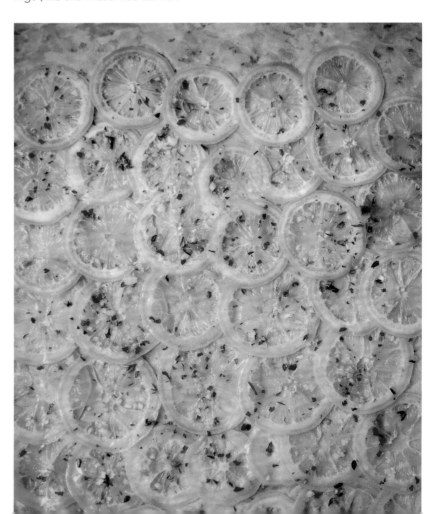

Line a baking sheet with parchment paper and arrange the lemon slices in an even overlapping pattern. When you have covered the surface of the baking sheet, sprinkle half of the sugar-and-salt mixture evenly on top of the lemons, then sprinkle half of the shallots, garlic, thyme, red pepper flakes, and olive oil evenly on top. Add another sheet of parchment paper right on top of the lemons and repeat with another layer of lemons and the remaining sugar-and-salt mixture, seasonings, and oil. Wrap the baking sheet in plastic wrap and refrigerate for 3 days. The preserved lemons should last 1 month in an airtight container in the refrigerator.

RADISH VINNY

Makes ½ cup (125 ml)

2 tablespoons vermouth vinegar
2 red radishes, minced (about 2 tablespoons)
Kosher salt and freshly ground black pepper
⅓ cup (80 ml) olive oil

In a small bowl, whisk together all of the ingredients. Refrigerate in an airtight container for up to 3 days.

SAGE BROWN BUTTER

Makes 1½ cups (120 g)

This nutty butter gives a kick to potatoes and polenta.

½ cup (125 g) unsalted butter
1 tablespoon chopped fresh sage
1 tablespoon aged balsamic vinegar
A pinch of kosher salt

In a small saucepan over medium heat, melt the butter and cook until browned. Remove from the heat and stir in the sage, balsamic vinegar, and salt. Refrigerate in an airtight container for up to 1 week.

SEASONED BREAD CRUMBS

Makes about 1 cup (125 g)

1 cup (125 g) panko
1 tablespoon unsalted butter, melted
¼ teaspoon kosher salt
1 clove garlic, chopped
1 tablespoon chopped fresh flat-leaf parsley

Preheat the oven to 350°F (180°C). In a bowl, toss the panko with the butter, salt, and garlic. Spread on a baking sheet and toast until GBD (golden brown and delicious), about 5 minutes. Toss in the parsley and serve. These are best enjoyed the day they are made.

SEMOLINA ONION RINGS

Serves 2 or 3

5 cups (1.25 l) neutral oil
2 sweet onions, cut into ¼-inch (6mm) rings
Kosher salt
2 cups (340 g) semolina flour
2 teaspoons all-purpose flour
2 teaspoons sugar
½ teaspoon baking powder
½ teaspoon baking soda
2 tablespoons cornstarch
2 eggs, lightly beaten
6 tablespoons vegetable oil
1½ cups (375 ml) club soda

In a deep fryer or large pot, heat the neutral oil to 350°F (180°C). Season the onion rings with salt. In a bowl, sift together the semolina and all-purpose flours, the sugar, baking powder, baking soda, cornstarch, and 2 teaspoons salt. Add the eggs, vegetable oil, and club soda to the dry ingredients and whisk just until incorporated; do not overmix.

Using tongs, dip the onion rings into the batter and then add them, in batches of about 10 rings, to the oil. Fry until golden and crispy,

6 to 8 minutes. (If you're using a deep fryer, shake the basket periodically). Transfer to a plate lined with paper towels and season lightly with salt. Repeat with remaining onion rings and serve immediately.

SESAME OIL VINNY

Makes ½ cup (125 ml)

1 teaspoon balsamic vinegar
1½ teaspoons rice wine vinegar
¼ cup (60 ml) neutral oil
¼ teaspoon sesame oil
½ teaspoon honey
A pinch of kosher salt

In a small bowl, whisk together all of the ingredients. Refrigerate in an airtight container for up to 1 week.

SHELLFISH CRÈME FRAÎCHE

Makes 1 cup (250 ml)

This is great served with pasta. It gives any dish that perfect hint of the sea.

2 cups (500 ml) Shellfish Stock (below)
1 cup (250 ml) crème fraîche

In a saucepan over medium heat, reduce the stock to a thick glacé, about 2 tablespoons. In a bowl, stir the shellfish glacé into the crème fraîche. Refrigerate in an airtight container for up to 2 days.

SHELLFISH STOCK

Makes about 4 quarts (4 l)

Always save your shellfish shells! Making a large shellfish platter is worth it just to save the scraps for this stock.

¼ cup (60 ml) neutral oil
5 pounds (2.25 kg) shrimp, crab, or lobster shells
1 cup (250 g) tomato paste
1½ cups (210 g) diced yellow onion
½ cup (80 g) diced carrots
½ cup (80 g) diced celery
½ cup (70 g) diced fennel
1 cup (250 ml) brandy
1 bottle (750 ml) white wine
1 tablespoon white peppercorns
1 bunch tarragon
1 teaspoon paprika
½ teaspoon cayenne pepper
1 lemon, halved
12 quarts (12 l) water

In a large, heavy pot over very high heat, heat the oil until it begins smoking. Carefully add the shellfish shells; stand back, as they will splash and spit. Smash the shells with a mallet or rolling pin to break them up as much as possible. Yes, it's messy breaking up the shells in the pot, but at least the mess is contained.

Add the tomato paste and stir with a wooden spoon until caramelized, about 2 minutes. Add the onion, carrots, celery, and fennel and cook for 3 minutes, stirring continually. Add the brandy and wine and cook, stirring, for 5 minutes. Add the peppercorns, tarragon, paprika, cayenne pepper, lemon, and water and bring to a boil. Reduce the heat to a low simmer and cook, occasionally skimming any froth from the surface with a ladle, for 2 hours.

Strain through a fine-mesh strainer, using the bottom of a ladle to push as much of the liquid through as possible. Discard the solids. Let the stock cool, then refrigerate in an airtight container for up to 1 week or store in the freezer almost indefinitely.

SHISO OIL

Makes ½ cup (125 ml)

1 handful fresh flat-leaf parsley
1 handful shiso leaves
½ cup (125 ml) neutral oil
Kosher salt

Combine all of the ingredients in a blender and puree until smooth. Refrigerate in an airtight container for up to 2 days.

SWEET AND SOUR RADISHES

Makes 2 cups (325 g)

We serve these with duck breast, but they would be fantastic on their own as a side, especially in the spring, when radishes are their best and brightest.

1 large bunch radishes, quartered
2 tablespoons red wine vinegar
2 teaspoons honey
2 teaspoons Moscatel vinegar
¼ cup (60 g) sugar
½ teaspoon kosher salt
2 tablespoons unsalted butter
¼ cup (60 ml) water

In a small saucepan over medium heat, combine all of the ingredients. Bring to a simmer and simmer until the radishes are just tender, about 10 minutes. Remove the radishes from the pan and continue to cook the liquid down until it has the consistency of maple syrup, about 5 minutes more. Add the radishes back to the pan and toss to glaze them. The radishes are best eaten the day they are made.

Once Gabriel decided he wanted to make taquitos for the staff meal, so he bought two paint cans full of enchilada sauce. As you can see, the sauce has never been used, with the exception of using the cans to press sweetbreads.

TITULAR ISLAND DRESSING

Makes ¾ cup (180 ml)

Thousand Island dressing, named for the thousand islands located between the United States and Canada on the Saint Lawrence River, is a variation on rémoulade. When we made our variation of Thousand Island dressing we *titularized* it (see sidebar on page 14), and so there was only one thing to call it.

¼ cup (60 ml) Aioli (page 321)
¼ cup (60 ml) LP Ketchup (page 324) or purchased ketchup
1 teaspoon Worcestershire sauce
1 teaspoon chopped cornichons
1 teaspoon chopped capers
¼ teaspoon chopped green peppercorns
A dash of Tabasco
Kosher salt

In a bowl, whisk together all of the ingredients. Taste and adjust the seasoning if necessary. Refrigerate for at least 30 minutes before using. Refrigerate in an airtight container for up to 4 days.

TRUFFLE VINNY

Makes 1 cup (250 ml)

This gets better with age.

1 shallot
1 teaspoon soy sauce
2 teaspoons good-quality balsamic vinegar
1 teaspoon sherry vinegar
¼ teaspoon white truffle oil
6 tablespoons extra-virgin olive oil
1 teaspoon chopped black truffle

In a bowl, whisk together all of the ingredients. Refrigerate in an airtight container for up to 2 weeks.

VEAL STOCK

Makes about 4 quarts (4 l)

I've always worked in kitchens where stock was at a premium and there was never enough. If you wanted to play around with some, it was most likely already allocated. That is why I decided to dedicate a whole freezer to extra sauces and stocks, such as this one.

5 pounds (2.25 kg) veal shank bones
2 tablespoons neutral oil
1 yellow onion, quartered
3 carrots, peeled and halved
3 celery stalks, halved
¼ cup (60 g) tomato paste
10 quarts (10 l) cold water
½ bunch thyme
¼ head garlic
3 bay leaves
1 teaspoon black peppercorns

Preheat the oven to 450°F (230°C). Place the bones on a heavy baking sheet and roast for about an hour, turning them every 15 minutes. They should be very brown.

Meanwhile, in a sauté pan over medium-high heat, heat the oil. Add the onion, carrots, and celery and sauté until the onion is translucent, 2 to 3 minutes. Add the tomato paste and stir well with a wooden spoon. Cook until the vegetables have caramelized and the tomato paste is the color of rust, about 5 minutes. Transfer the vegetables to a large stockpot.

Return the sauté pan to the heat and deglaze with 2 cups (500 ml) of the water, using your wooden spoon to scrape all the good bits off the pan. Add the liquid to the stockpot.

Remove the bones from the oven and transfer to the stockpot. We want to get all of the shank goodness into the stock, so deglaze the

baking sheet with 1 cup (250 ml) of the water and add it to the stockpot too.

Fill the stockpot with the remaining 9 quarts plus 1 cup water. Add the thyme, garlic, bay leaves, and peppercorns and place over high heat. When the stock comes to a boil, reduce the heat and simmer for about 4 hours, skimming as you go. Continually taste, as cooking times really vary. You will know the stock is ready when it has an intense veal flavor and a slightly viscous body that coats your tongue; you will end up simmering off about a quarter of the stock.

Strain through a fine-mesh strainer into a large plastic container and refrigerate. This stock will keep for up to 2 months in the freezer in an airtight container.

ABOUT THE AUTHORS

GABRIEL RUCKER is the chef and co-owner of Le Pigeon and Little Bird. At eighteen, Gabriel began his career by dropping out of the Santa Rosa Junior College culinary program to work in his hometown of Napa at the Silverado Country Club. He left California for Oregon in 2003 and landed a job at the highly regarded Paley's Place in Portland, where he would stay for the next two years. After soaking up as much as he could from the Paleys, he moved on and up to become the sous-chef at the Gotham Building Tavern. There he began combining straightforward American standards with classic French technique to resounding approval.

In June of 2006, Gabriel started at Le Pigeon, where his notoriety and career achieved warp speed. *Food & Wine* named him one of the country's Best New Chefs in 2007. And in 2008, 2009, 2010, and 2011, his name popped up on yet another high-profile list of overachievers, as a nominee for the James Beard Foundation's Rising Star Chef. After three years of loserdom, Gabriel finally brought home the goods, winning the Rising Star Chef award in 2011. Though the award was a great honor, it was second to the birth of his son, Augustus Lee Lightning Bolt Rucker, also

a 2011 surprise. When not at the restaurant, Gabriel can be found at home (usually watching the San Francisco Giants) with his son and his wife, Hana.

MEREDITH ERICKSON has written for the *New York Times*, *Elle,* the *National Post,* and *Lucky Peach*. She has worked as an editor and production manager for various magazines, campaigns, and television programs and was editor of *The Family Meal* by Ferran Adria. She is also the coauthor of *The Art of Living According to Joe Beef.* She splits her time between Montreal and London.

LAUREN FORTGANG found her calling early. After high school, Lauren left her hometown of Anchorage, Alaska, and headed to San Francisco and the California Culinary Academy. In San Francisco, she worked at Greens, where she developed her love for both pastry and working with fresh seasonal produce. Then she went back to Alaska as pastry chef at the Marx Brothers restaurant. In 2001, she moved to New York and joined the opening team of Tom Colicchio's restaurant, Craft. She worked there as assistant pastry chef, then held the pastry chef position at Hearth restaurant from its opening in 2003

Gabriel, Meredith, Andy, and David

until moving to Portland with her husband, Andrew, in 2007. She first worked as the pastry chef at Paley's Place, before taking the pastry chef position at Le Pigeon and Little Bird. Since the birth of their daughter, Dora, Lauren has made Le Pigeon (and Dora) her focus.

Lauren

ANDREW FORTGANG is the co-owner, manager, and sommelier of Le Pigeon and Little Bird. Born and raised in New York City, he began cooking at Gramercy Tavern at the age of sixteen. Following stints in the kitchens of Jean-Georges and Aureole, and upon the completion of his studies at the Cornell School of Hotel Administration, he returned to Gramercy Tavern as a floor manager and director of the cheese program. He then moved to Craft restaurant, where he served as the beverage director overseeing the wine list and helped develop the beverage programs at Craftbar, Craftsteak New York, and Craft Dallas. Tom Colicchio not only hooked Andrew up with a job, but he also (inadvertently) hooked him up with his wife, Lauren, who

worked at Craft when Andrew was at Gramercy Tavern. Andrew and Lauren live with their daughter in Portland.

DAVID L. REAMER is a food and lifestyle photographer whose images have appeared in *Bon Appetit*, *Food & Wine*, and *GQ*. Born and raised in New Jersey, David cooked for thirteen years before finally trading his chef's knife for a camera. He first met Gabriel Rucker in 2001, when they cooked together at a small bistro in Aptos, California. Luckily, David convinced Gabriel to leave his home state in search of greener pastures in Oregon. The rest, as they say, is history. David lives with his wife, Meredith, and their dog, cat, and two chickens in Portland.

ACKNOWLEDGMENTS

GABRIEL RUCKER: In the year spent writing, cooking, and collaborating on this book, I have come to have a great respect for the hard work and dedication it takes to create a cookbook. Through this process I have grown as a chef, boss, businessman, father, and husband. I would like to thank all of the chefs and cookbook writers that paved the way for us to join your ranks.

Thanks to my mother and father, who never pushed me too hard in one direction or the other and let me find my own path in life. And to my wife, Hana, who was by my side through the highs and lows of writing this book and continues to stand by my side through the highs and lows of life. Thank you. I love you with all of my heart.

Working on this book has been a blessing and a journey in both making new friendships and strengthening old ones. Thank you, Meredith Erickson, for helping to put my scatterbrained ideas and concepts into a beautifully written book. It was truly a pleasure to work with you, and I'm happy to think of you as a friend first and a colleague second. To my longtime friend and one of the most talented young photographers out there, David Reamer, it has truly been amazing to watch you grow and come into your own. I'm so proud

of you for getting off the hot line and realizing your dreams. Hopefully you will be reading your name in many more book acknowledgments in the years to come. Thank you for making my food beautiful.

To the city of Portland and the amazing diners who live here, thank you for your continued support and patronage of our restaurants. You are the ones who keep me going and inspire me. My favorite part of my job is seeing one of your smiling faces out in the dining room.

I don't think I will ever meet anybody who is a better yin to my yang than Andy Fortgang, my business partner and friend. Le Pigeon would not be where it is today if you hadn't walked through our door. Your dedication and professionalism have set a benchmark that keeps me motivated day in and day out. Thank you, sir, and cheers to many years to come and many bottles of Burgundy shared together.

To my partner in crime Erik Van Kley, wow, where to begin? We stood next to each other for so many years that we were kind of joined at the hip, and if you have to be joined at the hip with one person, well, I got pretty fucking lucky. You have been my greatest inspiration as a cook—always pushing yourself, causing me to push myself. I am happy to call you my partner in Little Bird and one of the most amazing chefs not only in Portland but also in the entire country. Keep it up, and thank you.

To Paul Brady, thanks for giving a twenty-five-year-old kid a shot at letting me do my thing. You are a true Portlander and one of the kindest, most generous humans on the planet.

Thank you to all of the cooks, servers, dishwashers, and stages who put in the hard work and long hours: Su Lien, Bones, Core Cakes, Nathan, Mace, Connor, Taffy, Amish Turk, Sunday Turk, Fistopher, Lunch Box, Basement Bunny, Muffin Boots, Grant, Isaac, Puma, Jessica, and everyone else who has ever clocked in or spent a day peeling carrots just to be in the kitchen.

Thank you to Lauren Fortgang for collaborating with me and sharing the great recipes for the desserts in this book, as well as for every day at Le Pigeon and Little Bird. Your hard work, passion, and dedication are an inspiration to everyone. Congratulations for turning me around on cheesecake; I didn't think it could be done.

A special thanks to Lars Norgren and Steve Jones for taking time out of their busy days to contribute to this book, spread the enjoyment of all things foraged and fine cheese, and truly help us capture the Portland spirit.

To my mentors, Vitaly Paley and Tommy Habetz, thanks for nurturing, pushing, teaching, and putting up with me. It is an honor to put both of your names on my resume.

Thank you to all of our purveyors, who constantly strive to bring the best meat, fish, bread, and vegetables through our doors: Nicky USA, Ken's Artisan Bakery, Sheridan Fruit, Pacific Produce, Viridian Farms, Newman's Fish, and Seafoods.com.

Thank you to all of our friends and family who tested recipes and gave us great feedback: Sarah and Jon Noble, Jacob Simms, Michelle Simms, Ben Stutz, Trevor Stutz, Zanna Stutz, Linda Chartrand, Yvonne Mathieu, Victoria Katayama, Megan Blackman, Patrick Monroe, Nancy Reinke, Paul Brady, Tracy Pendergast, David Rucker, and Laurie Rucker.

And finally, thank you to all of my peers, the cooks and front-of-house employees in this great city: you all are what make the heart of Portland beat and keep me full of great food and drink. When I'm not working in one of my restaurants, I am at home in one of yours.

Finally, this is dedicated to my son, Augustus Lee Lightning Bolt Rucker.

MEREDITH ERICKSON: First, I would like to thank Gabriel and Andy for being such lovely people to work with; you're absolute gems. Thank you for bringing me into your homes and allowing me to be a part of the story. Gabriel, thank you for your complete devotion to the project and endless meals and laughs. Andy, thank you for your organization and the endless bottles!

To David Reamer, for his tireless devotion and willingness to capture the times.

To Hana Rucker, who gave up her home and her time for the project. Your jokes and all-around good vibes gave me another reason to love this project, and moreover, Portland.

To Lauren Fortgang for her time and precision with the dessert recipes.

To Lars Norgren, for his words and for showing me the wilder side of the Pacific Northwest.

To Steve Jones, for agreeing to contribute to our book, and for so many wonderful afternoons at the Cheese Bar. To Tommy Habetz, for pitching in, and to Chad Crowe, for the illustrations.

To the entire Le Pigeon and Little Bird crews. Without you, this wouldn't be possible. I feel fortunate to be so welcomed in your dining rooms. Thank you, thank you.

To all of our testers. The sheer volume of this group is a testament to the LP network. Your input was crucial. You saved our asses on more than one occasion. We thank you.

To Ten Speed Press (for the second time). Specifically Aaron Wehner, for believing, and the ever-dependable Julie Bennett, for being such a pro. A big thanks (again!) to Katy Brown.

To Kim Witherspoon, Allison Hunter, and the entire Inkwell team.

To my parents and grandparents, for supporting an unusual path.

To Oliver Sasse, always.

A big thank-you to the staff at the Hotel Deluxe for letting me express my inner Eloise. To Portlanders Michael Russell and Karen Brooks, for your welcoming words, shared beers, and the shoulders to lean on.

Thank you to the city of Portland for being such a kind home away from home. I often landed after a ten-hour flight and instantly felt energized by your mountains, people, and, yes, restaurants.

LAUREN FORTGANG: I couldn't begin to thank all of the people in my life who have helped me get to where I am. Luckily, that's not what this cookbook is about. It's about Le Pigeon and I have many people to thank for being able to play the role there that I do.

First, I have to thank my daughter, Dora Jean. You were around for the production of this whole cookbook even though you were born halfway through its creation! Thank you for being so patient before you even knew what that was.

To my husband, Andy, thank you for being the most encouraging, supportive, and understanding person I could ever imagine. I couldn't get through each day without your love and patience. I'm so happy that we have managed to work together without killing each other!

Gabe, thank you for making Le Pigeon what it is. It is a joy to come into work, and I have really enjoyed taking a collaborative approach on the dessert menu. I look forward to many years of our families and the restaurants growing together.

There is a man behind the magic when you dig into a dessert at Le Pigeon: Eli Gregory, you have been so amazing this past year and a half. Coming back from maternity leave while working on the book was not easy for me, but you always kept my head above water. Your power is strong and will take you far.

Julia Moore, you are such an essential asset to both Le Pigeon and Little Bird. Thank you for being so flexible and for being able to decipher my cryptic notes.

A special thank-you goes to all of the pastry chefs who came before me: Bunny, the German, and Lunchbox, and to Megan Mitchell, for helping me through my first year here. I couldn't have helped open up Little Bird without you holding down the fort at LP.

David Reamer, thank you for coming to my house to shoot so many of the dessert photos. Whether it was because my daughter was going to be born any second or we had to work around nap schedules, you always made it work. It was such a pleasure to work with a friend—and a talented one at that.

Meredith, thanks for being able to crack the code on what makes Le Pigeon tick . . . that's not any easy undertaking for someone living half a world away. Thanks also for always keeping us on task!

Last but not least, I have to thank my parents for being supportive even when they didn't want to be. You always let your kids be who they wanted to be, and for that and so much more, I am forever grateful. Thank you.

ANDREW FORTGANG: Thank you. I say it all the time, but I cannot say it enough to the following people:

To my wife, Lauren. Not only did you write a whole chapter of this book, but we never even would have moved to Portland had you not opened my eyes to the fact that one *can* live west of the Hudson River. You support me

and challenge me, and I thank you for both of those things. Dora, my sweet daughter, I love you.

Thank you to my parents for helping me become who I am today. Thank you for teaching me to explore and question, and to discuss and debate. Thank you for teaching me to take the high road and to do what is right. An additional thank-you to my mom for starting me on this whole restaurant career path. I wanted something different for dinner, and you told me to cook it myself. Well, I did, and look at me now. Thank you also to my sister, Rachel, for all her support, and for joining us in Portland. Thanks to my Grandma Syvia, who taught me many rules for life, and to all of my family.

Thank you to my oldest and dearest friends, Graham, Karen, and Alexander.

A special thank-you to Tom Colicchio. It was dumb chance that a friend of his brother's passed along the phone number of this teenager who was interested in cooking. Lucky for me, he chose to call and invited me in to stage. (Full disclosure: at the time, I didn't know what Gramercy Tavern was, and I complained to my mom that I wanted to work in a restaurant, not a bar!) He let me keep coming back and offered me my first real job; he helped me get into kitchens like Jean-Georges and Aureole; and he trusted me to manage Gramercy Tavern and Craft. He also taught me that it never pays to raise your voice (a furrowed brow and disappointed glance are much more effective). Thank you.

Another thank-you to three people who put up with that teenager: the sous-chefs at Gramercy back in 1995, Payson Dennis, Matt Seeber, and Johnny Schaefer. I learned more from you than you realize. I must also mention Paul Grieco, who piqued my interest in wine. He introduced me to German riesling with a '76 Prum Auslese when he visited me at Cornell. I offered him a bong hit in return (he declined).

There are too many people from the Gramercy Tavern and Craft families for me to mention them individually. If I were to try to do so I would fail, because I would surely miss someone important to me. Thank you all so much.

That takes me from birth to 2007, and moving to Portland. Thank you to Gabriel and Paul for getting Le Pigeon started without me. Gabriel, brother, it is truly a pleasure and honor to call you partner. Thank you to everyone at Le Pigeon for the hard work you do every day. I am never prouder than when I think of the team we have here—how you care for the restaurant and for each other. An additional thank-you to the team at Little Bird. Le Pigeon casts a long shadow, but you all sidestepped it and made everyone take notice of how special Little Bird is. One special thank-you to Devin Haskell. You are the mortar between the bricks at Little Bird. So much of what I do is possible because of what you do.

Thank you, Meredith, for taking all of our thoughts and ideas and pulling them together to make this book happen. Special thanks to David Reamer, whose pictures really do speak a thousand words. Thanks to Kim Witherspoon, our literary agent, and to Julie Bennett, our editor. Thank you to the folks who tested some of our recipes to make sure they translate to the home kitchen: Juliana Santos, Joey Alvarez, Tatiana Mac (for tackling the profiteroles), Judi Dawson, Mike DeWitt, Jim Everitt, Sean O'Conner, Cyan Bott, Martha and Scott Wright, John House, Arlo Crawford, Paula Miller (caviar isn't normally a substitution for bottarga, but you may have improved the dish), Samantha Novak, Lindsay and Patrick Dawson (yes, we suppose "dickhead" prosciutto will have to do if you can't find "nice" prosciutto), Joe Moura, and Dana Frank. Also, an extra thank-you to the Stutz family for all their testing help.

INDEX

Library of Congress Cataloging-in-
Publication Data:
Rucker, Gabriel, 1981–
    Le Pigeon : cooking at the dirty bird
/ Gabriel Rucker, Meredith Erickson,
Lauren Fortgang, and Andrew Fortgang;
photographs by David Reamer.
        pages cm
    Includes index.
1. Le Pigeon (Restaurant) 2. Cooking—
Oregon—Portland. 3. Restaurants—
Oregon—Portland. I. Erickson, Meredith,
1980– II. Fortgang, Lauren, 1979– III.
Fortgang, Andrew, 1979– IV. Reamer, David.
V. Title.
    TX715.R9245 2013
    641.59795—dc23
                                    2013008703

Hardcover ISBN 978-1-60774-444-3
eBook ISBN 978-1-60774-445-0

Printed in China

Design by Katy Brown

10 9 8 7 6 5 4 3 2

First Edition